Michael Twaddle
1966

I. WILLIAM ZARTMAN, the author, received his Ph.D. from Yale University in 1956. He is Associate Professor of International Studies at the University of South Carolina and Visiting Professor of United Nations Affairs at New York University. He has lived in North Africa for three years, traveled in North and West Africa during 1962-63 on a Rockefeller Foundation research grant, and has written three books, co-authored six books, and published numerous articles dealing with African politics, society, and international relations.

*International
Relations in the
New Africa*

International Relations in the New Africa

I. WILLIAM ZARTMAN

Prentice-Hall, Inc.   A SPECTRUM BOOK   *Englewood Cliffs, N. J.*

to
Arnold Wolfers

PREFACE

This book examines the development of foreign relations among the new states of North and West Africa between 1956 and 1965. The choice of the subject involves a number of assumptions. The first such assumption concerns an unorthodox choice of areas: North and West Africa—Tunisia, Algeria, Morocco, Mauritania, Senegal, Gambia, Mali, Guinea, Sierra Leone, Liberia, Ivory Coast, Upper Volta, Niger, Dahomey, Ghana, Togo, and Nigeria—have been treated together and called Western Africa. There is no intent to suggest that the two areas or their component states are identical; all that is assumed is their comparability and their interaction. There is no doubt that a wave of independence has swept across the Sahara and that the new states on either side of the desert have had —after independence, as well as before—an effect on one another's policies, calling forth responses and reactions. There is no doubt, too, that all the states in the area of Western Africa are, in differing degrees, underdeveloped, not only socioeconomically, but also in the particular aspect of politics that involves foreign policy. Their reactions to this underdevelopment can be mutually enlightening.

Second, it is assumed that a meaningful study can concentrate on the relations of these states among themselves. Again, this does not suggest that their relations with other African states are unimportant, or that Western Africa does not have significant ties to and reactions toward Europe, or that the area does not have a place in the Cold War context, in the Afro-Asian group of states, or in the United Nations. These considerations will be brought in where necessary. But just as a meaningful study can be made of intra-European relations, or even of intra-Six relations in Western Europe, so it is important to investigate the development of interaction and reaction among the seventeen states of Western Africa. A state's primary area of interest in foreign relations is with its neighbors; even if a clear policy toward neighbors does not immediately appear, it is eventually imposed by the necessity of getting along with them. In fact, patterns have appeared in Western Africa, and they were to some extent self-contained (although a claim for complete self-containment is, of course, not made), partly because other parts of Africa were slower in attaining independence or were preoccupied with their own regional relations. Hence, this study is concerned with relations among the seventeen, for which the shorthand term *intra-African relations* will be used for convenience only.

Third, it is assumed that it is possible to analyze the area as a whole. This too does not imply that studies of individual states' foreign policy would be fruitless; on the contrary, it is hoped that this area study will stimulate attention to the foreign policies of the individual states and that some of its ideas, concepts, and methodologies may be useful in these analyses. Where appropriate, individual foreign policies will be mentioned and analyzed.[1] Moreover, general statements in this area analysis are the distillation of comparative analyses of the experiences of each of the seventeen states, made during the preparation of the study. As in any study of international relations, however, the focus here is less on the foreign policies and processes of the individual states than on the relations of the area in general. This approach has been consciously chosen in order to take advantage of insights derived from past studies in international relations; an attempt has been made to apply theoretical ideas from international relations to a new area, to test their applicability and at the same time to develop a clearer understanding of the theories themselves, for possible reapplication elsewhere. This approach also has reference to African area studies, for it is a systematic comparative study of former British and French, Black and Arab territories and their relations. Hence, this study is concerned with international relations as well as with foreign policies.

Fourth, it is assumed that the tools of diplomatic history can be applied to new nations as well as to old. Although notions of behaviorism, communications analysis, and decision-making have been employed as tools, this study begins with a simple historical approach that tries to ascertain what happened when and why. Obviously, as in any historical subject, there is no claim that interpretations given here are definitive. In Africa, perhaps more than elsewhere, truth tends to become relative and personal. Oral tradition is still a major source of information, and oral tradition combines elements of both history and literature. The telephone has perpetuated the oral tradition, for it is easier to operate than the typewriter. It is therefore crucially important to record what has happened on the basis of the knowledge available, even though all the dust may not yet have settled.

Fifth, it is assumed that relations among the states in the area began to develop even before independence. It is one of the anomalies of Western Africa that there were foreign relations—even foreign policies—before there were states. In fact, it is maintained here that understanding of the relations of the sovereign states is impossible without a knowledge of the relations among the political movements that waged the successful struggle for independence and then legitimized the new state. The anomaly is explained, in part, by the fact that the French West African territories attained autonomy in 1958, two years before they gained independence, the trusteeship territory of Togo had active relations with the United Nations and its members before it attained sovereignty, and those states, such as Algeria, that had an organized independence movement—and even a provisional government—very definitely had a foreign policy with clearly defined goals long before they won formal independence.

Sixth, it is assumed that the development of international relations is a legitimate, discrete concept. Although economic, social, and political development is an inseparable whole, its components can be analyzed separately as long as their intrinsic unity and interrelation are constantly recalled. The political aspects of development, for instance, constitute a formidable array of problems; the one that has received least attention is that which deals with effective use of the instruments, the goals, and the concepts of foreign relations. Elements of national power, criteria of national interest, instruments of national policy, and sources of national and international tension are all related to other economic, social, and political aspects of development; together, they form the perimeters of a valid area of focus for this study.

Although I alone am, of course, responsible for the material in this study, I would have been in no position to undertake it without the help of many people. I am most grateful to the Rockefeller Foundation for a grant to conduct research in Europe and Western Africa for fifteen months in 1962-63, during which time I worked in Tunisia, Algeria, Morocco, Mauritania, Senegal,

Guinea, Mali, Ivory Coast, and Ghana, as well as in France and England. I am also grateful to the University of South Carolina for granting me a leave of absence and additional support during the same period. Abroad, I enjoyed the hospitality and cooperation of the University of Tunis, the University of Dakar, the National Institute for Research and Documentation in Guinea, the University of Ghana, and the Overseas Organization for Scientific and Technical Research (ORSTON) in Ivory Coast. I am also grateful to the foreign ministries of the host countries for their very helpful cooperation—and particularly the foreign ministers of Morocco, Senegal, Mauritania, Mali, and Dahomey, who gave generously of their time and assistance. I owe a particular debt of gratitude to Mekhtar ould Daddah, president of the Islamic Republic of Mauritania. I am also very grateful to several ambassadors and their staffs throughout the area, including those of the United States, France, Morocco, Tunisia, and Liberia, who here and there "adopted" my wife and me during our travels. A list of others who were helpful in interviews would be long and perhaps unnecessary; I only hope that I have faithfully reflected their confidence and insight. Africa is a young, exciting area, filled—like any frontier area—with brave people but inspired by a confidence and solidarity all its own. These qualities cannot but impress the visiting foreigner and leave him with the sense of humility and respect that is necessary to understanding.

During the preparation of the manuscript, I have amassed further debts of gratitude. I appreciate the conferences and colloquia organized by William H. Lewis of Georgetown University, Vernon McKay of the School for Advanced International Studies, Rober C. Good of the Department of State, and Richard L. Walker of the University of South Carolina, in which I was able to exchange ideas and receive comments. I owe particular gratitude to Michael Crowder, David Hapgood, Russell Howe, Stephen Low, Mohammed Megdiche, Raymond A. Moore, Benjamin Nimer, Albert Tevoedjre, and Claude E. Welch for the time they spent reading the manuscript, and for their comments on it. Barbara Gene Murphy and Edward V. Roberts, Jr., were most helpful in preparing tables and gathering details. I am grateful to (and sometimes awed by) the speed, efficiency, and understanding of Mrs. Cloris DeGroot, who typed the manuscript (several times). Finally, I owe much gratitude to my wife, Danièle, not only for her constant help in many ways throughout the project, but also for her cheerful company as we bounced along the trails of Western Africa in our 1955 2CV.

I.W.Z.

[1] A few studies of individual states' foreign policies have been undertaken. They include Claude S. Phillips, *The Development of Nigerian Foreign Policy* (Evanston, Ill.: Northwestern U.P., 1964); Habib Bourguiba, Jr., "The Foreign Policy of Tunisia," and James A. Coleman, "The Foreign Policy of Nigeria," in Joseph E. Black and Kenneth W. Thompson (eds.), *Foreign Policies in a World of Change* (New York: Harper, 1963); Henry L. Bretton, "The Emergence of Ghana," in Andrew Gyorgy and Hubert S. Gibbs (eds.), *Problems in International Relations*, 2nd ed. (Englewood Cliffs, N.J.: Prentice-Hall, 1962); and L. Gray Cowan, "Nigerian Foreign Policy," in Robert O. Tilman and Taylor Cole (eds.), *The Nigerian Political Scene* (Durham, N.C.: Duke U.P., 1962). See also the foreign-policy sections in Charles F. Gallagher, "Tunisia," Ernest Milcent, "Senegal," L. Gray Cowan, "Guinea," Virginia Thompson, "The Ivory Coast," and J. Gus Liebenow, "Liberia," in Gwendolen Carter (ed.), *African One-Party States* (Ithaca, N.Y.: Cornell U.P., 1962), and in Virginia Thompson, "Dahomey," in Gwendolen Carter (ed.), *Five African States* (Ithaca, N.Y.: Cornell U.P., 1963).

CONTENTS

ILLUSTRATIONS

*International
Relations in the
New Africa*

1 THE HISTORICAL BACKGROUND: PARTY, STATE, AND ALLIANCE

Relations among the states and states-to-be in Western Africa in the years between 1956 and 1965 were directed toward three primary goals: independence, unity, and development.[1] Although there was a distinguishable hierarchy among these values, they were essentially symbols in search of a meaning: not only the ways of attaining independence, unity, and development, but also the very definition of these concepts were the subject of continual search and debate. These efforts did not take place in the seclusion of the salon or classroom; they were part of major historic movements that were later to engulf the entire continent. One was the birth of sixteen new states in Western Africa, in a wave that formed in Tunisia and Morocco and is still rolling southward. Another was the scramble for allies after independence, as new states and parties sought to strengthen their positions, soften the isolation of independence, and tackle the problem of unity. A third was the settling-in process, during which the new leaders tried out their newly won state machinery and thereby began the development—even if not always the attainment—of political stability. Thus, while Western Africans were seeking to understand the concepts of independence, unity, and development, they were also striving to achieve these imprecise goals in reality.

The study of the development of foreign policy in Western Africa requires some conceptual readjustments. The study of foreign policy in established states assumes the coincidence of three units of interest and identification: the territorial (country), the popular (nation), and the organizational (party government). Although Western African states, like any others, do possess territory, population, and government, neither these three components nor their interrelations are fully developed, nor is their underdevelopment mutually commensurate. In Western Africa the party existed before it had a country to govern; even since independence governmental authority has been felt unevenly throughout the territory, and government ties with the people in terms of interest, identification, and allegiance are still in the process of formation.

INDEPENDENCE AND UNITY
IN THE MAGHREB (1956-58)

When Morocco and Tunisia attained their independence in March, 1956, they faced a choice of foreign policies: they could focus on national independence and internal development, following a foreign policy geared to their national interests and to the promotion of their domestic well-being, or they could seek revolution and regional unity, considering their own independence incomplete until all North Africa was free of colonialism. The choice between independence and unity, or between state and revolution, was not clear-cut. Revolution was, of course, one way of creating a new political and social structure for the state, and unity usually implied independence, rather than a Eurafrican ensemble or a Franco-Maghrebin federation. Similarly, independence—formal equality in the world community and membership in the United Nations—provided an advantageous position from which to aid Algerian independence and North African unity. Like the alternatives, the answer of both states turned out to be ambiguous. But their choice leaned most heavily toward independence, and even a precocious awareness of national interest.[2]

In Morocco, the dominant Istiqlal party was split. Many of the original leaders, representing the nationalist middle class, agreed with what to King Mohammed V seemed a natural option: the establishment of a nation-state that would abide by classical rules of diplomatic procedure and defend its national interests. The appointment of Ahmed Balafrej, secretary-general of the Istiqlal, to the post of foreign minister put Moroccan foreign relations firmly in the hands of this school of thought. But Allal al-Fassi, the leader of the party, declared that "Moroccan independence is incomplete as long as the entire Arab Maghreb is not liberated."[3] This position was supported by Abdulkrim al-Khattabi, the Rif Republic warrior of the 1920s who (from his Cairo exile) refused to consider Morocco independent until all French troops had been withdrawn, and also by his son-in-law, Algerian-born Abdulkrim Khatib, chief liaison leader of the Moroccan Army of Liberation (ALM), a guerrilla force which had been operating in the Rif and Atlas mountains since November 1955 in close liaison with the Algerian Army of National Liberation (ALN).

In Tunisia, support for a revolutionary policy came from the dissident wing of the Neo-Destour. In September 1955, the secretary-general of the party, Salah ben Yussef, returned from Cairo to oppose the Franco-Tunisian conventions of June, which had established Tunisian internal autonomy. When he was disavowed by the party in November, his followers took to the hills of southern Tunisia and the Algerian border region, and established close contact with ALN units in the same area. The Neo-Destour, and then the independent Tunisian government, cooperating with the French army, cleared out these *fellagha* groups early in 1956, and ben Yussef was forced to flee to Tripoli and then back to Cairo. There he continued to meet with Khatib and with Ahmed ben Bella, chief arms procurer for the ALN, but his influence on Tunisian policy was slight. For the first sixteen months after independence, Neo-Destour President Habib Bourguiba was his own foreign minister, and the policy of progressive acquisition known as *Bourguibism* characterized Tunisia's foreign relations as well as its domestic affairs. Unlike Mohammed V of Morocco, who was content to play a paternal, nonpartisan role by laying out general lines and arbitrating among political forces, Bourguiba actually made policy. His methods—recurrent pressure, coercion and conciliation, and evolution—were often the antithesis of a revolutionary foreign policy, and were aimed at the constant goal of complete independence for Tunisia. Foreign policy was therefore intimately tied to the process of building the Tunisian nation.

Despite their preference for a conventional foreign policy directed to the consolidation of their own independence, the leaders of Morocco and Tunisia —by interest as well as by sentiment—could not divorce their fate from that of Algeria. Cultural and colonial similarities were reinforced by personal experiences common to the North African nationalists, including planned coordination by the ALM and the ALN, and the exile of several Tunisian, Moroccan, and Algerian leaders together in Cairo. Furthermore, the innumerable border incidents where Moroccan and Tunisian territory was the scene of fighting between French and Algerians and the continued occupation of both independent states by the French army could never be brought to an end until the Algerian war was over. Morocco and Tunisia were engaged in helping the FLN—Algerian National Liberation Front—by every possible means except direct military intervention. Arms from Egypt, Spain, and Eastern Europe were carried from Moroccan Atlantic and Mediterranean ports by the Moroccan army and the ALM to ALN bases in northeastern Morocco. Egyptian arms were also carried across southern Tunisia enroute from Libya to Algeria. By late 1956, in addition to nearly 10,000 ALN troops, there were 200,000 Algerian refugees crowded into camps and villages along the Tunisian border. In Tunis, a radio program, "Voice of Sister Arab Algeria," used extremist language more typical of Cairo's "Voice of the Arabs" than of a Tunisian broadcast.

The pro-Algerian policies of Tunisia and Morocco, however, frequently conflicted with their need to control and defend their own territory. Tunisia was crisscrossed by private arms traffic; government control over the south and west of the country had not yet been consolidated; French troops from Algeria pursued the Algerians to their Tunisian camps and French army units in Tunisia and Morocco were known to be carrying out intelligence operations at least.[4] ALN units stationed in Tunisia exercised too little control over their own troops and too much over the Tunisians. In western Tunisia, an Algerian-occupied zone, there were frequent incidents between the troops and the population and a growing potential for challenging the government in Tunis. In Morocco, during 1956 and 1957, central government authority along the Algerian border was largely ignored by both the French army and the ALM-ALN, living side by side in their camps and bases.

Support for the revolutionary foreign-policy alternative and the seat of the FLN's External Delegation both were found in Cairo. Morocco and Tunisia felt vague ties of sentiment to Nasser's Egypt, which had aided their independence movements, but both were extremely wary of his attempts to dominate their independent policies. It was natural, therefore, that the two independent neighbors of Algeria should want to regain predominant influence over the FLN, and end the dangerous war on their borders, by winning over the

Cairo-based Algerian leadership to the idea of a negotiated, gradualist settlement and to a united Maghreb.

The moment was propitious for both policies in mid-1956. FLN declarations had already mentioned North African unity as an important goal.[5] France and the FLN had also made a number of attempts at negotiation in Cairo, Brioni, Belgrad, and Rome between March and September. They disagreed over the question of recognition of independence as a precondition; the French had proposed autonomy and one-man-one-vote elections, while the FLN insisted on the formation of a provisional government and a declaration recognizing Algeria's right to independence.

The possibility that Morocco might lend its good offices to these negotiations was officially mentioned immediately after independence.[6] The idea fit well with the sultan's concept of Morocco's position as a "hyphen" or bridge between different states and cultures. But his Oujda speech in September 1956, when he spoke of a "North African entity," was so diplomatically worded that he was obliged to send the prince, the foreign minister, and the new Moroccan ambassador to Paris, Abderrahim Bouabid, to emphasize Morocco's interest in the Algerian problem; in response, French Premier Guy Mollet reiterated his interest in negotiations. The prince had had contacts with ben Bella in April in Seville; in June, he had spoken in Cairo of a Franco-Maghrebin federation. Mohammed V therefore felt that it was time to meet the Cairo leaders of the FLN and also coordinate Moroccan policy with that of Tunisia, which until then had merely approved Moroccan moves from a distance. In late October, Mohammed Khider, ben Bella, and their associates came to Nador and Rabat, where they were persuaded by Mohammed V to accept Bourguiba's invitation to meet in Tunis and devise a common policy. Ben Bella does not seem to have been convinced of the advisability either of an organic link among the three countries or of dropping the precondition (independence) to a negotiated settlement with France, but he had no reason either to break off negotiations or to reject the interest of Mohammed V and Bourguiba.

It was France, however, that broke off the negotiations, for the plane carrying ben Bella and Khider from Rabat to Tunis was ordered to land in Algiers on October 22nd, and the Algerians were sent to French prison. The kidnapping removed the most important of the Cairo-based leaders, but the brutal rupture of negotiations also nullified any progress that Bourguiba had been able to make in persuading FLN leaders to drop independence as a precondition for a settlement. Thus ended the first phase of North African foreign policy; the possibilities of mediation, of special ties (still undefined) with France, and of a moderate Algerian government all gave way to a period of deep wounds and difficult relations. Probably the only positive effect of the visit of the sultan, Balafrej and Moroccan Premier Mbarek Bekkai to Tunis was the agreement to develop cooperation and permanent contacts, to serve the common interest of the sister nations of the Maghreb, and to draw up a treaty of cooperation and alliance.

The hardening of both sides in the Algerian war made it more necessary than ever for Tunisia to devise an arrangement which would render the ALN presence on its soil compatible with its regular diplomatic operations and internal consolidation. After the kidnapping of ben Bella and Khider, the arrest of the Algerian interior leader, Larbi ben Mhidi (in February 1957), and the subsequent collapse of terrorism in Algiers, FLN leadership required reorganizing. Belqassem Krim and Amar Ouamran, the two leaders who had dominated the interior, moved out of Algeria to Tunis, and in March 1957 Bourguiba and Ouamran signed the first formal treaty ever made by the Algerian nationalist movement. The terms were satisfactory to both sides. The FLN agreed not to meddle in Tunisian internal affairs and to confine its presence to areas designated as ALN camps. Tunisia agreed to accept Algerian wounded in local hospitals and to use its National Guard to handle the arms traffic across Tunisia. Because Tunisia would deliver arms only to FLN-accredited units, the FLN and Tunis both gained control over their dissident groups. By mid-April, Bourguiba succeeded in moving the FLN seat of command from Cairo to Tunis, where it was subject to his moderating influence and removed from the revolutionary policies of Nasser.

While dealing with his own problems with Algeria, Bourguiba also continued to seek North African cooperation and to increase chances of peace in Algeria by moderating the FLN's stand. Morocco supported his point of view; in February 1957, Moroccan officials had met the head of the FLN External Delegation in Madrid to discuss the Algerian position. In March, Morocco's Premier Bekkai joined Bourguiba in an attempt to convince the FLN to endorse free elections, but Mohammed Lamine-Debaghine, head of the FLN External Delegation, publicly reiterated his insistence on the precondition of independence and the rejection of United Nations control of Algerian elections. A week after Bekkai's visit to Tunis, Bourguiba was in Rabat to consolidate relations with Morocco by means of the alliance outlined the previous October. The treaty, a conventional diplomatic agreement to cooperate in several fields, was signed by Bourguiba and Mohammed V on March 30, 1957. Most of the negotiations, however, were devoted to a joint communiqué on Algeria; the final communiqué spoke of "a just solution" and "the right of self-determination" rather than of independence. Bourguiba's influence was evident in both documents.

Within four months, before either party had ratified the treaty and before any complementary accords had been negotiated, the Morocco-Tunisian alliance nearly dissolved. Morocco interpreted the Tunisian proclamation of a republic headed by Bourguiba as an implicit threat to its own monarchy; Bourguiba's repeated calls for North African unity "from Sollum to Casablanca" were considered presumptuous and dangerous. Continuing policy disagreements within the FLN, plus the occasion to exercise North African influence offered by the coming visit of Mohammed V to Washington, aroused Bourguiba to another attempt at policy coordination with Morocco. There was a growing sense of urgency in Tunis, for in late August the French defense minister had publicly announced that the right of hot pursuit into Tunisian territory would be applied, and a number of incidents had followed soon after. In November, therefore, Bourguiba was again in Rabat to meet with Mohammed V, whose Speech from the Throne had just ended six months of silence on Algeria with a mention of "independence." The result of the meeting, coordinated with the FLN, was a new offer of good offices from Tunisia and Morocco.

The time, however, was less opportune than the year before. In Morocco, a foreign-policy debate in the National Consultative Assembly suddenly replaced the King's "hyphen" concept with the tougher neutralist slogan of "nondependence." In Algeria, while the uncompromising attitude of Lamine-Debaghine dominated the FLN's stand, the French accelerated their military campaign and continued to pursue ALN bands into Tunisian territory. In mid-September, the Morice Line on the Tunisian border was completed, sealing off a no-man's-land in Algeria from Bone to Tebessa. It was effective in reducing the flow of arms supplies to the FLN in Algeria, but it did not stop rebel attempts to cross the border and it did not, of course, protect Tunisia against the French army. Instead, it caused more refugees and ALN units to settle in western Tunisia, thus increasing Bourguiba's dilemma. The crowning incident came on February 8, 1958, when French planes retaliated against an ALN raid by bombing the Tunisian border town of Sakiet Sidi Yussef, where ALN units were stationed. When the matter was taken to the United Nations, both France and Tunisia accepted Anglo-American good offices, but with conflicting aims. Tunisia sought, at least, protection against further French incursions—although refusing a border control which would have denied the Algerians sanctuary in Tunisia—and, at most, mediation to end the Algerian war. France sought a border control which would cut off the ALN from the sanctuary so necessary to guerrilla warfare. The proposals made by Britain and the United States in mid-March covered a number of points in dispute, but ignored the border issue; to FLN leaders, it seemed that Tunisia was using the Algerian crisis to solve its own problems with France. In mid-April 1958, however, the French National Assembly rejected the proposals; the government fell, and a series of crises began that came to a head a month later with the collapse of the Fourth Republic.

The events of the preceding six months, however, did not diminish the desire of Morocco and Tunisia to gain predominant influence within the FLN. In early March, both Bourguiba and Mohammed V formally espoused (and the FLN executive approved) the idea of a North African federation, although this would remain a foreign-policy dream until the Algerian state was free to federate. From time to time since 1956, there had been moves to create an Algerian government-in-exile and the FLN threatened to establish such a body in Cairo "within thirty days" if Bourguiba gave in to French demands on the border in April 1958. But such a solution would have served only to perpetuate Egyptian predominance within the FLN, make any negotiation with France much more difficult, and render Bourguiba's moderate position untenable. The common denominator was thus to be found at the party level, and the Istiqlal undertook missions to Tunis and to the FLN in Cairo in order to prepare a conference of the three North African political movements. One of the principal aims of the conference was to be the creation of an Algerian Liberation Committee in order to facilitate negotiations and bypass the problem of a government-in-exile. The Tangier conference of the Istiqlal and Neo-Destour parties and the FLN ended on April 30th with recommendations for the creation of a North African federation, and the immediate formation of a common consultative assembly and a permanent secretariat. It also agreed to the formation of an "Algerian government," but only after consultation with Tunisia and Morocco, and it included side agreements to harmonize foreign policies and augment common war efforts (although these stopped short of total commitment to a revolutionary policy). In return for these important concessions, the Algerian delegation, which did not include Lamine-Debaghine, agreed to insist only on the *"right* to sovereignty and independence" as a precondition to negotiations.[7]

The conference, widely hailed as a turning point in North African relation, was merely a prelude to further diplomatic ups and downs. The proposed assembly was never constituted. The first meeting of the permanent secretariat, called for May, was held in June in Tunis, and was marked by the ratification of the 1957 Morocco-Tunisian alliance; implementing conventions, however, were not negotiated until the following year. The FLN renewed its pressure for the formation of a government-in-exile, but the hesitations of the two neighboring states again prevailed, largely because the uncertain position of the new French government made any dramatic action unadvisable. Scarcely a month after the meeting ended, relations between Tunisia and the FLN were embittered by a violent dispute over Tunisia's agreement to the construction of a pipeline carrying Algerian oil to the Tunisian port of Skhirra. A second meeting of the permanent secretariat was called by the FLN in Tunis, where, at the end of August, the participants' energies were successfully turned away from the pipeline dispute to the problem of the Algerian war. Two weeks later, on September 19, 1958, creation of the Provisional Government of the Republic of Algeria (GPRA) was announced by Ferhat Abbas, its premier, in Cairo. At the same time Abbas declared that the GPRA was "ready to begin negotiation." The Algerian war had reached a turning point. During the first eighteen months of the revolt, the FLN, with help coming largely from Egypt, had aided the cause of Moroccan and Tunisian independence by diverting French military attention from the two protectorates.[8] In the three years that followed, Morocco and Tunisia repaid their debt in kind—giving arms and sanctuary to the guerrillas, helping to keep alive the External Delegation when the fortunes of war failed in the interior, and extending political and diplomatic support to a war that was eventually to be won in the political arena rather than on the field of battle. In the process, Tunisia and Morocco were gradually winning over the FLN to a negotiated settlement and away from predominant Egyptian influence.

The change in government in France made possible a number of improvements in relations with Tunisia and Morocco, that strengthened their position in counseling moderation to the Algerians. Most notable were the decisions to evacuate some of the French bases in Morocco, particularly those along the Algerian border, in October 1958, and all French bases in Tunisia (except Bizerte) in June 1958. Of even broader significance was the referendum of September 27th, which opened new possibilities of negotiation to Algeria and independence to French West Africa. To understand the effect of this event on Western African diplomacy, attention must shift to preceding events south of the Sahara.

PRE-INDEPENDENCE ALLIANCES IN AOF (1956-58)

The establishment of political institutions in French West Africa (*Afrique Occidentale Française* or AOF) posed conflicting criteria of political interest and identification for the local populations. Whereas in Tunisia and Morocco the colonial territorial unit (country) and the nationalist organizational unit (party) existed side by side and competed for allegiance before independence, in AOF the organizational unit came into being long before the state. It was only with the passage of a *loi-cadre* (enabling law) on June 23, 1956, and the holding of legislative elections on March 31, 1957, that the first African governments were formed in the eight territories of AOF—Senegal, Mauritania, Soudan, Guinea, Ivory Coast, Upper Volta, Dahomey, and Niger. Once the governments were established, the third unit—the popular (nation)—could be developed in earnest. Until then, the geographic framework of the nation and the party had been ambiguous, and there was no clear modern replacement for the tribe (the traditional nation) as the unit of interest and identification. The *loi-cadre* therefore was important in providing an institutional stimulus to the formation of eight new states, giving parties and nations a territorial framework. In the process, despite the fact that the territories of AOF were still French colonies and not sovereign entities, the basis for foreign relations—both with France and among the territories—was also established several years before actual independence.

Relations among the party-governments of French West Africa were thus protoforeign relations, and their evolution from the mid-1950s foreshadowed their development after independence.[9] Two types of situations existed in 1957. In a number of territories, a single party was in firm control, with a geographic and institutional base from which to develop a national consciousness, conduct external relations, and make alliances with other West African parties and governments. In other territories of AOF, there was a struggle among parties for control of government and country. In these cases, local parties operated as branches of federal party alliances, which were in turn dominated by the established party-governments in the single-party territories. Party-governments in these states were not free to consolidate their nations, to act purely on the basis of their territories' national interests, or even to carry out their own foreign relations, for they were preoccupied with the problems of achieving power at home.

In 1957, territories in the single-party category were Ivory Coast, Guinea, and Soudan, where the Ivory Coast Democratic Party (PDCI) led by Felix Houphouet-Boigny, the Democratic Party of Guinea (PDG) led by Sekou Touré, and Soudanese Union (US) led by Modibo Keita, had won all or nearly all the territorial assembly seats in their respective countries. Each of these parties was a territorial section of the African Democratic Rally (RDA), headed by Houphouet-Boigny. The long-awaited third congress of the RDA in Bamako at the end of September 1957, like the legislative elections of that year, showed clearly the relation between the territorial sections and the federal party. The three sections were essentially political machines, each grouped about a charismatic leader who expressed his party's peculiar attitudes, policies and philosophies; the federal party was the ensemble of these machines, united only at the summit by the common experiences of the leaders and by their periodic meetings. One of the major accomplishments of Bamako was simply the prevention of a split between Houphouet-Boigny and the other two major leaders.

The Bamako meeting of the RDA alliance made possible the formulation of a few common stands, the coordination of aid to minority territorial sections in difficulty, and negotiations with opposing parties for the realization of West African unity. In the first category of achievements were resolutions favoring negotiations between France and the "authentic representatives of the Algerian people" to "build a vast community of people" respecting the "Algerian personality." In the third category, the RDA's own precarious unity and past abortive attempts at talks with rival party leaders convinced RDA chiefs that unity could be achieved only from the base. The congress favored pursuing the subject, but the RDA's own successes at the polls in March 1957 led it to look more to absorbing other parties than to merging with them. Unlike North Africa, French West Africa had both a precedent and an institution for unity: the AOF Federation and its Grand Council, which met at Dakar. But the *loi-cadre*, by creating territorial governments rather than a federal executive, had favored the separate evolution of the eight protostates instead of one federation; the RDA, with its territorial bases and its policy disagreements over the very issue of federation, was in no position to use its predominance in the Grand Council for any purpose but to hinder the development of regional unity.

The center of the other alliance was Senegal. The government of Mamadou Dia was made up of members of the Senegalese People's Bloc (BPS), the strongest territorial section of Leopold Sedar Senghor's federal party: the African Convention. The Convention was an alliance, founded in January 1957, of several territorial parties, and its statutes provided for its disappearance upon the final unification of all rival West African political groups. Senegal, with Dakar as the main port and capital of AOF, was most strongly in favor of federation, but as the territory of Dia, Senghor, and the African Socialist Movement (MSA) leader, Lamine Gueye, it was the strongest opponent of the RDA, even though divided among several parties. The RDA had already suggested to Senghor that unification begins at home, and the opening session of the new Grand Council, at which the African Convention and MSA were thrown together in the opposition, provided the opportunity for an initial step in this direction. When, in response to a mandate given by the RDA congress at Bamako, Houphouet-Boigny called a meeting of all AOF party leaders in Paris in February 1958, a further occasion was provided for the Senegalese to push the complementary ideas of territorial federation and party unification. The meeting vaguely endorsed federation, placing it within the context of a larger federation with France and the right to independence, but the RDA soon let it be known that any party unification would be acceptable only within its own organization. However, the next unity meeting, in Dakar in March, did bring about the unification of the Convention and MSA alliance systems into a single African Regroupment Party (PRA), the unified Senegalese section of which was to be the Senegalese Progressive Union (UPS). The long history of competition within Senegalese politics, reflecting divisions within the Senegalese nation, was finally—although only superficially—overcome.[10]

The last single-party territory of the AOF was Mauritania, which presents a special case of geography and foreign relations.[11] Three quarters of the Mauritanian population are Saharan Arabs, many of them nomads; the rest, living in the Senegal river valley, are black Africans like the other peoples of west Africa. Political activity began among the Arabs in 1946, with the election to the French National Assembly of Horma ould Babana, candidate of the radical nationalist Mauritanian Entente party. With the help of the colonial administration, the Qadiriya brotherhood, and conservative tribal chiefs, ould Babana was defeated narrowly in 1951 and more decisively in 1956. In March 1956, he fled to Rabat, and then, in the company of Allal al-Fassi, to Cairo, where they presented a claim on behalf of Morocco over all of Mauritania. Ould Babana then returned to Rabat, where he took up residence; in August, at the head of two hundred Mauritanian tribal figures, he was received briefly by the sultan. The Mauritanian government was therefore driven to seek support for its independent existence through association in the French West African federation; yet it was wary of too close an association because of its fundamentally different ethnic composition and because of its fear that a federal party would favor minority rule by the black Africans over the Arabs. The government party joined neither of the two federal alliances, RDA or PRA. Instead, it sought primarily to consolidate its own national basis. After winning the March 1957 territorial elections, the party absorbed remaining elements of the Mauritanian Entente at the constituent congress of a new Mauritanian Regroupment Party (PRM) in May 1958.

As poorer, weaker territories, Niger, Upper Volta, and Dahomey were fields of conflict for the two federal party alliances rather than centers of influence. Niger's vast area, sparse population, and tribal divisions were reflected in its numerous small parties and personal factions, and this multiplicity of organizations was further accentuated by a split in the territorial section of the RDA into one faction that was affiliated with the federal party (led by Hamani Diori) and one that was not (led by Bakary Djibo). In July 1956, Djibo unexpectedly issued a call for external allies, appealing to Houphouet-Boigny and Senghor to unite the parties of AOF, including his own. Houphouet-Boigny refused, and instead strengthened the approved RDA section by dispatching help to Diori. After municipal elections in November 1956, Djibo made an alliance with the Niger Socialist Movement (MSN) and was elected mayor of Niamey, and then assistant secretary-general of the federal MSA. His external ally was Lamine Gueye rather than Houphouet-Boigny or Senghor. In the territorial elections of March 1957, the MSN won two thirds of the seats and Djibo formed a government. A political-warfare campaign, including a teachers' strike in November 1957 and bloody riots the following April, was launched by the RDA alliance to discredit the government and bring the territory back into the RDA camp. The MSN government won additional allies, however, when the MSA and the African Convention united to form the new federal PRA. At the first PRA congress at Cotonou in July 1958, Djibo was elected secretary-general. Yet Niger's appearance as a single-party territory safely in the PRA camp was deceptive; the territory was situated far from its allies and the vulnerability of the government weakened the whole PRA alliance system.

Upper Volta was another political battleground.[12] It had come back into existence only in 1947, after fifteen years of partition among Ivory Coast, Soudan, and Niger. It too was divided by numerous tribal rivalries, notably between the dominant Mossi nation, whose partisan unity was disintegrating by 1956, and other smaller tribes, which had been organized by the RDA section, the Democratic Voltaic Party (PDV). In the legislative elections of March 1957, a new coalition—the Unified Democratic Party (PDU)—succeeded in uniting both some Mossi and smaller tribes, won a bare majority, and formed the territorial government. Most of the other assemblymen belonged to the Mossi-supported Voltaic Democratic Movement and the rest were followers of the non-Mossi and anti-RDA African People's Movement. None of these groups, except Ouezzine Coulibaly's PDV members of the PDU coalition, had ties to a federal party alliance as yet, and the others resented the tactics of the RDA, which tried to incorporate the PDU in September 1957 and destroy the other parties. In December 1957, these parties tried to unseat the PDU government, charging the RDA had broken an electoral agreement by contesting seats in their fiefs, but they failed. The two opposition parties then strengthened their position by uniting to form the local section of the PRA. When Coulibaly died in September 1958, there was no leader popular enough to unite the tribal factions, which were further split over the question of federation. Maurice Yameogo, who succeeded Coulibaly as RDA leader, temporarily united the RDA and PRA sections, and formed a coalition government. Unity on all levels, however, was not yet consolidated.

Finally, in Dahomey, tribal antagonisms between the north and the south also contributed to create a battleground for alliances.[13] The southeasterners had their own party, the Dahomeyan Republican Party (PRD) of Sourou Migan Apithy, and the northerners supported the Dahomeyan Republican Rally (RDD) of Hubert Maga. In the legislative elections of 1957, the PRD won a slight majority and formed a government with the RDD. The government was apparently strengthened in mid-March when the PRD, the MDD, and other smaller groups in the coalition united to form the Dahomeyan Progressive Party (PPD), local section of the federal PRA. Apithy now had all the territorial legislators behind him except those of the Dahomeyan Democratic Union (UDD) of Justin Ahomadegbe, a local section of the RDA and the party of the southwestern tribes. Apithy's solid support was in reality only a regional coalition; as in Upper Volta and Niger, tribal differences made it impossible to maintain a durable majority, invited interference from the interterritorial RDA and PFA alliances, and upset the tenuous coalitions when the ideological issues of federation and independence erupted in 1958.

Thus, by the beginning of 1958, pressure for unification of the territorial political organizations had resulted, ironically, in the division of AOF into two alliance systems, each competing for unity on its own terms. The split was widened by the introduction of an ideological issue, the problem of federation or the unification of the geographic units, posing a choice between a federal executive to control the territorial governments and the separate development of individual states through direct—but separate—ties with Paris. Guinean and Soudanese attachment to the idea of federal unity, against the wishes of Houphouet-Boigny and Ivory Coast's PDCI, nearly broke up the RDA's Bamako congress. The Guinean PDG defected the following April, when Touré cosponsored a motion in the AOF Grand Council calling for "the urgent necessity of creating a federal executive." The motion was voted by acclamation, in the absence of all but one Ivory Coast councillor. The PDCI reaction was to "withdraw" from AOF and request the establishment of direct bilateral ties with France. Before the temporary isolation of Ivory Coast could turn into a permanent *renversement des alliances* on the part of Guinea and Soudan, the bureau of the RDA's Coordination Committee met in Paris, in mid-April 1958, to arrive at a compromise on federal unity. The agreement appears to have been based more on sentimental attachment to RDA unity than on concrete consideration of territorial interests; Guinea and Soudan, unable to compel the rich Ivory Coast to share its revenue with the other territories of AOF, made the greatest concessions. The accord was unstable and contradictory; it recognized the primacy of the "territorial personality," the possibility of an "executive delegation" instead of a federal executive, and the right of each territory to determine its own relations with France.

The entire situation changed with the introduction of a new ideological element: independence.

THE INDEPENDENCE IDEA IN WEST AFRICA (1957-58)

Ghana (formerly the Gold Coast) attained its independence on March 6, 1957. The event was overlooked in the electoral campaigns being waged in the neighboring AOF territories, yet it was to affect the relations of all West Africa. Prime Minister Kwame Nkrumah believed that "our independence is meaningless unless linked up with the total liberation of the African continent." [14] Nkrumah came to power with a foreign-policy goal so strong that it was tantamount to a personal mission: the union of Africa. His main obstacle, besides colonial rule, was the gulf of incomprehension that separated French from British territories. The Bamako congress of the RDA hardly mentioned the independence of the new West African state, nor were observers from British West Africa or Liberia present or invited. However, Ghana's independence celebrations in 1957 did provide an opportunity for Nkrumah to sound out some delegations on his immediate and longstanding dream, that of holding a Pan-African conference in Africa; within five weeks, letters proposing the meeting were sent to the heads of government of all eight independent African states.[15] At the same time, Nkrumah took his first official trip abroad, to neighboring Ivory Coast, where he talked briefly and inconclusively with Houphouet-Boigny and Touré and was publicly challenged by his host to compare—in ten years' time (that is, in 1967)—the merits of independence against those of colonial cooperation. If there was a positive lesson to be drawn by Nkrumah from his trip, it was that immediate possibilities of Ghanaian leadership in West Africa were limited.

Unlike the territories of AOF, Ghana had not had extensive relations with other African parties—not even with those of British West Africa—before independence. Unlike the Maghreb, West Africa was not torn by a military conflict—not even the independence "struggle" of AOF—which could have limited the new states' freedom of action. Ghana was therefore essentially free to follow its own policies, interests, and sentiments. Yet, even more than the states of the Maghreb and the territories of AOF, Ghana was torn between its nature as a territorial unit (a newly independent state) and an organizational unit (a revolutionary political party). Rather than resolve the dilemma, Ghana proceeded to base its foreign policy on its dual nature. Nkrumah's participation in the Commonwealth conference of June 1957 in London gave double impetus to this activity. There he met his old mentor, George Padmore, the elder statesman of Pan-African socialism, whom he appointed his special advisor on African Affairs in November;[16] there too he set in motion the machinery to plan a Pan-African conference. It is significant that all the preparatory work of 1957 took place in London among the eight African ambassadors, and that not until February 1958 (when a Ghanaian delegation led by Ako Adjei and Padmore visited participating states) did the scene of preparation move to the African continent. Negotiations centered on the Ghanaian dilemma: Was the conference a diplomatic meeting of independent states, now that Ghana was sovereign? Or was it a meeting of African nationalist organizations, since the Convention Peoples Party (CPP)-government was the marching wing of the Ghanaian nation, spearhead of the African people? Ghana was facing the same alternatives of state and revolution that North Africa had confronted.[17] Because the African ambassadors in London represented sovereign states, it was natural to decide that the conference should be limited to independent Africa. In March, however, the Ghanaian government announced that it would also sponsor (but not "as a country") a later meeting of African political organizations, the first Pan-African congress on free African soil.[18]

The first Conference of Independent African States (CIAS) was held in Accra on April 15-22, 1958, the week before the Tangier conference of North Africa.[19] It was independent Africa's first formal diplomatic conference, and its success showed the wisdom—frequently to be forgotten in later meetings—of careful preparations. Its immediate value lay in the attendance, which revealed that countries north and south of the Sahara, Arab and black African nations, ex-French and ex-British colonies all considered themselves African and could agree on common policy guidelines. These policies included support of Moroccan and Tunisian good offices in Algeria; "the right of the Algerian people to independence"; use of negotiations, conciliation, and mediation to solve intra-African conflicts; promotion of economic cooperation; constitution of their United Nations representatives into "a Permanent Machinery for consultation, cooperation," and preparation of a second conference two years later at Addis Ababa. There was concern that the conference, without an effective permanent secretariat, would lose momentum (as had happened in the case of the 1955 Afro-Asian Conference at Bandung). During the month of June, Nkrumah attempted to enhance the newly won cooperation by a series of state visits to the participating countries, but the results were largely ceremonial.

Another resolution gave support to the Juvento party of Togo, which presented a brief at the conference. Although the British portion of the Togo Trusteeship territory had (by a narrow margin) voted in favor of union with Gold Coast in May 1956 and had attained independence a year later as an integral part of Ghana, the French portion continued its separate course and, in an October 1956 referendum, acceded to the new status of autonomous republic.[20] Legislative elections in April 1958 resulted in an unexpected victory for Sylvanus Olympio's Togolese Unity Committee (CUT), parent group of Juvento; the Accra conference resolution, coming as it did a week before the elections, strengthened the CUT campaign. The CUT had a strong following among the Ewe tribe (which was divided among Togo, Togoland, and Gold Coast) and was dedicated to the independence of a united Togo. In early May, Olympio publicly requested an open customs frontier with Ghana; Nkrumah acceded to the request the same month. Thus it was through Togo, with its ethnic border problem and its special trusteeship status, that a window was opened between British and French territories, through which the idea of independence could penetrate French West Africa. Togo's foreign policy as a buffer state was thus early established.

Ideas of federalism and independence were also given encouragement by events in another British territory. Two weeks before the 1957 territorial assembly elections in AOF and a week after Ghana gained independence, elections were held in Nigeria's eastern region; by the beginning of August, both the eastern and the western regions had acceded to self-government, a status similar to the autonomy that was to be proposed for the French West African territories.[21] The same month, however, a federal executive for Nigeria was also formed, under Prime Minister Abubakar Tafawa Balewa. Continuing the British colonial policy of federal unity, Nigeria took the measures advocated by the French West African federalists. At the same time, it took steps toward independence; the constitutional conference of May-June 1957, which decided on autonomy and federalism, also prepared the way for a reconvened conference in September-October 1958, that set October 1, 1960, as the date for Nigerian independence. In the interval between the two conferences, the ways to independence were debated in the federation of Nigeria as they were in the federation of French West Africa, but language and cultural barriers kept the two discussions in their separate geographic locales, with no interaction.

In the midst of these events, the overthrow of the French Fourth Republic and the preparation of a constitution for the Fifth Republic opened AOF not only to thoughts of independence but also to action toward it. The RDA Bamako congress, like the Maghreb Tangier conference, had cited "the inalienable right of independence" but, under pressure from Houphouet-Boigny, had made a neo-Leninist distinction between the right and its exercise. By mid-1958, such philosophical distinctions were no longer germane, and the new French constitution was considered as providing an opportunity for France to fulfill the pledges of the old one: "to lead to a state of freedom the peoples of whom . . . [France] has assumed charge." The PRA Cotonou congress—which grouped the ruling parties of Senegal, Dahomey, and Niger with other, lesser parties—in an attempt to undercut the RDA subscribed to the idea of "immediate independence" and confederation between France and a West African federation. When the draft French Constitution was announced, however, neither option appeared to be among the three—status quo, departmental status, or autonomy—offered to the African territories. PRA delegates returning home, particularly to Senegal and Dahomey, found themselves prey to their own doubts and to pressures from France over the wisdom of immediate independence, although their primary preoccupation with West African federation continued.

By the end of de Gaulle's trip through Africa in August 1958, the two ideological issues upon which the African territories placed so much emphasis were clearly understood in the choice offered by the referendum.[22] Independence could be obtained simply by voting *Non*, but it would exclude the emerg-

ing state from the new Franco-African Community. Unity could be negotiated after the referendum among like-minded states who wished to enter
the Community on a group or federal basis. But unity and independence at
the same time were not possible. The ideological choice completely disrupted
the two party alliances. Each alliance contained one supporter of immediate
independence—Guinea's PDG in the RDA and Niger's MSN in the PRA—and
one supporter of immediate federation—Soudan's US in the RDA and Senegal's
UPS in the PRA. The PDCI of Ivory Coast was the strongest opponent of both
choices. The *renversement des alliances* which followed on Ivory Coast's isolation was consummated, marking the lowest ebb of Houphouet-Boigny's
foreign-policy fortunes.

The situation was immediately reversed by the referendum of September
27, 1958. It was now Guinea which, by its *Non* vote and subsequent independence on October 2nd, found itself isolated in West Africa. France's ex-
communication of Guinea was reflected, and partially caused, by a similar
attitude on the part of the RDA leaders, particularly Houphouet-Boigny. But
within the two weeks after independence, Guinea had been visited by special
delegations from the two other independent states of West Africa, Ghana and
Liberia, and the latter had offered food supplies. A week later, Guinean missions were sent to Monrovia and Accra, and a month later, a delegation led by
Touré visited the same capitals. The meeting in Monrovia was restrained, and
ended with a communiqué pledging "to safeguard [the two countries'] national independence, sovereignty, and territorial integrity" and to erase a
longstanding border dispute. The meeting in Accra was ebullient, terminating
in the proclamation of a Guinea-Ghana Union. The declaration was ambiguous and the two parties' concepts of their creation conflicted, but the action
brought Guinea an ally and a $28 million loan. A return mission from Ghana
the following week began the process of drawing up a constitution and negotiating economy, foreign-policy, and communications coordination. For all
the vagueness of the "union," a major shift in West African alliances had
occurred, and the barrier between French and British Africa had been
breached.

The other party-government to favor independence in the 1958 referendum,
the Sawaba (formerly the MSN) of Niger, was beaten by the combined activities of Ivory Coast and France. The vote in Niger had several aspects: it
was not only a contest between PRA and RDA sections, but also a contest between the influence of Ivory Coast and that of Ghana. Initial contacts were
made with Padmore at the PRA Cotonou congress, and then with Nkrumah
after the first-anniversary celebrations of Ghanaian independence. Again in
Accra a month before the 1958 referendum, Sawaba leaders were the only
AOF politicians who coordinated their *Non* campaign with the Ghanaian government. The return envoy of Ghana, however, was able to give the Sawaba
only promises, not material support, and the campaign ended with no effective help from Accra.[23] The RDA of Houphouet-Boigny was in a far better
position, for it provided personnel and financial aid to the Niger RDA section

with the assistance of the French colonial administration. After the referendum, the Sawaba government resigned under pressure from the French, and after new elections in December the RDA, benefitting again from French and Ivory Coast support, formed the new Niger government under Diori.

In the other territories of AOF, the political forces favoring independence were only minimal splinter groups, in special need of allies. The Conference of Independent African States had declared that the problems of colonial Africa were not the exclusive domain of the European powers but "the responsibility . . . in particular of the Independent African States," and it called on these states to assist the African struggle for independence and to offer training and education facilities to nationalist groups working toward freedom. A conference specifically devoted to these organizations was a cardinal point of Ghana's foreign policy. Preparations had begun among representatives of British Africa during the first-anniversary celebrations of Ghanaian independence at Accra, and continued within the African Affairs Bureau set up under Padmore. The first all-African Peoples' Conference, held in Accra on December 5-12, 1958, set the tone for the radical foreign-policy line in West and North Africa. The conference was a Pan-African affair, although the RDA, strong from its referendum victory, was scarcely represented. Working under the theme of African unity, the conference looked to an eventual African commonwealth, endorsed aspirations for federations in West and North Africa, and denounced artificial colonial frontiers. It supported African freedom fighters, both nonviolence and defensive violence to attain independence, and the creation of a volunteer African Legion. It also established a permanent All-African Peoples' Organization (AAPO) with a Freedom Fund, located at Accra. The Accra conference, even more than the Tangier conference of the same year, was an attempt at "peoples' foreign policy," seeking to conduct and determine intra-African relations on the basis of political organizations, independent of state action. The fact that government parties were frequently represented did not alter this characteristic, for the AAPO was to have its greatest activity—in the absence of any real effectiveness—among splinter groups opposing colonial or independent African governments. The AAPO, and the Ghanaian Bureau of African Affairs which worked closely with it, attempted to be the alliance center for radical African political organization—Ghana's counterpart to the RDA and PRA headquarters.

ALLIANCES AND COUNTERALLIANCES IN WEST AFRICA (1959-61)

There were two major reasons behind the drive for alliances and regional unity in West Africa between 1959 and 1961. One was the ideology of unity, expressed as federation in AOF and as African unity by Ghana and other radical states. The other was the desire to avoid isolation, made particularly sharp in West Africa because of the interdependence and powerlessness of the states. Of all the classical ways to increase national power rapidly, the

AFRICAN GROUPS AND CONFERENCES

READ DOWN FOR STATES.
READ ACROSS FOR DATES.
GROUPS INDICATED BY BOXES.

Column headers (read across): Pan-African Conferences | Liberia | Sierra Leone | Nigeria | Togo | Ivory Coast | Niger | Upper Volta | Dahomey | Mauri-tania | Senegal | Mali | Guinea | Ghana | Morocco | Algeria | Tunisia

Pan-African Conferences

1957 — Accra, April 15 (CIAS 1)

1958 — Accra, December 5 (AAPO 1)

1959 — Sanniquellie, July 19 ; Monrovia, August 4 ; Tunis, January 25 (AAPO 2)

1960 — Addis, June 15 (CIAS 2)

1961 — Cairo, March 23 (AAPO 3):

AOF / African party conferences (Ivory Coast column)

Dakar, January 11 (African Convention)
Bamako, September 25 (African Democratic Rally—RDA)
Dakar, March 26 (African Regroupment Party – PRA)
Cotonou, July 27 (African Regroupment Party—PRA)
REFERENDUM, September 28 (Autonomy—November 24 to December 18)
Bamako, December 28 (Federalist Conference)
Dakar, January 14 (Constituent Assembly)

Mali Federation

Dakar, March 24 (PFA)
Dakar, April 4
Dakar, August 19

Entente

Abidjan, April 4
Abidjan, May 29
Paris, February 24
Bobo, March 8
Cotonou, April 15
Abidjan, May 20
Abidjan, August 8
Cotonou, September 28
Abidjan, October 9
Niamey, December 23
Ouagadougou, January 5
Niamey, February 18
Ouagadougou, March 17
Abidjan, August 10
Abidjan, October 21

UAM

Abidjan, October 24
Brazzaville, December 15
Dakar, January 30
Yaounde, March 26
Tananarive, September 7

UAS

Accra, November 24
Conakry, May 1
Accra, July 11
Conakry, December 24
Accra, April 27
Bamako, June 25

Group (Casablanca)

Casablanca, January 4
Accra, February 22
Cairo, May 3
Conakry, July 10
Cairo, August 28

Maghreb

Tangier, April 27
Tunis, June 17
Tunis, August 30
Rabat, October 6

Group (Liberia)

Monrovia, May 8
Dakar, July 17

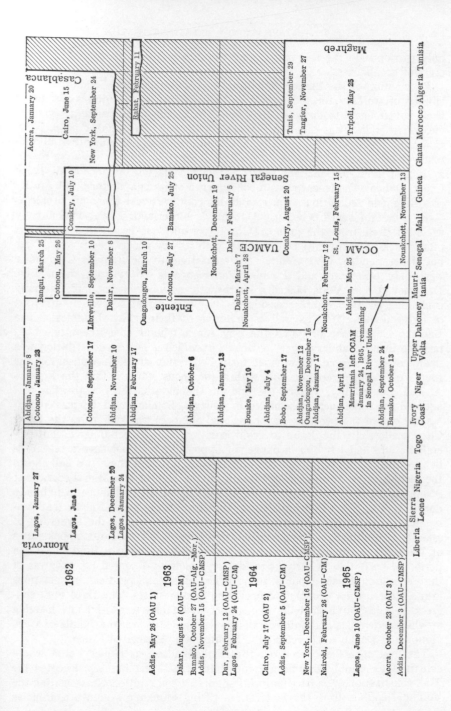

only two open to the new states were the manipulation of symbols and the creation of alliances.

Ratification of the French constitution gave Senegal and Soudan the possibility of working for federation, as their territorial assemblies instructed their governments to do when they voted to accede to autonomy. A conference of federalists was called in Bamako for the end of December 1958. Ivory Coast and its like-minded RDA ally, Niger, were absent, but four other autonomous states of AOF were represented. The Senegal-Soudanese initiative meant a shift of allies for Soudan, which abandoned its RDA alliance with Ivory Coast. Dahomey's presence was a consequence of its PRA alliance, but Apithy also sought in federation an answer to his country's real economic problems —an uncertain venture because Dahomey's hinterland, Niger, had already excluded itself from the group. Dahomey would not be contiguous to the other federal territories if Upper Volta, with its key geographic position, was not also a member. Upper Volta's representatives to the Bamako Conference were only observers, and Premier Yameogo was not among them. Like Dahomey, Upper Volta lacked a charismatic national leader, and its many competing political figures considered the prospects of federation in terms of its economic effects as well as in terms of their political interests. The Bamako Conference prepared the way for a federal constituent assembly meeting in mid-January 1959 in Dakar, at which a federal constitution was unanimously accepted. It provided for a Federation of Mali, made up of the four West African republics and with autonomous status within the Franco-African Community. Before the end of the month, the constitution was adopted by constituent assemblies in Senegal, Soudan, and Upper Volta.[24]

Only one of the two reasons for regional alliances was shared by the Ivory Coast leadership: the desire to avoid isolation. Houphouet-Boigny's antifederalist stand had left him in danger of opposing all formal governmental alliances and relying simply on RDA organization ties. But these ties had shown themselves to be outmoded and fragile in the face of the Mali Federation; Soudan and Upper Volta were following their own path, as Guinea had already done. At the risk of inconsistency, therefore, Houphouet-Boigny had announced as early as October 1958 that he was considering the formation of a loose, nonpolitical, economic-cooperation formula for the autonomous states of West Africa, including a customs union and a solidarity fund.[25] After a period of hesitation in early 1959, during which he observed the progress of the Federation, he set about to turn his RDA alliance of political organizations into a structure for economic cooperation among states. The third PDCI congress, in mid-March, had the appearance of an interterritorial RDA meeting at which federalists and antifederalists presented their various points of view. Houphouet-Boigny again referred to his idea of a "Council of Union."

The first open defection from the Mali alliance was Upper Volta, whose constituent assembly, exactly a month after it had unanimously accepted the Mali constitution, by a bare majority adopted a constitution disassociating the Voltaic Republic from the Federation. Citing economic arguments, Premier

Yameogo declared that his country had revised its stand on the Federation because "it did not want to choose between Dakar and Abidjan." After a referendum approving the constitution and new general elections giving most of the assembly seats to the antifederalist wing of the local RDA section, Yameogo's strengthened government signed bilateral agreements on April 4, 1959, setting up a Council of the Entente with Ivory Coast. Upper Volta had chosen Abidjan. Three days later, its contiguity with Ivory Coast established, Niger followed suit. The new "anti-Federation" thus established was a flexible organization which provided for economic harmonization, political consultation, and a Solidarity Fund through which Ivory Coast could aid the poorer members.

In Dahomey Premier Apithy too had found himself opposed to the political exclusiveness and economic rigidity of the Mali Federation, which, he felt, was contrary to his federalist views and to the economic welfare and sovereignty of his country. His stand was supported, not by his own party or by the majority of the Dahomeyan assembly, but by the UDD, the local section of the RDA. At the end of January Apithy resigned from the Dahomeyan section of the PRA and reconstituted his old Dahomeyan Republican party (PRD) in opposition to the Mali Federation. When new elections were held in early April to choose the assembly and government that would decide on membership in the Mali Federation, the results were almost identical with those of 1957, for the country was gerrymandered into political fiefs. However, the UDD (RDA), which had received more votes than the winning PRD but less than a third the number of its assembly seats, claimed that the new government was illegal, demanded new elections, and occupied parts of the country to enforce its protests. Houphouet-Boigny sent in RDA Premier Diori from Niger to mediate the dispute; when that failed, he negotiated personally with Apithy's representative in Abidjan. As a result, new elections were held in late April on the basis of a predetermined PRD-UDD apportionment. The outcome, however, was a three-party deadlock, with the UDD (RDA) now refusing the good offices of Houphouet-Boigny's envoys. The party also rejected Apithy and turned instead to the leader of the third Dahomeyan party, the Dahomeyan Democratic Rally (RDD), Hubert Maga, who was finally chosen premier in mid-May. Maga had not been party to the May negotiations among Ivory Coast, Niger, and Upper Volta and had to be convinced of Dahomey's economic interest in the Entente. On May 29, 1959, Dahomey signed a multilateral agreement with the other three members of the Entente, and in October of the following year, the RDD asked to join the interterritorial RDA party alliance.

When the legislative assembly of the Mali Federation met in Dakar on April 4, 1959, only Senegal and Soudan were represented. Modibo Keita of Soudan was chosen to head the federal government, while Senghor was elected president of the assembly and of the new federal party. To avoid a deadlock between the separate political organizations of the two states, a conference had been held in Dakar at the end of March to create a combined

African Federalist Party (PFA). In addition to its Soudanese and Senegalese
sections, the PFA also included associated organizations outside the Federation: Sawaba in Niger, the PRA remnant in Dahomey, the leftwing RDA federalists and later a new National Voltaic Party (PNV) in Upper Volta, and a
new National Union Party (UNM) of the southern (Senegalese-affiliated)
population in Mauritania.[26] The *renversement des alliances* was thus complete; Senegal and Soudan, united in the Mali Federation, had a cautious
ally in Mauritania and weak movements to support in three other states.
Once the institutions of the new regional-unity organization were in place on
both the territorial and the political levels, the leaders of the Federation could
once more turn their attention to the demand for independence.

The Malian request for independence was not accepted by President de
Gaulle until December. The news caused Houphouet-Boigny again to consider an important policy reversal. The same month, in an Entente meeting
in Niamey, he promised that the four states would not be left behind by the
Malian move, if only they would stick together. Franco-Malian negotiations,
which began in January, ended in April with an agreement for independence
on June 20, 1960. In February, Houphouet-Boigny and Senghor met in
Paris to begin the process of *rapprochement;* the following month, missions
from the two Mali states visited Abidjan. At the end of May, Houphouet-
Boigny himself went to Dakar to declare his hope for "a broad union between Mali and the Council of the Entente"; soon after, he announced that
he would request immediate independence, with agreements with France to
be negotiated only after admission into the United Nations. Thus, on alternate days in the period August 1-7, 1960, Dahomey, Niger, Volta, and Ivory
Coast also attained their independence. The Council of the Entente, meeting
in Abidjan during the Ivory Coast independence celebrations, decided to harmonize the political and economic structures of the four member states and
to establish identical constitutions for each.

Although the Entente was strengthened in August through the achievement
of independence and some reinforcement of unity among its members, the
tensions inherent in the Mali Federation soon brought about its collapse.[27]
These tensions were partly organic: the hastily devised federal constitution
uniting only two states while providing no mediatory institution between
them, and the imbalance between richer, smaller Senegal and poorer, larger
Soudan. But the tensions were also ideological: Soudan, with a well-organized
party section, had announced as early as April 1959 that it favored a strong
unitary federal government. The Soudanese were radicals in economic and
foreign policy, while Senegal was liberalist and favorable to France. There
was also a rivalry between both the personalities and the beliefs of the leaders:
the Soudanese were opposed to Senghor as PFA candidate for federal president in the coming August elections. It was little wonder, then, that when
Federal Premier Keita of Soudan dismissed Defense Minister Mamadou Dia
of Senegal and declared a state of emergency on August 19, 1960, the Senegalese interpreted this as a Soudanese attempt to take over their country. On

August 20, 1960, Senegal declared its independence from the Mali Federation, arrested Keita and the Soudanese ministers, and sent them back to Bamako. On September 22nd, Soudan declared the Federation ended and proclaimed its own independence, adopting the name of Mali. Thus two new states in West Africa achieved their independence, but at the cost of unity, and both were now isolated from any allies.

Houphouet-Boigny's reaction was skillful. Although neither of the formerly federated states could admit the correctness of his predictions and join the Entente, both needed allies. Senegal's need was partially political, and Ivory Coast continued a gradual development of better relations that overlooked the PRA-RDA and Dakar-Abidjan rivalries of the past. Mali's need was economic, and Houphouet-Boigny made an unpublicized visit to Bamako immediately after the rupture to assure Mali of his support, despite the bad blood that the RDA rupture had caused earlier. An Ivory Coast mission and then an exchange of visits by the premiers of the two states in early September completed the negotiation of arrangements whereby Abidjan would replace Dakar as Mali's supply port. The agreement benefited both sides, but it was made with a minimum of offense to Senegal.

The members of the Ghanaian alliance system did not have to contend with problems of independence, but they encountered other basic obstacles to successful unity. Like the defunct Mali Federation, the Guinea-Ghana Union contained only two members. The states were not contiguous (they were separated by Ivory Coast), but the gulf between them was more than geographical: they spoke different languages; their two strong leaders were potential rivals; their levels of modernization and their systems of government were different; and they profoundly misunderstood and sometimes even mistrusted each other. Only their common radical ideology and their similar party structures provided grounds for agreement. The fragility of this agreement was revealed in the Conakry declaration of May 1959, negotiated during Nkrumah's trip to Guinea. The statement of "Basic Principles of the Union of Independent African States" was couched mainly in terms of policy coordination and made no provision for common political institutions.

Talk of union disturbed President Tubman in Monrovia. After the initial Guinea-Ghana announcement of 1958, a Guinean mission had to be dispatched to Liberia to assure Monrovia of Conakry's intentions and to negotiate a counterbalancing treaty of friendship, commerce, and navigation. In response to the 1959 Conakry declaration, Tubman called a conference of the heads of the three independent West African states to clarify the problem of unity. (Another stimulus to a West African meeting was the impending French atomic test in the Sahara, announced in early July 1959.) The resulting Sanniquellie meeting of mid-July dashed Nkrumah's hopes for concrete measures of union; a ten-point declaration proposed a Community of Independent African States similar to the union of the Conakry declaration, with no political institutions, and with national identity, constitutional structure, and future policies and relations specifically excluded from unification.[28]

The community idea, according to which all African states would simply seek friendly and harmonious relations among themselves, was Tubman's view of African unity. It had been reflected in his emphasis on mutually beneficial economic ties with Guinea, and it was in sharp opposition to Ghana's drive for leadership of African political unity. Nkrumah felt that he had been betrayed by his ally, Touré, but he did agree to place the declaration before a proposed Special Conference of Independent African States.

Despite the weaknesses of their union, Ghana and Guinea continued to cooperate in spreading independence during the following months. Like Ghana, Guinea also carried on its West African policy at two levels. Groups such as the National Committee for the Liberation of Ivory Coast, the Study Group for the Questions of Benin and the Committee of Dahomeyans in Guinea carried out political warfare and open pressure against the Entente states from Guinean sanctuary. To an increasing extent, however, Guinea also developed conventional diplomatic influence in neighboring states through visits and agreements. In May 1960, Tubman came to Conakry to strengthen frontier and economic agreements, and in July Touré went to Accra and Lomé to confer on unity and economic cooperation. As independence spread throughout West Africa in 1960, Guinea's diplomatic contacts increased and the causes for bad relations with other states in the region fell away. In Abidjan on the way home from Accra, Touré even suggested that he would be willing to meet Houphouet-Boigny. A rapid return visit by an Ivory Coast minister prepared the way for a border meeting between the two former RDA leaders in September. Guinea, however, was not ready to go further by shifting alliances and renouncing its radical ideology.

The same duality of methods continued to characterize Ghanaian policy. Surrounded by states that were not independent until mid-1960, and thereafter by governments that were suspicious if not hostile, Ghana's radical regime saw itself the focus of a colonialist and then neocolonialist encirclement that aggravated its sense of isolation. Between the Ivory Coast elections of April 1959 and Houphouet-Boigny's public warning to Nkrumah in January 1960 to cease intervention in neighbors' affairs, Ghana armed and aided the dissident Sanwi movement in southeast Ivory Coast. Beginning in October 1959 and continuing after Togolese independence on April 27th, Ghana accelerated its campaign to annex Togo, turning formerly sympathetic Olympio sharply against Nkrumah. A Ghanaian attempt at *rapprochement* with Ivory Coast was coincident with and as limited in scope as Guinea's. After Nkrumah indicated in July that he was ready to meet Houphouet-Boigny, an important Ivory Coast delegation was sent to Accra in August, the two heads of state met briefly on the border in mid-September, and diplomatic relations were opened in October, although the proposed state visit of Houphouet-Boigny to Accra never took place.

The breakup of the Mali Federation in August 1960 had important repercussions on the Guinea-Ghana Union and on the trend of moderation in the two states. Economic assurances from Ivory Coast did not solve the problem of political isolation for the radical regime of the new Mali Republic. In November 1960 in Bamako and again in early December in Siguiri, Touré and Keita met to discuss unity between the two states and with Ghana[29]; on Christmas Eve the heads of the three radical states met in Conakry, where Ghana offered a $11.2 million loan to Mali. A committee was instructed to prepare the accession of Mali to a revised and strengthened Guinea-Ghana Union, and the second meeting of the three heads of state, in Accra at the end of April 1961, ended in the creation of a new radical alliance: the Union of African States. Institutions were to include a political preparatory committee and an economic committee, with the supreme executive organ being quarterly conferences of the heads of state. The significant characteristic of Union—borrowing a page from the RDA and the PRA-PFA experiences—was the provision for a coordination committee for mass organizations (parties, women's groups, trade unions, and youth movements) to develop "a common ideological orientation which is absolutely necessary for the development of the Union." The counter-Entente was expanding, breaking the isolation of Ghana and supporting its ideological bent.

In order to eliminate completely Ghana's isolation and at the same time cut off Ivory Coast from its allies, it was necessary to reverse the ties of alliance held by Upper Volta and join it to the UAS, thus achieving contiguity among the three UAS members. Nkrumah lost no time in putting this strategy into effect, aided by the current dissatisfaction of Volta with the economic arrangements of the Entente.[30] At the end of June, at the frontier town of Paga, Nkrumah and Yameogo knocked down a wall (specially constructed for the purpose) to symbolize the establishment of a customs unions between them. However, neither Guinea nor Volta's neighbor, Mali, took part in this arrangement (there was no customs union between them or with Ghana), and there is much reason to believe that Yameogo was merely using his Ghana agreements to strengthen his hand with Ivory Coast; by August, he had achieved a favorable revision of financial arrangements with Ivory Coast and reaffirmed his solidarity with the Entente. This rebuff to Ghana's efforts to consolidate the UAS was followed by a letdown in the activities of the Union itself. The three heads of state met in late June 1961 in Bamako, but never again within the framework of their alliance. "Mass organizations" were never unified, and the preparatory and economic committees made no progress toward unification. The only effective bond among the three states was their radical ideology, manifest internally in their African Socialist economies and mobilization parties, and externally in their suspicion of continuing European influence. Nevertheless, after four years of foreign-policy maneuvering and reversals, the West African alliance structure had crystalized into two interlocking systems, with Ghana, surrounded by the four Entente states, allied to Guinea and Mali in the UAS. Coastal powers large and small —such as Senegal, Liberia, Togo, and Nigeria—conducted their foreign policy without allies, only with enemies, looking for ties with other West African states but unable to accept or qualify for membership in either of the two alliance systems.

IDEOLOGY AND THE WESTERN AFRICAN ALLIANCE SYSTEM (1960-63)

There are three courses of action open to a foundering alliance: it can be strengthened internally; it can be scrapped; or it can be held together as the core of a new, large ensemble. It has been characteristic of Western African relations that most alliances have never really been tested; as soon as weaknesses have appeared, the alliances have been discarded or replaced by a new, larger model, and only less frequently have they been the subject of concerted efforts internally to overcome the weaknesses. It has also been characteristic, as already noted, that foreign policy has been largely spent in a continual search of allies, allies to avoid much-feared isolation, but a continual search because the alliances were often issue-bound and crisis-racked and their members were often incompatible.

The ideological issue posed by the split in the newly independent Congolese government in 1960 is often considered the cause of the competing alliance systems of West and North Africa during the following three years. Although the Congo question brought the ideological division between the two African groups to a head, the roots of the two groups antedate Congolese independence and reach back into the earlier alliances of West Africa. The Sanniquellie conference of July 1959 had made two proposals for future meetings, one on the foreign ministers' level in August to consider recognition of the Algerian provisional government (GPRA) and the other presumably on the heads-of-state level in 1960 to draw up a charter defining *African unity*. Both proposals came from Tubman, who did not want to decide either question alone with the two West African radicals. Yet the special Conference of Independent African States which met in Monrovia in early August 1959 was, for the most part, a prefiguration of the radical African group to be formed two years later. Guinea, Ghana, Morocco, the Algerian GPRA (a full member for the first time), Libya, and Egypt joined Tunisia and Liberia to discuss a number of African problems.[31] The foreign ministers called for active support and recognition of the GPRA, urging France to admit Algeria's right of independence and to withdraw all its troops prior to negotiations. They protested against use of African troops in the French army in Algeria and against French atomic tests in the Sahara, and supported the right of African territories "to autonomy and independence." The conference had no direct follow-up, although in the second All-African People's Conference (AAPC) in Tunis the following January, a recommendation was again made for all African states to recognize the GPRA and to aid in creating an African volunteers corps for Algeria. The AAPC had the effect of impressing Tunisia with its African vocation, as it also impressed Algeria with the force of African solidarity.[32]

In June 1960, as scheduled, the second Conference of Independent African

States was held in Addis Ababa. Its most important characteristic was the list of participating states. In line with the Monrovia decisions, territories with a fixed date for independence were invited; thus Nigeria was eligible to join the independent states, but not the members of the Entente. Ten nationalist movements from South and East Africa attended, and the GPRA was recognized as a full member. Yet the final roster showed a heavy predominance of moderates, most actively represented by Liberia, Nigeria, and Ethiopia, for many of the former French territories were not represented. Only diplomatic and material support—not recognition—of Algeria was recommended, and the major task of the conference—the elaboration of a charter on the basis of an acceptable definition of *African unity*—was not even attempted. Instead of adopting even the moderate Sanniquellie declaration, which Nkrumah advanced, the final resolution put off discussion of political unity until the next Conference of Independent African States (scheduled for Tunis in 1962), as Liberia and Nigeria advocated, and concentrated on economic cooperation, as Ethiopia wished. The conference marked the entrance of Nigeria on the scene of African relations, four months before its independence, and showed the continued moderating effect of Liberia's policy. Had it been postponed for four to six months, so that the majority of the continent could be independent and present, it might have been able to arrive at a definition of *unity* and the creation of an international relations system based on it. On the other hand, the differences in outlook on independence—policy toward Algeria—and unity were already the cause of division and dissatisfaction. Meeting when it did, with the states that participated, the second Conference of Independent African States had little effect on African relations. In August, a special meeting of most of the Addis Ababa participants in Leopoldville at the invitation of Congolese Premier Patrice Lumumba arrived at the same ineffectual result.

This characteristic ineffectiveness was recognized by Houphouet-Boigny, one of the Addis Ababa uninvited, who also felt that the sudden increase of African members in the coming United Nations session made a united stand on Algeria imperative. He therefore set about preparing a new African conference, inviting states who could be expected to agree with each other. Beginning with the August 1960 meeting of the Entente, and broadening his consultations to include Senegal and Nigeria, he prepared with care and caution. The meeting was held at the end of October in Abidjan, its participants and its agenda unannounced until its success had been fully assured.[33] It brought all French-speaking states of West Africa except Guinea and Togo (Mali sent an observer) together with the rest of former French Africa. As seen in earlier meetings and as foreseen by Houphouet-Boigny, the attendance foreshadowed the results. The group planned to use its good offices to urge direct negotiations between Algeria and France, as Morocco and Tunisia had attempted earlier; Dia and Diori were immediately sent to Tunis to meet Bourguiba and Abbas, while Senghor and Houphouet-Boigny went to Paris. The meeting also supported Mauritania against Morocco and Kasavubu against Lumumba, and refused to oppose French atomic tests in the Sahara. A second meeting was scheduled for Brazzaville in December 1960. There, the twelve states studied the Congo in detail and reaffirmed their previous stands, strengthening the Algerian resolution to include a demand for immediate cessation of the war and application of the principle of self-determination by 1961. In addition to examining issues, they attacked the problem of unity by empowering a commission to meet in Dakar in January 1961 and study the possibilities of economic cooperation. From these preparations came, in Yaounde in March and in Tananarive in September, the formation of an alliance of moderate, French-speaking African states, the African and Malagasy Union (UAM), supported by organizations for close harmonization in the fields of economy, telecommunications, air transport, and defense: the African and Malagasy Organization for Economic Cooperation (OAMCE), the African and Malagasy Post and Telecommunications Union (UAMPT), Air Afrique, and the African and Malagasy Defense Union (UAMD).

If the foundation of the UAM had results, it also had repercussions. Mali's position of the fringe of the Abidjan meeting and outside the Brazzaville meeting was seized on by Guinea to bring Mali into the Guinea-Ghana Union. The success and strength of the moderates—particularly on the Congolese question—worried the West African radicals, who feared isolation in a minority position. The sudden appearance of a bloc of states resolutely opposed to irredentist claims on Mauritania caused Morocco concern. The absence of support from the new French-speaking African states for the strong Afro-Asian resolution on Algeria in the United Nations disturbed the GPRA, just as the absence of a protest against French atomic tests bothered certain littoral states of the Sahara. Morocco, scarcely a radical state, had an additional reason for uneasiness: the monarchy, which had taken over the cabinet and premiership from the left wing of the Istiqlal in May, felt itself particularly pressed by its internal, progressist opposition. The question of the Congo, therefore, was merely a detonating incident in a critical context that included the search both for allies and for a definition of *unity*, and also a number of narrow, divisive issues on which individual North and West African states wanted support. In December 1960, invitations to attend a nonaligned summit conference at Casablanca were sent out to the non-UAM states and to leading Asian neutrals. Several states from West Africa did not attend. Nigeria, newly independent, was still cautious in its foreign policy; its colonial history and its own federal system did not give it the sense of need for regional alliances that the French-speaking states felt, and its internal divisions and its moderate stand on African unity did not permit the missionary drive that impelled Ghana. In North Africa, Tunisia's highly principled foreign policy insisted on recognition of Mauritania's right to self-determination, and, in November, Morocco recalled its ambassador from Tunis over the issue.[34] Of the remaining Western African states, those most active in foreign affairs, being most sensitive to their sudden minority position, came to Casablanca in early January 1961 in search of allies:

Morocco, Algeria (GPRA), Guinea, Ghana, and Mali, plus the United Arab Republic (UAR), a Libyan minister, and a Ceylonese ambassador.

As at Abidjan, the attendance foreshadowed the results.[35] In addition to mutual assistance on the individual national issues (not acquired without tempering some members' positions), the conference gave its support to Lumumba, declared the participants' intention of withdrawing their troops from the United Nations Operational Command in the Congo, and proclaimed its ideas of African unity in the Casablanca charter. The charter set up a political committee of heads of states or their representatives meeting periodically, an economic and a cultural committee, a joint African high command, and a permanent secretariat, and, like the earlier Tangier conference, looked to the creation of a consultative assembly. Not only were some of the most dynamic states of Western Africa present, but, had the Algerian political unit—the GPRA—also controlled the territorial unit—Algeria—the Casablanca Group would have stretched in a solid band from the Mediterranean to the Gulf of Guinea, with only Ghana and Egypt noncontiguous. Unlike the Abidjan and Brazzaville meetings, however, the Casablanca Conference was hastily thrown together, and its participants had little in common to make it last.

As long as Congo and Algeria were issues on the agenda, they overshadowed unity and kept the states of Western Africa divided into rival groups. But the years following the establishment of the two competing alliance systems were also filled with numerous small incidents between individual members which helped to maintain the ideological split. Some of these disputes were ground out of old mills. The Senegal-Mali rupture, hardened by the Malians' deep sense of hurt pride, provided material for some of the most acrid exchanges between West African neighbors; the Dakar-Niger railroad, Bamako's lifeline, rusted in idleness. Competition between Ghana and Ivory Coast over Upper Volta's loyalties lasted throughout much of 1961 and caused a temporary breakdown of Entente cooperation during that year. The most serious dispute concerned Moroccan irredentist claims on Mauritania. In West Africa, the National Council of the Mauritanian Resistance, headed by ould Babana in Rabat, organized its supporters to operate from Malian territory, after tribal disputes in the frontier region had produced raids on Mali at the end of 1960.

In Morocco, the death of Mohammed V in February 1961 and the ascension of Hassan II brought a moment of reflection to Moroccan policy-makers. The new king realized that Moroccan policy had painted itself into a corner and that isolation threatened as a result. In June 1961, acting under the good offices of Premier Dia of Senegal, the Moroccan ambassador at Dakar presented President ould Daddah with a proposal for a heads-of-state meeting to establish a "fraternal union" between two sovereign states. Ould Daddah, strengthened by UAM support, insisted on prior recognition of Mauritanian independence, and was further vindicated, in the fall, by admission to the United Nations. Morocco was now in an embarrassing position; the king was committed before his domestic supporters to pursue the issue, while the Moroccan opposition castigated the government for fighting a battle it had already lost when other problems pressed. In North Africa, the Mauritanian issue kept Moroccan and Tunisian diplomatic relations suspended until mid-1964. Bourguiba and Abbas met amicably with Hassan II during Mohammed's funeral in March, and Algerian aid and Moroccan support were offered to Tunis during the Bizerte crisis in July; the North African summit meeting foreseen in the heat of the Bizerte summer took place in January 1962 in Rabat, but only Hassan II and Abbas' successor, GPRA president Benyussef ben Khedda, were present. The conference created an interministerial commission of the Arab Maghreb with three Algerian members and four Moroccans to work for the creation of North African unity, reserving outstanding problems for diplomatic settlement after Algerian independence. But the commission, like the Tangier Secretariat and the UAS quarterly conference, did not last beyond the year of its birth.

The paradox of the Casablanca-Brazzaville split was that both groups, originally created to discuss African issues, claimed to be representative of all Africa and attempted to define the content of African unity. Their separation was to some extent a reflection of their ideological makeup, but it was also the consequence of continental issues and local incidents which kept individual members apart and committed their allies with them.[36]

These four elements—general ideology, search for African unity, Congolese and Algerian problems, and local incidents—were both contradictory and complementary in their effects, for they provided both reasons for the alliances and strains within them. Against these strains, there was a natural attempt to strengthen the alliances, again either by internal consolidation or by enclosing the original alliance within a new, larger ensemble. Once the African alliance system had left its purely West African phase and had expanded to North Africa and beyond, both means of preservation began to be employed.

As the Brazzaville meeting led to the Casablanca conference, so the latter led to a counterattempt to enlarge the moderate alliance.[37] Such states as Liberia, Sierra Leone, Togo, and Nigeria sought to avoid isolation, but did not feel at home among the radicals of Casablanca or the Gaullist Frenchspeakers of Brazzaville. Immediately after the Casablanca conference, Tubman discussed with Touré and Keita his idea of acting as host for a truly Pan-African summit. Senghor paid personal calls to Monrovia, Lagos, and Accra, urging that a conference be called by the unallied states to discuss a common African policy for Congo. Houphouet-Boigny prepared for the meeting within the Entente and the UAM. Nigeria's Tafawa Balewa, in March 1961, also called for an African summit conference, proposing Liberia, Nigeria, Mali, and Ivory Coast as inviting powers. There was no intention of creating a new group; rather, it was hoped that a Pan-African summit of all states and alliances could be arranged. In an effort to be ecumenical, the inviting group was enlarged to seven sponsoring states: Ivory Coast and Cameroun from the UAM, Guinea and Mali from the Casablanca Group, and

Nigeria and Togo, plus Liberia (the host), from the unallied countries. All states but Congo and Algeria, the subjects of discussion, were invited. Ghanaian pressure at the last moment, however, forced out the new UAS allies at the charter meeting of the alliance in late April; Morocco stayed away because of Mauritania's presence; and the Casablanca Group, protesting the exclusion of Algeria, also demanded a postponement of the meeting until a proposed protocol to the Casablanca charter could be drawn up, to serve as a basis of discussion. The states that attended the founding meeting of the Monrovia Group in early May 1961 thus included all the non-Casablanca Group states of Western Africa, plus the other members of the UAM, and Libya, Ethiopia, and Somalia. In line with the procedure already put forward by Houphouet-Boigny at the Abidjan and Brazzaville meetings, the conference limited itself to basic principles but scheduled a second meeting in Lagos to work out concrete details of an African unity charter, hoping for larger attendance at that meeting. The principles, however, included one of the ideas of Bandung—noninterference in internal affairs—in response to the continuing use of conspiracy and subversion; a commission to facilitate the peaceful settlement of disputes was also proposed. The resolution on Algeria was moderate, calling for early Algerian independence through negotiations. The resolution on the Congo deplored assassination as a means to attain political power (referring to Lumumba's murder), but also castigated subversion of one African state by another. In accordance with Monrovia decisions, a conference of experts met in Dakar in mid-July to elaborate technical details of cooperation.

As expected, the Casablanca Group's reaction took the form of a series of meetings to consolidate the alliance. The foreign ministers of the member states met in Cairo in the days preceding the Monrovia meeting. The protocol adopted developed the Casablanca charter in some detail, establishing the secretariat at Bamako under a Moroccan secretary-general; an accompanying statement gave "absolute" support to the GPRA, particularly in the matter of territorial integrity, and also to Antoine Gizenga, Lumumba's successor in the Congo. A schedule for future committee meetings was established. The economic committee met as scheduled in July 1961 in Conakry, where a hasty but detailed plan for an African common market was proposed by the Moroccan delegate, to go into effect on January 1, 1962. Unable to expand its membership, the radical group sought rapidly to reinforce its structure.

The Monrovia Group quietly continued its attempts to reinforce and expand the alliance. Tafawa Balewa went to Guinea and planned a later trip to Morocco, in an effort to bridge the gap between the blocs. Houphouet-Boigny visited Mali, and ould Daddah traveled to Accra. All independent African states were invited to a new meeting in Lagos. The GPRA, however, was again omitted, on the ground that an invitation to Algeria would open a Pandora's box of all insurgent movements throughout the continent; a resolution of the subsequent conference, strongly advocated by the majority Brazzaville Group, called for complete Algerian independence but indicated that Algeria would not be invited to any Monrovia Group meeting until it had attained sovereignty. Despite the furious battle of criticism waged by Ghana's press against the Monrovia meeting and the counterattack launched by Nigeria's press against Nkrumah's pretentions to African Messianism, Ghana announced that it would attend, and the rest of the Casablanca Group with it. When an informal meeting of foreign ministers caucussed in Lagos prior to the meeting, however, it was unable to satisfy the Arab states' demands (presented by Morocco, Tunisia, Libya, and Sudan) that Algeria be invited, without reversing the firm stand of the UAM states. First Sudan, then Tunisia and Libya, withdrew from the meeting, and the Casablanca Group members, waiting in Accra, also refused to join for the same reason. Attendance at Lagos was therefore limited to Black Africa, although the number of participants remained twenty (Tanganyika and Congo replacing Tunisia and Libya).

The business of the Lagos conference of January 1962 was as important as the attendance. Sixteen proposals were submitted from the Dakar experts' conference, and an African charter was presented by Liberia, with provisions similar to the rival Casablanca charter except for the omission of the supranational institutions such as the proposed African consultative assembly and joint military command (but including a less rigid and more realistic African common market). In keeping with the spirit of careful preparation that characterized the formation of the Group, participants decided to take home the proposal for study. In the meantime, another effort could be made to bring the rest of Africa into the deliberations. The charter was discussed by the UAM at its meeting at Bangui in late March; small changes were made, and accepted at the Libreville meeting in mid-September. Meanwhile, all the Monrovia Group's foreign ministers met again in Lagos in early June, approved the charter, and passed it on to the heads of state.[38] In mid-December, the twenty Lagos participants met again in the Nigerian capital, still unable to augment their numbers, and decided to call a subsequent meeting in Addis Ababa for final signature.

With no possibility of extending its membership and with rising difficulties in strengthening its structure, the Casablanca Group was experiencing troubles.[39] Its heads-of-state conference of mid-June 1962 met in Cairo without Nkrumah and without an agenda; for the most part, it reaffirmed decisions already made, except to further postpone the opening date for the common market to January 1, 1963. One important decision was made, however; Touré, who came with a renewed proposal for a continental conference, was authorized to sound out African leaders on the prospects of such a meeting. When Foreign Minister Adjei brought the results of the Cairo meeting back to Ghana, Nkrumah called for a preparatory meeting of African foreign ministers at Addis Ababa and set about drawing up a comprehensive plan for an African political union, which was then circulated to all heads of state.[40] In the meantime, Touré proposed a committee of seven, cutting across ideological differences, to prepare the African summit. Guinea, Ghana, and Mali all sent extensive missions throughout the continent between mid-1962 and early 1963.

A third series of preparations for an All-African meeting was also taking place. The only Western African state outside both the Brazzaville and the Casablanca Groups, Tunisia, had been chosen in 1960 (before the formation of the two alliances) as the site of the third Conference of Independent African States. The meeting was scheduled for April and then postponed to September to avoid the Algerian issue. After it became evident that African states were looking to Addis Ababa instead, an attempt was made in December and in January 1963 to turn the Tunis meeting into a preparatory foreign-ministers' conference. This too became unsatisfactory and the biennial Conference of Independent African States disappeared as an institution. Nevertheless, preparatory efforts by Tunisia helped build up pressure for the Addis Ababa summit. The fourth area whose preparations contributed to the African summit was the Maghreb, where Tunisia's role was also important. For the first time, a formal conference of the three states' foreign ministers took place, in mid-February 1963 in Rabat. North African unity and the avoidance of disputes—such as the rupture of relations between Tunis and Algiers the previous December over a plot to assassinate Bourguiba—were discussed.

The Tunisian difficulties in arranging the Conference of Independent African States also clarified problems of preparation for Addis Ababa. The need for a preliminary foreign-ministers' meeting was generally recognized, but so fragile were the summit's chances of success that the preliminary meeting would have to take place immediately before the plenary conference so that no new problems could arise to disturb the atmosphere. The Abidjan and Monrovia approach was agreed to be inapplicable for Addis Ababa; once the heads of state were present, the prestige of the occasion and the expectation of results would be too great simply to end with an agreement to reconvene later and elsewhere. It was also clear, however, that the moment was auspicious for a dissolution of the competing alliances. On one hand, the major problems that had separated the two sides had faded away; Algeria became independent on July 3, 1962, and the Congolese problem was eased by a new government that was neither Gizenga's or Tshombe's. The local issues, too, were less important, and when not combined with the two major problems so easily definable in ideological terms, they tended to lose their weight for others than the parties immediately concerned. Specifically, the visits of Houphouet-Boigny and Senghor to Guinea and of Touré to Senegal, and the signature of an agreement between Mali and Senegal in February 1963 on the disposition of the Mali Federation's assets prepared the way for smoothing over the feuds among the four neighbors.[41] In fact, the approach of the long-awaited summit seemed to pressure those states with quarrels to reconcile themselves before coming to the meeting.

Despite the careful preparations, an issue did arise between 1962 and the

Addis Ababa conference. In the current context, however, it was of a nature to favor the breakdown of old alliances without catalyzing the formation of new ideological splits—hence to aid, rather than obstruct, the success of the conference. On January 13th, President Olympio of Togo was assassinated under circumstances which gave initial credence to rumors (never proven) of Ghanaian interference. Except in Senegal, the reaction of the UAM, which all during the past year had insisted on noninterference in internal affairs, was violent and dominated the Ouagadougou meeting in March, but the most serious outburst came from Guinea. The incident kept Togo away from the final summit conference, but it also isolated Ghana, so weakening its position that it could no longer pose a threat of predominance over the meeting, and it caused the final breakup of the Casablanca Group. To the latter effect, other causes also contributed; Morocco's insistence on its Mauritanian policy isolated it too and finally brought about its absence from Addis Ababa, while Algeria's independence cooled its interest in the Casablanca Group, which for the FLN had been above all a source of support during its struggle for independence. Guinea and Mali lost interest in the Group when the possibility of a universal summit appeared. The UAM, meeting at Ougadougou, prepared to go to Addis Ababa as a group. The meeting of the Casablanca Group's political committee was postponed from December 1962 but vigorous efforts by the secretary-general, Thami Wezzani, finally gathered agreement for a date in early May. At the last minute, ben Bella, meeting with Nasser, declined to attend a final Casablanca meeting, and the Casablanca Group collapsed. The Brazzaville-Monrovia Group had the good sense not to gloat, and in fact the members of both alliances could claim a large hand in paving the road to the summit.

REGIONAL RELATIONS WITHIN THE OAU (1963-65)

The Addis Ababa summit meeting of May 22-26, 1963, marked a turning point in the foreign policies of Western Africa, as of the entire continent. Previous ideological differences by no means disappeared, but they were submerged in the combined atmosphere of euphoria and seriousness that reigned at the meeting. When they appeared later, they were contained within the institution set up at the conference, the Organization of African Unity (OAU), and were subject to a number of ground rules for keeping intra-African disputes on a manageable level.[42] These rules all reflected the dominant position of the moderates, solidly organized in the UAM alliance and its Monrovian outgrowth. They included notably a declaration against subversion, political assassination, and interference in internal affairs, taken from the Lagos charter, and provision for an arbitration commission for the peaceful settlement of disputes, along the lines of a detailed Tunisian proposal. In exchange for the predominance of moderate theses on intra-African relations, the radicals obtained greater attention to the problems of colonial Africa, particularly the Portuguese territories and South Africa. A Liberation Coordination Committee of nine—Guinea, Algeria, Senegal, Nigeria, Tanganyika, Uganda,

Congo, Ethiopia, and the UAR—was established to administer aid to anti-colonial liberation movements. In this exchange, the Ghanaian federalist thesis of African unity was left by the wayside. The OAU was established on the basis of an Ethiopian draft, along lines drawn from both the Casablanca and Monrovia charters, and it included an annual summit meeting, a council of foreign ministers, a secretariat, and a number of special commissions. Liberia, Nigeria, and Ethiopia were most active in drawing up the charter, and the definition of *unity*—solidarity and cooperation among sovereign and equal states—vindicated the ideas consistently expressed by Western Africa's oldest independent state since Tubman's first meetings with Touré in 1958.

Four elements made for the success and impact of the Addis Ababa meeting. One was the careful preparation, resulting from the efforts of the Casablanca and Monrovia Groups almost from their beginnings and from Tunisia's work toward North African harmony and a third Conference of Independent African States. A foreign-ministers' meeting at Addis Ababa immediately preceding the summit meeting set up an agenda and completed the year of preparations. Another element was the nearly universal attendance, which indicated that the local issues of the past had been relegated to a second level —although by no means resolved—and that the traditional divisions between Black and Arab Africa, between English and French-speaking states, between radicals and moderates, and among rival personalities were not important enough to prevent a common meeting. Furthermore, the impressive attendance imposed on the delegates the need to come to some agreement. In the middle of the conference, when spirits had begun to flag because of an apparent lack of harmony, a speech by Emperor Haile Selassie reminded the heads of state that the foreign press, only too conscious of the failures of past attempts at unity, was scornfully predicting failure again at Addis Ababa. The speech roused the delegates and impressed them with the need for more than formal attendance.

Third, the results of Addis Ababa combined the aims of previous groups, alliances, and organizations, eliminating rivals by absorbing their purposes. Goals of political consultation, economic cooperation, and assistance to independence movements were taken over from the Conference of Independent African States, the Casablanca and Monrovia Groups, and the AAPO. In June, Touré, who called for the abolition of all subgroups, announced the dissolution of the UAS; the collapse of the May meeting of the Casablanca Group brought the end of this alliance. The Entente and the UAM both faded and then changed in nature, and the Monrovia Group dissolved into the OAU.

Finally, the Addis Ababa meeting meant an effective resting place in the search for African unity. Agreement on a specific formula did not destroy the arguments of those states—like Ivory Coast—which wanted no interference by a supranational institution, nor of those—like Ghana—which believed in the creation of a Pan-African federation. But it did establish an initial consensus, and working institutions based on that consensus. Only when these had been tried and tested for several years could it be determined whether or not they were adequate to the needs and wishes of their members and to the changing African situation.

Western African relations immediately put the OAU institutions to the test. Most serious was the outbreak of hostilities between Morocco and Algeria over their undelineated border. Initial military action along a frontier that had been troubled by incidents for several months broke out in early October 1963, and continued despite bilateral negotiations and attempts at mediation by Tunisia, Ethiopia, and the Arab League. Later in the month, on the suggestion of Algeria, the matter was carried before a special quadripartite summit meeting of the OAU at Bamako, where Hassan II, ben Bella, Keita, and Haile Selassie worked out a cease-fire agreement. The Bamako declaration also called for an urgent meeting of the OAU foreign ministers at Addis Ababa in mid-November to create a special arbitration commission. The commission—composed of Mali, Senegal, Ivory Coast, Nigeria, Sudan, Tanganyika, and Ethiopia—met at Abidjan in early December, in Bamako in late January and late April, and in Casablanca and Algiers in May. The "Africanization" of the problem brought several results: it symbolized North Africa's membership in the African world, and showed the greater vitality of the OAU over the Arab League. By giving the new organization of Addis Ababa something to do, the border war both put it to the test and prolonged its life. The OAU succeeded in stopping the war because the rest of Africa was more deeply committed to unity than to either belligerent, and because an armistice fit in with both Morocco's goal (to bring the unsettled border to Algeria's attention) and Algeria's aims (to end the war that it was losing). The OAU did not succeed in establishing the frontier because it was impossible to make a technical decision either on the border or on the "war guilt," and because it still did not have the authority to make a political decision on either matter.

The work of the Liberation Coordination Committee was less effective in Western Africa. Meeting in Dar es-Salaam in late June, the Committee of Nine drew up a report recognizing the government-in-exile of Holden Roberto as the authentic Angolan nationalist movement and requesting a budget of $4.2 million for support of nationalist movements. But no agreement was to be had on recognition of a single movement in Portuguese Guinea, although a subcommittee (Algeria, Guinea, Senegal, Nigeria, and Congo) interviewed representatives of rival Portuguese Guinean groups in Conakry in late July, and recommended the formation of a United Action Front based on the militant African Independence Party (PAIGC). Senegal disagreed and vetoed endorsement of the Conakry-supported PAIGC when the matter came up before the foreign-ministers' conference of the OAU in Dakar in early August. The Committee of Nine had also made the decision to turn over coordination of support to the exiled movements' host countries (in most cases, Congo or Tanganyika), thus giving up most of its functions. This position caused increased dissatisfaction among radical states, culminating in an open attack on the committee in the Ghanaian press—an attack immediately endorsed by Algeria. When the new state of Gambia became the seventeenth independent state in Western Africa in mid-February 1965, it was not as a result of any action by the OAU.

The existence of a continental organization challenged the *raison d'être* of the remaining alliances of Western Africa. The UAM held its first meeting after Addis Ababa in Cotonou in late July, under attack from Touré, who felt that all alliances should give way to the OAU and who preferred to deal individually with the former members of AOF. The results were ambiguous. Togo was admitted as the fourteenth member and Ivory Coast was proposed as a member of the United Nations Security Council, but the UAM office in the United Nations was dissolved in favor of an OAU caucus and the "evolution" of the Group in relation to the OAU was proposed. Most of the smaller members remained dependent on the alliance for security and thus were interested in its continuing existence; a period of reflection was therefore granted before scheduling a new meeting in 1964 in Dakar. The heads of state met in the Senegalese capital in early March, without Houphouet-Boigny and the presidents of Equatorial Africa. Particularly after the initiative provided by the host, Senghor, and the current president of the UAM, Yameogo, the "evolution" was begun: the political organization—UAM—was dissolved as unnecessary, and the institutions for harmonization of economic and communications matters were reconstituted as the African and Malagasy Union for Economic Cooperation (UAMCE). Foreign ministers of the states in the new organization met for the first time in Nouakchott in late April, but the absence of the ministers of the three Entente states and the Centrafrican Republic prevented the final signing of the new charter. Another time of reflection was scheduled before a second meeting in Nouakchott in 1965.

Within the Western African membership of the UAM, old rivalries were also pressing toward new constellations. Most important was the long-standing political and economic competition between Dakar and Abidjan. The Entente fell into somnolence after Addis Ababa. During 1963, plots against the president were discovered in Ivory Coast, the RDA government of Maga was overthrown in Dahomey, and a quarrel broke out between Dahomey and Niger. Entente meetings were held among only Houphouet-Boigny, Diori, and Yameogo in Abidjan in late 1963 and throughout 1964. Ignoring Dahomey and the Entente, Houphouet-Boigny turned to his old RDA allies, and in April 1964 invited Diori, Yameogo, Touré, and Keita to Bouake to discuss means of controlling internal subversion; in September, he brought Diori and Yameogo with him to meet Senghor in Bobo-Dioulasso. In mid-August, on Tubman's suggestion he also met in Monrovia with Touré and Albert Margai (who had succeeded his late brother as premier of Sierra Leone), to study the possibility of a West African free-exchange zone; important ministerial delegations of the four countries met again in the Liberian capital to continue negotiations in mid-February 1965. Senegal too was preoccupied with internal economic and political problems incident to the consolidation of Senghor's new regime, after a confrontation between Senghor's and Dia's followers in December 1962 led to the imprisonment of the premier. But Dakar also moved to restore its commercial and political leadership in West Africa, beginning first with a *rapprochement* with Mali and then by promoting economic cooperation among the four Senegal River states: Senegal, Mali, Guinea, and Mauritania. Senegal's interest in an economic UAM was part of its campaign to make the organization acceptable to Guinea and Mali, and bring them back into cooperation with their former AOF partners. The rivalry between Dakar and Abidjan concerned primarily these two states, which lay between Ivory Coast and Senegal and could serve as markets for both; unfortunately, they could serve as close allies for neither, for their basically radical attitudes clashed with the more moderate outlook of both Senghor and Houphouet-Boigny. Economic rivals but political allies, Senegal and Ivory Coast failed to realign the basic elements of West African affinities and conflicts in 1963 and 1964.

Probably the most important shift in policy on regional cooperation after Addis Ababa concerned the outlook of newly independent Algeria. After coming to power in the fall of 1962, ben Bella followed the patterns of sympathy formed during his stay in Cairo (before his capture by the French), and turned to developing a close relationship with the Arab Middle East and especially with Nasser's Egypt. Missions to Cairo by Khider, Defense Minister Haouri Boumedienne, and Foreign Minister Mohammed Khemisti in late 1962, however, brought back disappointing impressions. Nasser's visit to Algiers in May 1963 was a festive occasion and Egypt aided Algeria in time of need, notably during the Algero-Moroccan war, but ben Bella looked elsewhere for a primary field of action. His experience at Addis Ababa, selected African support for the FLN during the Algerian war, and the apparent opportunities for action and Algerian leadership in Africa—all combined to turn his attention to his own continent. Disappointment was not long in appearing. The Liberation Coordination Committee temporized, the OAU in general was dominated by the moderates, and the African states proved little susceptible to Algerian leadership. If Addis Ababa marked a turning toward Africa by Algeria, the Dakar meeting of the OAU foreign ministers in August, at which ben Bella (then Algeria's foreign minister) could observe for himself the bickering and indecision, was the beginning of a turning away. More promising were possibilities of North African cooperation, despite the border war with Morocco. Algeria perceived that unity was more meaningful and more likely through a functionalist (or economic) approach than through a federalist (or political) one. The economic agreements concluded with Tunisia in September and November 1963 were the first result of bettered relations with one neighbor. They were followed by the meeting of ben Bella, Bourguiba, and Nasser at the celebrations over the French evacuation of Bizerte in mid-December. Hassan II stayed away in protest over the border affair, and although this conflict slowly lost fire, relations were kept strained by the infiltration of armed bands from Algeria into Morocco. Nevertheless, Algeria used new opportunities, such as the problem of relations with the European Common Market, to move toward greater economic cooperation with its two neighbors. In late November, Morocco, Algeria, Tunisia, and Libya met in

Rabat and Tangier to try a new approach to Maghreb unity. Using the OAMCE as a model, the four states planned their unity on economic lines, creating a permanent consultative committee of economic ministers and a center for industrial studies.

Many of Western Africa's problems found a fitting denouement in the second OAU summit held in mid-July 1964 in Cairo. As had become customary at such meetings, the occasion was used for the reconciliation of bickering states. Bourguiba brought together Hassan II and ben Bella. (It was not until ten months later, however, that the two heads of state finally met on their own soil, in the Moroccan town of Saidia, and that ben Bella at last agreed to study the frontier issue.) Hassan's presence at the conference, in alphabetical order next to Mauritania, marked a noticeable relaxation of Moroccan irredentist pressures, and permitted the two delegations to agree on the cessation of radio propaganda.

On the other hand, the 1963 Togo incident had its parallel in 1964, when Congo's new premier, Moise Tshombé, was banned from attending. Unfinished business at Cairo consisted mainly of strengthening and completing the original structure of the Addis Ababa organization problems which the foreign ministers had not tackled at Lagos and Addis Ababa and had not solved at Dakar and Cairo. A resolution specifying the legitimacy of colonial frontiers was introduced by Touré and passed, and a renewed plea for immediate political unity by Nkrumah was turned into a weaker resolution recommending study of the Pan-Africanist approach. Agreement was finally reached on three matters: the site of a permanent seat (Addis Ababa in preference to Dakar or Lagos), the choice of a permanent secretary-general (Guinean Telli Diallo in preference to the UAM candidate, Émile Zinsou) with four assistants (from Nigeria, Algeria, Dahomey, and Kenya), and the location of the third heads-of-state meeting (Accra, in September 1965). A potential item of unfinished business that received little attention was the matter of the undissolved regional units. Partly because their value was recognized, partly because there was increased interest in new regional groupings, and partly as an antidote to Nkrumah's insistence on continental political unification, organizations of regional cooperation were spared from attack.

Despite the reconciliations and the progress achieved at Cairo, one dispute —Congo—continued to worsen. The national government of Tshombé, facing widespread dissidence from the Congolese Liberation Movement (MLC), turned to mercenaries for support when an appeal for troops addressed to other African governments (including Nigeria and Liberia) was rejected; the MLC rebels, in turn, benefited from military and diplomatic aid from Algeria, Ghana, Guinea, Mali, and others. The issue at stake involved more than a simple personality or government; it was a clash between two basic ideological concepts. One claimed the right to interfere in the internal affairs of another state in the name of a higher value, "Africanity," and saw in Congo an overt colonial threat against the entire continent; the other rejected subversion and interference in the affairs of a sovereign state and viewed the African system as a concert of states designed to defend the new independence from any threat. Broadly, the argument between unity (orthodoxy) and independence (sovereignty), or between the revolutionary and conventional policies, had broken out again over Congo.

The effects were evident in a number of policy changes. For Ghana, there was a return to the tools of subversion (after it had apparently suspended their use upon appeals in the OAU). For Algeria, there arose a new opportunity for leadership in Africa, which was added to continued policies of cooperation in the Maghreb; this basic orientation was not changed by the military coup of June, 1965, that replaced ben Bella with his former vice-president, Col. Haouri Boumedienne. For the Entente, the need to tighten cooperation became evident, and active efforts were made to solve the Dahomey-Niger dispute by recalling Dahomey to the fold instead of merely giving support to Niger; in a meeting of the Entente states in mid-January, Ahomadegbe met with the delegates of the other three states and the alliance was complete for the first time in over a year. Houphouet-Boigny proposed common citizenship and increased cooperation (although they were not implemented before the target date of July 1965) and overtures on membership were favorably greeted by Togo, which was also undergoing a period of tense relations with Ghana.

The most significant changes concerned the UAMCE. When the heads of member states met in Nouakchott in mid-February to sign the new organization's treaty, they were confronted with a strong group of Entente allies who had returned to play their original role of a core group in the larger organization and who were now convinced by the weakness of the OAU and the upsurge of radical, subversive activity in Africa that a political bloc of moderates was necessary. The UAMCE was scrapped before it was inaugurated, and in its place was established an Afro-Malagasy Common Organization (OCAM) "to strengthen cooperation and solidarity . . . in order to speed up political, economic, social, technical, and cultural development." The same final communiqué condemned Ghanaian subversion by name and supported the legal government of Tshombé in Congo. Immediately after Nouakchott, the moderate group went to Nairobi for the OAU foreign ministers' meeting. There their number was large enough to block any radical proposal for official support to the rebels, although not quite enough (largely because of absences) to push through full approval of Tshombé. Instead, they used OCAM for the purpose, admitting Congo to membership at a meeting held in Abidjan in May (total membership remained the same, however, because Mauritania withdrew in disagreement with both the fact and the manner of Congo's joining).

In 1965, the new states of Western Africa were beginning a second distinct stage in their developing relations. By its universality and its modest charter, the OAU created at Addis Ababa embodied a temporarily satisfying definition and institutionalization of the elusive unity slogan, while at least outwardly legitimizing and consolidating the independence of the participants. Western Africa had become part of a continental system of international relations, of which it was the initiator. The frantic search for alliances to overcome isolation was temporarily arrested as the states digested their newly found unity. By 1965—as at the 1960-61 midpoint of the previous stage—the unity idea was again torn by ideological differences triggered by an outside event. Instead of looking for unity as the highest goal, radicals and moderates —split on the new Congo question—looked for unity on their own terms and were unanimous only in deploring the ineffectiveness of the OAU. Unlike 1960-61, however, the second year of the OAU did not see the formation of rival groups. Toward the end of the year, the three major conferences to which Western Africa was host—the Arab League meeting in Casablanca in September; the Afro-Asian or "second Bandung" conference in Algiers, postponed from June to November and then *sine die;* the third OAU summit in Accra, postponed from September to October—all had notable defections and meager results. The development of intra-African relations by 1965 showed also the durability of the inchoate, artificial, colonial-inherited state. This durability was not inherent, for much of the leaders' foreign effort (and a good part of their domestic activities) was required to shore up their new creation. But at least the states lasted, creating their own legitimizing mythology, while regional or continental unification faltered, despite a mythology already established.

NOTES

[1] Where not specifically attributed, historical events are taken from the following newspapers and periodicals: *New York Times, West Africa* (London), *Le Monde* (Paris), *Africa Report* (Washington), *Al-Istiqlal* (Rabat), *La Nation Africaine* (Rabat), *Petit Marocain* (Rabat), *L'Avant-Garde* (Casablanca), *Révolution Africaine* (Algiers), *El-Moudjahid* (Algiers), *Jeune Afrique* (Tunis,), *Mauritanie Nouvelle* (Nouakchott), *L'Unité Africaine* (Dakar), *Agence France Presse-Guinée* [AFP-G] (Conakry), *Horoya* (Conakry), *Essor* (Bamako), *Agence France Presse-Côte d'Ivoire* [AFP-CI] (Abidjan, *Abidjan Matin, Fraternité* (Abidjan), *Ghana Times* (Accra), *Daily Ghanaian* (Accra).

[2] For Moroccan and Tunisian preindependence diplomacy, see Charles-André Julien, *L'Afrique du nord en marche* (Paris: Juillard, 1952); Robert Rezette, *Les partis politiques marocains* (Paris: Colin, 1955); Allal al-Fassi, *The Independence Movements of North Africa* (Washington, D.C.: American Council of Learned Societies, 1954); Lorna Hahn, *North Africa: Nationalism to Nationhood* (Washington, D.C.: Public Affairs Press, 1960); Roger LeTourneau, *Évolution politique de l'Afrique du Nord musulmane 1920-1961* (Paris: Colin, 1962); Stéphane Bernard, *Le Conflit franco-marocain 1943-1956* (Brussels: Editions de l'Institut de Sociologie, 1963), 3 vols.

[3] *Petit Marocain,* April 25, 1956. The same feelings were repeated by former ALM members revolting in the Rif in 1958-59, and even later Mehdi ben Barka of the activist wing of the Istiqlal suggested that Morocco should not even have accepted independence without that of Algeria; "The Unity of the Maghreb," *Africa South in Exile* (London), V, 2 (January-March 1961), 99-100. For an amplification of these foreign-policy schools

in North Africa, see I. William Zartman, "Foreign Policy Since Independence," in L. Carl Brown (ed.), *State and Society in Independent North Africa* (Washington, D.C.: Middle East Institute, 1965).

⁴ At the time of the kidnapping of ben Bella, a French army unit penetrated into Tunisia as far as Beja—halfway from the Algerian border to Tunis; *New York Times*, October 26, 1956.

⁵ See the platform of the Soummam Congress of August 20, 1956, in *El-Moudjahid* (clandestine), (November 4, 1956), also reprinted in André Mandouze, *La Révolution algérienne par les textes*, 3rd ed. (Paris: Maspéro, 1962), p. 82. On FLN diplomacy, a subject still much in need of research and analysis, see Serge Bromberger, *Les Rebelles algériens* (Paris: Plon, 1958); Jacques C. Duchemin, *Histoire du FLN* (Paris: La Table Ronde, 1962); Michael K. Clark, *Algeria in Turmoil* (New York: Grosset, 1960); Friedrich-Wilhelm Fernau, *Arabischer Westen* (Stuttgart: Schwab, 1959), pp. 127-54, 165-75.

⁶ Al-Fassi, *Le Monde*, April 10, 1956; Bouabid, *Al-Istiqlal*, May 11, 1956.

⁷ See *Maghreb arabe uni* (Rabat: Presidency of the Council, 1958). The Tunisian account is less complete; *La Conférence de l'unité* (Tunis: Secretariat of State for Information, 1958).

⁸ A good exposition of this point is found in Bernard, *op. cit.*, I, 263, 311, 339-40, 379, 384; II, 110-11, 271.

⁹ The political history of this period is found in Ruth Schachter Morgenthau, *Political Parties in French-Speaking Africa* (New York: Oxford U.P., 1964); James S. Coleman and Carl G. Rosberg, Jr. (eds.), *Political Parties and National Integration in Tropical Africa* (Berkeley: U. of California, 1964); William J. Foltz, *From French West Africa to the Mali Federation* (New Haven: Yale U.P., 1965); Thomas Hodgkin, *African Political Parties* (Baltimore: Penguin, 1961); Gil Dugué, *Vers les États-Unis d'Afrique* (Dakar: Lettres Africaines, 1960); Ernest Milcent, *L'AOF entre en scène* (Paris: Temoignage Chrétien, 1958); André Blanchet, *L'Itinéraire des partis africains depuis Bamako* (Paris: Plon, 1958); Aristide Zolberg, *One-Party Government in the Ivory Coast* (Princeton, N.J.: Princeton U.P., 1964); Michael Crowder, "Independence as a Goal in French West African Politics," in William H. Lewis (ed.), *French-Speaking Africa: The Search for Identity* (New York: Walker, 1965); *La Semaine en AOF* and *La Semaine en Afrique Occidentale* (Dakar: High Commission), 62 weekly issues ending April 6, 1959.

¹⁰ On Senegal and its rather unique divisions, see Michael Crowder, *Senegal: A Study in French Assimilation Policy* (New York: Oxford U.P., 1962).

¹¹ On Mauritania, see Alfred G. Gerteiny, *The African Hyphen, or Mauritania's Destiny* (New York: Praeger, 1966).

¹² The best account of Voltaic politics, with a special ethnic focus, is Elliot P. Skinner, *The Mossis of Upper Volta* (Stanford: Stanford U.P., 1964). No study has yet been made of the modern history of Niger.

¹³ Dahomeyan politics are treated by Virginia Thompson, "Dahomey," in Gwendolen M. Carter, *Five African States* (Ithaca: Cornell U.P., 1963), and Robert Cornevin, *Histoire du Dahomey* (Paris: Beiger-Levrault, 1962).

¹⁴ Kwame Nkrumah, *I Speak of Freedom* (London: Heinemann, 1961), p. 107.

¹⁵ Alex Quaison-Sackey, *Africa Unbound* (New York: Praeger, 1963), pp. 63-64. See also the insightful introduction by A. K. Barden, director of Ghana's Bureau of African Affairs, to *Awakening Africa* (Accra, n.p., n.d. [1962]), which includes records from the conference. South Africa was invited but declined.

¹⁶ See George Padmore, *Pan-Africanism [Or Communism]: The Coming Struggle for Africa* (London: Dennis Dobson, 1956). For the excerpts from the London draft memorandum, see Thomas Hovet, *Africa in the United Nations* (Evanston, Ill.: Northwestern U.P., 1963), pp. 27-28.

¹⁷ The problem of Algerian representation was posed by Tunisia, foreshadowing the coming ideological split on the issue; *Daily Ghanaian*, February 24, 1958. This was the time

of the Sakiet Sidi Yussef incident, which exerted pressure on Tunisian foreign policy. The FLN eventually attended as an observer. On the effect of the Algerian war on AOF, see Blanchet, *op. cit.*, pp. 3, 51-52, 145, 154; Milcent, "Senegal," in Carter (ed.), *African One-Party States* (Ithaca: Cornell U.P., 1962), pp. 103, 137-38.

¹⁸ The numbering of the Pan-African conferences has posed difficulties. Colin Legum, in *Pan-Africanism: A Short Political Guide*, 2nd ed. (New York: Praeger, 1965), considers the London conference of 1900 as the first, whereas Padmore, in *Pan-Africanism . . .* , *op. cit.*, considers the Paris conference of 1919 as the first. The second (third) congress was held in London and Brussels in 1921, the third (fourth) in London and Lisbon in 1923, the fourth (fifth) in New York in 1927, and the fifth (sixth) in Manchester in 1945. A subsequent (sixth or seventh?) congress on a smaller scale took place in Kumasi in 1953; see Philippe Decraene, *Le Pan-africanisme* (Paris: Presses Universitaires de France, 1961 [Que sais-je? Series, No. 847]), pp. 27-28.

¹⁹ For resolutions at this and subsequent conferences through 1964, see Legum, *op. cit.* See also the series of documents on the conference published by the Ghanaian government, 1958, and Barden, *op. cit.*, for speeches and resolutions. See Hovet, *op. cit.*, pp. 79-84, for the work of the United Nations Permanent Machinery. For a good interpretive study of African alliances up to Addis Ababa, see Doudou Thiam, *The Foreign Policy of African States* (New York: Praeger, 1965).

²⁰ On Togolese politics and pre-Independence diplomacy, see James S. Coleman, *Togoland* (New York: Carnegie Endowment for International Peace, 1956 [International Conciliation Series No. 509]), and Robert Cornevin, *Histoire du Togo* (Paris: Beiger-Levrault, 1962).

²¹ On Nigerian politics, see James S. Coleman, *Nigeria: Background to Nationalism* (Berkeley: U. of California, 1958); Michael Crowder, *Short History of Nigeria* (New York: Praeger, 1962); Richard L. Sklar, *Nigerian Political Parties* (Princeton, N.J.: Princeton U.P., 1963); Richard L. Sklar and C. S. Whitaker, Jr., "Nigeria," in Coleman and Rosberg (eds.), *op. cit.*

²² The best account of this process is found in the chapter on Sekou Touré in Jean Lacouture, *Cinq hommes et la France* (Paris: Seuil, 1961).

²³ From interviews with Bakary Djibo and Otto Makkonen.

²⁴ Federalist delegations had been sent in early January to Ivory Coast, Mauritania, Niger, and Togo to persuade their governments to join, without success; Hubert Maga (see below) was one of the delegates to Ivory Coast. *La Semaine en Afrique Occidentale,* January 3, 1959.

²⁵ The original interview was given to *Carrefour* (Paris), October 15, 1958.

²⁶ All the associated, minority parties except the UNM were soon to be charged with subversion. The UNM merged with the ruling PRM (which had an observer delegation at the Dakar PFA conference) after the Federation broke up. In addition, the small Guinea-based National Committee for a Free Ivory Coast also claimed association with the PFA; *La Situation politique en Côte d'Ivoire et l'indépendance nationale* (Conakry: Comité Nationale, 1959).

²⁷ This analysis, and the later section in Chap. III, subscribe to the causes of the breakup as described in Crowder, *Senegal . . . , op. cit.*, pp. 61-62, somewhat more than to the description by Thomas Hodgkin and Ruth Schachter Morgenthau in "Mali," in Coleman and Rosberg (eds.), *op. cit.*, pp. 241-46, particularly in the matters of direct French interference and of differences of opinion over the Algerian war. Hence, this analysis is closer—although not uncritically—to the Senegalese view, given in *Livre blanc sur le coup d'état manqué du 19 au 20 août 1960 et la proclamation de l'indépendance du Senegal* (Dakar: Ministry of Information, 1960), than to the Malian version, given in *Le Mali continue . . .* (Bamako: USRDA, 1960 [Extraordinary Party Congress Record]) and Modibo Keita, *Le Mali en marche* (Bamako: Secretariat of State for Information, 1962). For an insightful analysis on a different level, see Foltz, *op. cit.*

²⁸ A good review of events leading to Sanniquelli is found in Lawrence A. Marinelli,

The New Liberia (New York: Praeger, 1964), pp. 122-29, 187-98. Information has also been gathered from interviews with Fodé Cissé. For a full report of speeches, see *La Première conférence au sommet* (Monrovia: Liberian Information Service, 1959).

[29] Gabriel D'Arboussier had been sent by Senegal to Ghana in mid-September 1960 to secure Ghanaian neutrality in the aftermath of the Federation's breakup, but without success, since Keita had got there a week earlier.

[30] The *rapprochement* was aided by a flurry of diplomatic activity between Upper Volta and the UAS states. Yameogo visited Mali and Ghana and Touré visited Upper Volta in May; Malian and Guinean delegations visited Upper Volta in May and June. Mali claimed that Volta's rejection of military agreements with France made it "acceptable" to the UAS. But no multilateral ties were negotiated to buttress the Accra agreements of May 22nd and the Paga agreement of June 27th.

[31] There is some confusion over the name, officially the Conference of Independent African States even though the meeting was not part of the Accra-Addis(-Tunis) series and the delegations were only on the ministerial level. For proceedings, see Legum, *op. cit.*, pp. 165-69, and *Conference of Independent African States: Speeches* (Monrovia: Liberian Information Service, 1959). Because all other participants had already recognized the GPRA, the recognition resolution was directed against the host, which "continued to study the problem" until June 7, 1960, when de facto recognition was granted. On the various types of recognition, see Mohammed Bedjaoui, *Law and the Algerian Revolution* (Brussels: International Association of Democratic Lawyers, 1961), pp. 114-38.

[32] See *El-Moudjahid*, August 17, 1959.

[33] It appears that invitations went out to all former French African colonies and trusteeship territories; the Senghor–Houphouet-Boigny communiqué on October 9th declared that Touré and Olympio were in agreement in principle, and as late as two days before the conference they were expected to attend. Both leaders would have been ill at ease among the African Gaullists, however; Olympio later explained his refusal by the non-invitation of Morocco and Tunisia, whose absence, he feared, would make a discussion on Algeria either moderate or meaningless (*Afrique-Action* [Tunis], November 21, 1960), and Guinea vigorously doubted Houphouet-Boigny's intentions (*Afrique-Action*, October 31, 1960). Good accounts are found in Thompson, "Ivory Coast," in Carter (ed.), *op. cit.* pp. 304-307; Hella Pick, "The Brazzaville Twelve," *Africa South in Exile*, V, 3 (April-June 1961), 77-84.

[34] See *Livre blanc sur le différend entre le gouvernement de la République Tunisienne et le gouvernement Chérifien du Maroc* (Tunis: Secretary of State for Foreign Affairs, 1961).

[35] See Margaret Roberts, "Summitry at Casablanca," *Africa South in Exile*, V, 3 (April-June 1961), 68-74. Libya did not sign the charter, and never again attended the Group's meetings; Ceylon also withdrew. There is some doubt on the invitation list. It appears that, in addition to the seven governments represented, Tunisia, Nigeria, Liberia, Togo, Somalia, and Ethiopia were invited; see Thiam, *op. cit.*, p. 84; Alex Quaison-Sackey, *Africa Unbound* (New York: Praeger, 1963), pp. 94-95; Kwame Nkrumah, *Africa Must Unite* (New York: Praeger, 1963), p. 145. Marinelli, *op. cit.*, pp. 130-31, appears to be in error in giving a smaller list. Leading Moroccan foreign-ministry officials, in interviews, claimed that all Africa except Mauritania and the Union of South Africa were invited; Hassan II stated that only states with forces in the ONUC were invited (*Maroc Documents* [Rabat: Foreign Ministry, February 1963]). Both appear to be wrong. In addition to Ceylon, India and Indonesia were also invited.

[36] Another issue keeping the moderates and radicals apart—although not involving a Brazzaville Group member—was the Ghana-Nigeria feud, which had broken out into the open immediately after Nigeria won independence, at CIAS II at Addis Ababa, and which, by July 1962, was cited by Lagos radio as *the* divisive issue.

[37] While initiators from the UAM side looked for a larger alliance, one element of un-clarity in the original Liberian and Nigerian proposals was whether the conference would include only West Africa or the entire continent.

[88] The major issue under discussion concerned a difference of opinion between the minimalists of the UAM, who wanted simply an association of heads of state, and the English-speaking maximalists, who wanted a secretariat which would have political as well as administrative powers. The same argument has continued in the OAU and the UAM itself. The Monrovia-Lagos charter was edited by a committee of Liberia, Nigeria, Sierra Leone, Senegal, Togo, Cameroun, Congo (Brazzaville), Madagascar, Ethiopia, and Somalia.

[89] Groundless rumors in West Africa suggested that Sierra Leone would join in mid-1962, just as it had been suggested that Nigeria and Gambia might join the UAS. The only successful attempt to expand Casablanca group membership was Hassan's persuasion of Libya, in November 1962, to rejoin the coming political committee meeting, but this success was cancelled when the meeting did not take place.

[40] *Towards African Unity: A Proposal for the Consideration of the Independent African States* (Accra: Flagstaff House, 1963). Parts of the text are incorporated in Nkrumah, *Africa Must Unite, op. cit.,* pp. 218-21.

[41] Skillful Mauritanian diplomacy undercut the Moroccan position in the remaining issue of Western African division. Between August 1962 and February 1963, Mali was reconciled with Mauritania; at Libreville in September 1962, the UAM withdrew Mauritania's candidacy to the United Nations Security Council, so as not to offend the Casablanca Group.

[42] See Boutros Boutros-Ghali, *The Addis Ababa Charter* (New York: Carnegie Endowment for International Peace, 1964 [International Conciliation Series No. 546]); Marinelli, *op. cit.,* pp. 138-40.

2 CRITERIA FOR POLICY

Although there is little consensus on what constitutes national interest, it is at least agreed that it involves "national" (i.e., not class, regional, or party) "interests" (i.e., not whims, sentiments, or accidents). Beyond this, it is agreed only that the concept refers to the search for security of the national "self" (i.e., the territory and people, the way of life, and the standard of living of the state), the exact appreciation of *security* and *self* being properly a function of the national leaders' perception.[1] In Western Africa, ideology and personal interest are used more frequently than national interest as criteria for foreign policy.

THE PROBLEM OF NATIONAL SECURITY

The choice of criteria for foreign policy has an integral relation to the task of nation-building. Until the state and the nation are defined, subnational interests have an advantage, particularly if they are not specifically incompatible with efforts at consolidating the nation and the state. As long as party interests—such as the achievement and maintenance of power by a specific political elite—are the criteria for policy, national interest remains secondary. The process is self-perpetuating, for the predominance of subnational interests tends to prevent the formation of national criteria.

Nevertheless, national leadership, no matter how narrow its real base, is under pressure to justify its actions in terms of national considerations. This necessity is, in part, self-imposed, for the ruling party lives by the myth that it acts in the name of all the people, that its goals are for the good of all the people, and that its leader is the incarnate symbol of the new nation. By so doing, the national leadership denies potential rivals access to the same national symbols, and exposes them to charges of treason for acting as instruments of either external (usually colonial) or subnational (frequently tribal) interests. If the party-government fails to maintain its monopoly of national symbols, or is suspected of governing in the interest of subnational groups, an opposition party can seize the torch of unity and, sooner or later, the seat of legitimacy. This has already happened in Algeria, Togo, and Dahomey.

The situation, as well as the symbols, of the new national elite also tends to impose national criteria for policy-making. Before the new nations achieved independence, their nationalist leaders worked to overthrow the established political order; now, they are required to construct a new order and to defend it. Just as domestic policy is aimed at creating a viable polity, society, and economy, so foreign policy is, ideally, geared to the needs, values, and security of the state. Hence there is a presupposition that the national viewpoint serves as criterion and focus in intra-African foreign policy.

47

Although the focus is national at the current stage of development of African national interest, however, there is little conception of the specific interests involved. *National interest* may be a common phrase in Western African policy statements, but it is used mainly for its negative implication that policies shall no longer be decided on the basis of colonial, metropolitan, foreign, regional, or class interests. Like the national single party, the new state's foreign policy must represent the unified common interest of the indivisible nation, to the exclusion of any specific or subnational interests.[2] Thus the very use of the phrase and its implied meaning pushes the concept into a high level of generalization, reducing its value as a real guide for action. Because component interests are prohibited, the phrase excludes more than it defines. This somewhat curious phenomenon is an outgrowth of the developing nature of African politics and derives from the present necessity to assert and consolidate national identity.

The need of policy-makers to think and act in national terms is usually reflected in the matter of national security, traditionally considered the basic issue of foreign policy. To some extent, the concern of Western African states for their security has been expressed in indirect terms, and represents a general but "acute sensitivity of the small to possible encroachments on their independence."[3] These states, like other small states, voice frequent demands for the respect of their dignity. In Africa, this appeal is sharpened by memories of the injustices inflicted on the native populations during the period of colonial rule. The assertions of dignity that reverberate in the speeches of African leaders thus express a popular feeling inherent in nationalism, defend in high moral terms the fragility of their newly won independence, and reflect the sensitivity of any weak state to its general insecurity. It would be tempting to hypothesize further that any state must conceive of its existence in terms of security and invent specific threats if no identifiable ones exist. It would also be intriguing to speculate that, in Black Africa, the characteristic personal insecurity that accompanies the breakdown of tribal traditions and group identity[4] creates an atmosphere responsive to leaders' cries of insecurity for the state. A Nigerian deputy, for example, said that South Africa is his country's greatest security threat because South Africa feared Nigeria and "this fear is definitely going to drive the South African government to invade Nigeria if our policy supports Pan-Africanism." The alleged invasion was to be planned for early 1961, when Nigeria was "still finding her feet after independence."[5] It is likely that such cases merely reflect uncomprehending use of what was considered to be "normal" foreign-policy language.

With very few exceptions, the security of the new states of Western Africa has not been endangered by threats from neighbors. Yet, in a general sense, the very existence and stability of the new states is far more tenuous than the small number of incidents and symptoms in their early life would indicate. Insecurity is endemic, even if not always chronic. The threat is internal, rather than external. Yet such threats—whether they be political (instability), economic (underdevelopment), or social (revolution)—are troublesome for governments to admit publicly, difficult to combat effectively, and hard to identify precisely. Although leaders may recognize these problems to be internal (as many of them have), the very magnitude of the threat tempts them to see it as externally generated. The temptation and the confusion is compounded in Western Africa by another phenomenon: the insecurity is far more characteristic of the organizational unit than of the territorial unit. It is not the country that is in danger of attack or conquest, but the government that is in danger of overthrow or collapse. Insecurity is thus endemic, inherent, and political, rather than specific, external, and military.

The nonspecific nature of insecurity in Western African states has inevitably affected their formulation of foreign-policy criteria. As a defense against their general (but undefined) danger, the states of Western Africa have either invented scapegoats, remembered old threats, reacted instinctively, or attempted to minimize the effects of insecurity. The first two reactions take the form of an anticolonialist revival. It is natural that leaders whose careers were formed in the fight against foreign rule should continue their habits of thought and action after independence, although it is unlikely that the security of any state in the area (except possibly Guinea and Tunisia) was threatened after independence by a former colonial power. Fears of continuing colonialism are naturally strongest in the immediate postcolonial period and can be expected to fade away with time. The independence-day statements of Nkrumah and Touré—that Guinea and Ghana could not be secure until Africa was free of colonialism[6]—reflected a real fear that Britain and France might believe the colonial propaganda that Africans could not govern themselves and reverse their policy of decolonization. Nevertheless, ben Bella made similar statements in reference to Portuguese colonialism, over a thousand miles away, and Nkrumah has repeated his proclamation although any credible threat to Ghana has disappeared.[7] Two factors tend to keep this concept alive: the arrival of new independent states with their own fresh fears and the existence of suspected or substantiated attempts at colonial return. Algeria's recent achievement of independence and its great sensitivity on the colonial issue is an example of the first factor; Suez, Bizerte, and the Congo—particularly Katanga—were examples of the second. In addition, the positive value of anticolonialism is so strong and so unquestioned in Western Africa that it can serve a multitude of artificial purposes. It can be used to condemn a neighbor, to divert popular attention from domestic troubles, or to create a national hero; sometimes, as in Touré's running argument with Houphouet-Boigny between 1958 and 1962, all three goals can be achieved simultaneously.

Instinctive reactions, leading states to group together for security and against isolation, led to a kaleidoscopic pattern of alliances, *renversements,* and counteralliances between 1956 and 1963. These reactions were sparked, specifically, by Ghana's injection of the topic of unity into newly independent African foreign policy in 1957-58, and, more generally, by the efforts of the new states of AOF to overcome the unaccustomed separation forced on them by the disruption of their former common services. Real isolation (and resentment) was also felt by the chips and chunks of territory that made up former British West Africa, as their common services and currency too were broken up, at Ghana's request. In North Africa, where basic social and economic similarity exists alongside myths of political unity (unsupported by history), the fear of isolation was more specific to the individual states. Algeria sought massive African support for its long struggle for independence, while Morocco sought support for its Mauritanian policy. Both faced a reluctance to provide such support on the part of most former AOF states. In all cases, the redefinition of *self* and *neighbors,* implicit in the nation-building process, tends to increase awareness of isolation, and the relative powerlessness of the new states leads to a desire to increase power by one of the few ways available: alliances. Once a round of alliances is formed, the necessity for countermeasures against neighbors' efforts to overcome their own isolation leads to the alliance spiral. There is no doubt that the desire to overcome isolation was the major manifestation of insecurity in Western African foreign policy.

Given this fact, exceptions should be noted in the case of states that suffered isolation and were untroubled by it. Unlike most states in the area, Togo had no historical allies and no tradition of alliances; its heritage was a buffer policy. Tunisia put little stock in African alliances, even to the point of disdaining close ties with Morocco, its natural ally against pressure from Algeria. Sierra Leone has had so few problems of foreign relations that isolation has not bothered it; Liberia learned to live in isolation; and Mauritania, like Togo, followed a buffer policy, but with the UAM as reinsurance.

The fourth reaction to inherent but nonspecific insecurity involved conscious attempts to solve the problem by minimizing its effects.[8] These attempts were aimed at legitimizing the existing states through the creation of public consensus about certain "rules of the game" for African foreign policy. Thus the inclusion of the principles of noninterference, territorial integrity, and peaceful settlement of disputes in the OAU charter was designed to deal with the problem of insecurity at its source. In Western Africa, the state has no inherent legitimacy; rather, it has a presumption of illegitimacy because of its colonial origins. Nor does nationhood confer legitimacy, according to tenets of national self-determination, for the nation is at best only inchoate at the time of independence. It is the nationalist movement or party, the organizational unit—because it antedates all the others—that legitimizes the government and state, which then create the nation. This is quite the reverse of the "normal" Western experience. The result is a "state nation"—like a state religion or a state economy—rather than a nation-state. This inverted order of creation forms the very basis of Western African insecurity, and the legitimizing action of such documents of consensus as the OAU charter is designed to reduce this weakness until such time as the state can provide its own continuing legitimacy.[9] That the attempt succeeded at least temporarily is shown by the fact that the Addis Ababa meeting was able to arrest the sometimes seemingly frantic efforts to overcome isolation by alliance, for it reduced the source of Western Africa's peculiar type of insecurity, rather than simply reacting to it. The precedence of party-government over state and nation, however, poses more complex problems, for it tends to confuse state and regime and opens the way for action in the name of subnational party interests.

SUBNATIONAL INTERESTS AND NONCRITERIA

If threats to the security of the national "self" are absent, distant, or ill-perceived, other interests rise in importance. These interests may prevent the formation of national criteria; they may accede to pressures for national criteria by adopting a national garb; or they may simply be adopted by the entire nation. Subnational interests may be regional, tribal, class, party, or personal.

Interestingly enough, there are few examples of Western African foreign-policy actions based on regional interests, although centrifugal pressures are encouraged by the fact that many states have isolated border regions that are closer to neighboring centers of population than to their own national life. Thus, Tarfaya and Agadir province of Morocco look southward for trade and social ties, as northern Mauritania looks north; Oujda province has historically and economically been closer to Algeria than to the rest of Morocco and Tindouf has closer links to Morocco than to Algeria; the Gao region of Mali, the Malian Sahara, and the Kayes area have closer ties with Niger, the Algerian Sahara, and Senegal, respectively, than with the rest of Mali, while the Nema region of Mauritania shares its economic and social life with the Nara-Nioro region of Mali; the Hausa region of Niger around Zinder is further from the socioeconomic center in Niamey than from the Hausa region of Nigeria around Kano; the Senegalese region of Kedougou has closer ties with Guinea than with Dakar, but the Nzerekore region of Guinea is more a part of western Ivory Coast or northern Liberia than of Guinea. Other cases could certainly be cited; perhaps most striking is the case of Upper Volta, where migrant labor creates centrifugal tendencies toward its neighbors that put in doubt the very existence of the state. Yet representatives of most of these regions exercised no pressure on their central governments to improve relations with neighbors; exceptions, when delegates from the Moroccan Rif, Kayes laborers in Mali, and the Mauritanian Hodh petitioned for a change of policy toward neighboring states, had no effect on government actions. If anything, pressure toward nation-building required these regions to be "more nationalist than the nation" and to lead the campaign for support of the particular policy. The one case of regional foreign policy was the flurry of activity on the part of Sir Ahmadu Bello, Sardauna of Sokoto, premier of the Northern Region of Nigeria, who in 1960 and 1961, until reined in by his peers, carried out a Pan-Islamic and sometimes irredentist campaign toward parts of Africa and the Middle East.[10]

The pressure of class interests is more difficult to measure, for Western African leaders—if not all their followers—are nearly unanimous in asserting that there are no classes in their countries. An orthodox Marxist analysis, on the other hand, would doubtless reveal that policy in most of these states was determined on the basis of bourgeois nationalist or even "feudal" interests.[11] This is not the place to settle the argument. Not surprisingly, no Western African leader has justified his policy in terms of class interest. The omission can be explained partly by the pressures toward the use of national symbols discussed earlier, and also by the fact that subnational interests have usually not yet been organized in Western Africa except as party auxiliaries under government control. If the working class or the bourgeoisie have any organization, it is in the hands of the nationalists and not a class organization *per se*.

The existence of tribal criteria for policy-making, like that of class or regional criteria, depends on an awareness of tribal interests and their expression as such. The continuing existence of traditional nations in Western Africa is too sensitive a matter to be cited by leaders as the avowed basis of foreign policy in most cases. Instead, tribal interests have sometimes been adopted by the state and presented in national terms, and it may be possible to surmise that a particular leader would not have acted in a certain way had he not been a member of a given tribe. Nkrumah, a Nzima, supported the Sanwi movement, although he might also have supported other tribal dissidence on his border if it had existed. Mamprusi and Ewe desires for unification were taken over as Ghanaian state goals, just as Olympio, an Ewe, adopted the same unification goals for his state. Ben Bella, from the village of Lalla Maghnia on the Moroccan border, refused boundary talks that other Algerian leaders had promised. Mali espoused grievances of its border peoples following incidents with Mauritania in late 1960 and made tribal hostilities the basis of its attitude and policies toward Mauritania for three years. There appear to be no other examples of tribally based policy. It is particularly noteworthy that the new states of the area have not espoused traditional tribal rivalries—Songhai-Moor, Fula-Bambara, Fula-Hausa, and so on— although this may be explained to some extent by the fact that few tribes fit neatly into one particular state and that their traditional enemies are frequently inside the same state.[12] It is true that on numerous occasions states have reacted to protect members of their population who were expelled from neighboring countries or otherwise harmed by neighboring people, but the people in question were protected as citizens of the state, not as members of a particular tribe.

Among the subnational interests, it is the party interest that presents the most complicated picture. Western African parties maintained active foreign relations among themselves (including alliances and subversion), with the colonial power (including negotiations and aid), and with the external world (including attendance at international conferences and the United Nations) before independence. These policies were carried out in the parties' own interest, which can be summarized as the attainment of control over the territorial and popular units of government. With independence, the parties and their charismatic leaders, as the legitimizers of the new regime, made their own rules of operation, followed their own aims and interests, and set about to develop the state and nation in the image of their dreams. It is a moot question whether the party adopts the national interests or the state adopts those of the party. Obviously, policies that enhance the welfare of the nation may also work to keep the government in power, and policies to keep the government in power—such as the RDA alliance of the Entente governments—may also be in the national interest. The line between party interests and national interests may be very thin; frequently an action—or particularly a reaction —will differ only in timing or in form from one that another government at another moment would take in a similar situation. Thus, ben Bella's government met the Moroccan army in the border war of 1963, but the vigor and timing of his actions were largely influenced by his need for support against internal dissidence in Kabylia.

But there have also been distinguishable occasions when the elite used events or acts in order to stay in power, basing its actions on the same criteria of power consolidation that it used before independence. The clearest, if broadest, example of this type of action is the attitude of Western African governments toward political union; it is based to a large extent on reluctance to give up their own *situations acquises*, rational or justified as this reluctance may be. A more specific example is Morocco's initiative in calling the Casablanca conference and proclaiming a radical policy, just at the moment when Mohammed V felt particularly pressed by the activist opposition. Maga's consolidation of power in 1959-60, like Apithy's similar attempts in 1958-59, showed the use of alliances as a means of placating domestic opposition in Dahomey.[13] Nkrumah has frequently invoked external as well as internal threats in order to rally popular support; a notable case was the charge of an attack from Togo in March 1960, when he needed public support for the republican constitution and for his own candidacy as president. Olympio also discovered plots in time to consolidate government control over elections, and Tubman acted in a similar fashion.

Although there may be some relation between domestic and foreign politics, there is frequently too little relation between domestic and foreign policies. Western African relations are anything but "domestic policy pursued by other means . . . carried beyond the boundaries of the state."[14] Only if *policy* is understood as *ideology* may this be true; for the most part, intra-African foreign policy has little to do with domestic needs or purposes. Instead, it is often an exercise in pure politics—a struggle for external influence for its own sake—and at times has no other criterion than whim, emotion, or accident. This is something different from actions in the party interest against a threatening opposition. In few African states does the opposition have access to national symbols or an opportunity to organize public opinion to the point when it becomes necessary for the group in power to defend itself with a particular foreign-policy action. The unit of interest referred to here is purely personal. Summit meetings enhance the local prestige of the party-government leader (they may thus also enhance his value as a central symbol for nation-building). Good relations are based most firmly on personal friendships drawn from common experiences in school, politics, labor unions, or exile. *Rapprochement* is more frequently reached in terms of this common past than in terms of national interests. If there is no common past, *rapprochement* is contingent upon a personal meeting of the heads of state. An alliance functions when heads of state meet; when they do not—even if lesser figures do—the alliance is often considered to be foundering. Bad relations are revealed through nasty statements about the head of state—not about the state itself and sometimes not even about the rest of the government. Bad blood between Mali and Senegal (1960-63), Mali and Ivory Coast (1958-60), Guinea and Ivory Coast (1958-62), Upper Volta and Ivory Coast (1961), Ghana and Ivory Coast (1957-64), Ghana and Togo (1957-63), Morocco and Tunisia (1960-64), Morocco and Algeria (1962-64), and Tunisia and Algeria (1962-63), was either caused or prolonged by personal reactions of pride or anger, usually felt by the head of state. The tendency to speak of "Nkrumah's Ghana" or "Bourguiba's Tunisia," instead of "Ghana's Nkrumah" or "Tunisia's Bourguiba," is symbolic rather than inaccurate, especially in intra-African relations. Thus, whether the personal factor be interest or merely emotion, it is frequently the dominant criterion for relations in Western Africa.

The personal factor in determining policy also raises the importance of the role of accident, of which two types can be distinguished. The first is the pure accident or the accident of events, a fortuitous action which triggers an important reaction. A small border incident caused by Mauritanians at the time that Mali was invited to attend independence celebrations at Nouakchott began three years of bad relations between the two countries and—combined with Mali's predilection for African unity—resulted in Mali's membership in the Casablanca Group. Another example is found in chance press comments with no apparent relation to policy which often upset slowly bettering relations between Western African countries.[15] The second type is the accident of excuse or the "African U-2 incident." Senghor's ousting of Dia, which had nothing to do with Mali, was nevertheless seized on by Dakar and Bamako alike as a cause for *rapprochement;* the assassination of Olympio, which had nothing to do with the Casablanca Group or the UAS, was used by Touré as a cause of rupture with Ghana. In this type of accident, the desire is present and only the excuse is awaited; in the other type, the accident is a more fundamental cause for the foreign-policy action. In both cases, however, there is little control over policy or events, and frequently little purpose evident in the policy action.

In sum, it can be seen that the interests of subnational groups play a smaller role than might be expected as criteria for intra-African policy, but the personal nature of Western African relations places great importance on the interests and emotions of the heads of state and on the role of accidents. The commanding interests—whatever they may be—are expressed or assumed in terms of national interest. Thus the language of national interest is kept alive, although it may have neither reality nor meaning.

SENTIMENT AND IDEOLOGY AS THE NATIONAL "SELF"

In the twentieth-century Cold War world, the national "self" is construed more broadly than in terms of mere population and territory. It often includes a way of life, actual or proposed, without which the defense of the state and nation is considered meaningless and the welfare of its citizens unattainable. Ideological criteria are thus not matters of self-abnegation or of supranational interests, in which the state is bypassed in the name of a higher value;[16] rather, they are integral—in fact, basic and paramount—components of the ruling elite's perception of national interest, national security, and national welfare. Therefore, although an ideologically based foreign policy may be neither realistic, pragmatic, nor in the best interests of the state or its citizens when judged from a nonideological point of view,[17] it does form a coherent whole with domestic ideology and with domestic politics. It is more susceptible than nonideologically based relations to change and to reinterpretation when governments change. On the other hand, it may clash with domestic needs, for it can cause the leaders to neglect opportunities for profitable cooperation with ideologically undesirable states, and to embark on wasteful campaigns in areas where the state has no direct interest.

Ideological criteria tend to produce a purist, idealistic policy. Max Weber has written of two modes of ethical conduct: the purist ethics of "ultimate ends," and the compromising ethics of "responsibility." To the idealist, ideological goals are high on the list of policy criteria and must be kept untainted; to the realist, the necessity of making discrete choices for immediate needs involves pushing ideological criteria into the background and the long run, in order to gain real advantages in the present. Ideological goals have a place in both types of policies, for every state nurtures a number of dreams and hopes about the world in which it would like to live. In one group of Western African states, however, these aspirations are dominant over other considerations, both in forming the image of the state "self" and in determining foreign-policy actions. In other states, these aspirations are more distant matters.

If similar aspirations are shared throughout the area, what accounts for the differences in their importance as criteria for policy? Reduced to its simplest terms, the answer would seem to be that ideology is important as a foreign-policy criterion in those states where it is important as a domestic-policy criterion. In the struggle against colonialism, the mobilization of the masses and the formulation of slogans was one of the very few sources of power open to the nationalist movements. Because these movements succeeded in crumbling the walls of the major world empires mainly by blowing on ideological trumpets and parading around the citadels of colonialism, there is a continuing tendency to believe in the power of slogans and ideas. For a small number of states in Western Africa—Guinea, Mali, Algeria—independence came in circumstances that involved an emotional rupture with the colonial power and gave the new state a sense of revolt against its colonial past. This revolt imposed the need for a new, justifying code of values or national ideology. Also, these states saw a mass exodus of colonial minorities at the time of independence, thus setting off a revolutionary change in the societies.[18] Some states—Guinea, Ghana—were the first among their neighbors to achieve independence and hence developed a sense of mission that had to be codified into a body of ideas and goals. One state of North Africa—Algeria —experienced a violent struggle for independence that went far beyond the mere formulation of slogans and began a unique revolutionary upheaval.

In all these cases, the process of attaining independence was one of revolution, rejection, and replacement. The tearing down of old edifices and the search for indigenous substitutes creates a real human need for goals and guidelines, for a set of values that would give at least the appearance of solidity in time of upheaval and the assurance of a promised land on the other side of the desert. There is a rejection of present reality in exchange for a future ideal. At the same time, ideology in revolutionary-idealist countries becomes necessary as the legitimizer of the new government, for the colonial regime is so strongly rejected that it cannot serve as a justifying antecedent to the successor state. In the remaining states, revolution and rejection did not mark the process of attaining independence; therefore, idealistic, ideological policies have not characterized their relations with other African countries. In either case, the importance of ideology in the hierarchy of criteria for foreign-policy actions depends on the internal situation of the country, not merely on an isolated area of foreign relations.

Even in the revolutionary-idealist states, of course, ideological criteria are not the only determinants of foreign policy. No state can afford to be totally idealistic in its policy; the pressure of real, immediate problems is too great. The limits of ideological foreign policy are clearly shown by two incidents. In the Algero-Moroccan border war of 1963, Algeria defended its position in strongly ideological terms, speaking of a confrontation between "the guarantor of socialism, defender of the poor" and the "criminal tyrant" of Morocco when a simple call to the defense of national security and state territory would have sufficed. After the rupture of the Mali Federation, Mali did not hesitate to accept just as great a commercial dependence on the transportation system of Ivory Coast, which it had previously condemned for its "colonialist, un-African" government, as it had had on Senegal, now to be condemned in the same terms. Ideology cannot be an exclusive basis of foreign policy because its specific recommendations are limited and unclear. It can provide a unified context into which individual policies and actions can be fit, but it is not a plan for specific acts. Ghana's ideology does not say: "When in doubt, unite"; Ghana has "united" with other African states as much but no more than Ivory Coast. Algeria's ideology does not say: "Support any action that furthers liberation"; Algeria has been rather silent on the issue of liberating Spanish African territory and on some aspects of the question of French troops in Algeria. At best, ideology tells what *not* to do, and what to see: its effect on policy is therefore one of limitation, interpretation, and justification.

The uses of ideological criteria lie most frequently in these areas. On one hand, ideology affects the choice of allies and enemies. The three states of the UAS were able to agree on a list of principles, even if these remained largely unimplemented, because they had similar regimes based on similar ideologies. The three states of the Maghreb were able to concert their plans and actions only to the extent and at the time (1958) that their ideological orientation included common predominant values (a single nationalist movement, accent on liberation, regional unity); when internal developments and external circumstances changed, affecting these values, ideological similarities and the basis of cooperation fell apart. Even among the four states of the Entente ideological elements governed the choice of partners, reinforced before the fact by the establishment of sympathetic regimes in Ivory Coast's three allies and after the fact by constitutions and legislation reflecting the same points of view. Considerations of principle rather than interest are also invoked in the choice of enemies. Ideological reasons are cited for nearly every case of bad relations, although they may or may not be the primary causes. After their first meeting (1957), Houphouet-Boigny and Nkrumah went home convinced the other was a local imperialist and a colonialist agent, respectively, and subsequent relations between their two countries have proven each to be "correct"—in his own mind, at least. Diori and Soglo, and their followers, exchanged ideological insults during the half-year of bad relations between Dahomey and Niger (1963-64), calling each other "revolutionary" and "colonialist." Further examples could be given from every case of bad relations between two countries.

Ideological criteria are also used to justify actions. Policy announcements, joint communiqués, acceptances or rejections of invitations to meetings—all make reference to the major aspirations of Western African states: unity, independence, development, and their ramifications—anticolonialism, legitimacy, revolution. Ideological justification can be used to "sell" attitudes to local parties and to the people, to gain support, to undercut opposition, and to consolidate the state and nation. It can also be used to defend policies before foreign audiences, usually made up of leaders of other states, their parties, and (eventually) their people. This dual justificatory use of ideology makes it difficult to distinguish the cases in which principles are the real criteria of action from those in which they are merely the sugar-coating for less publishable reasons. In this, Western Africa differs little from other areas of the world.

The only purely African element lies in the particular principles used. The major goals of Western Africa are unity, independence, and development. The foreign-policy ideologies that derive from these goals can be called African Socialism, Pan-Africanism, and comprehensive anticolonialism.[19] Despite their loose structure and lack of doctrine, it is possible to present inductive models of these three ideologies from their proponents' pronouncements. Foreign policies justified in the name of African Socialism would be based on planned cooperation to further internal development, using socialist slogans as a unifying justification. "Rational planning and effective development imply an equally rational and active foreign policy."[20] The African Socialist approach also regards the party-state-nation as an indivisible vertical unit, complementary to the Pan-African idea of the horizontal indivisibility of African states. Proponents of African Socialism thus tend to consider their African policy to be a "people's foreign policy," with a popular base, national aspirations, and mass organizations closely associated with policy formation, all reminiscent of preindependence appeals. They also follow the Rousseauian concept of the general will and call for sacrifices in the name of the collectivity, which may in turn be used to support notions of national interest or to justify limitations on the state in the name of "the African people" and "the good of Africa." "In the end, there emerges another, perhaps deeper meaning of African Socialism: the natural demands of the poor in the midst of plenty, joining the clamor for justice voiced by the underprivileged throughout history."[21]

Pan-Africanist criteria refer to a particular aspect of the general aspiration to African unity: the creation of a homogeneous political union with common institutions, policies, and economies. It is not an ideology that foresees unity in diversity; rather, it proclaims a certain orthodoxy in interpreting events and prescribing policy, presents itself as the only valid interpretation of African interests, and casts doubt on the independence and legitimacy of states that do not agree.[22] There is a difference, however, between prescribing orthodoxy and extending domination; although Pan-African ideologues seek general acceptance of their ideas and common action on their policies, Pan-Africanism is not necessarily a hegemonistic policy. Pan-African criteria for policy do equate the interest of the state with that of the continent and the voice of the leader with the aspirations of "true" Africans. They are also considered necessary to obviate the boundary disputes and development rivalries that weaken the new states and to defend their fragile existence: "We must unite or perish, for no single African State is large or powerful enough to stand on its own against the unbridled imperialist exploitation of her men and resources and the growing complexities of the modern world."[23] Finally, although Pan-Africanism inveighs against regional and territorial balkanization and against counter-schemes that challenge its orthodoxy, it can also be used to justify partial and potentially divisive attempts at unity and to boycott unorthodox approaches.

The intra-African aspects of a foreign policy based on comprehensive anticolonialism derive from the notion of "complete" independence. This ideal has both a horizontal and a vertical dimension. It emphasizes the liberation of remaining colonial territories (even through violence), for the independence of any single state is not considered secure as long as parts of Africa remain under foreign rule; it also seeks to achieve the "total" independence of the state from all foreign influence. Formal independence is therefore only a minimal precondition for—sometimes even a distraction from—"real" independence. There is a tendency to regard the enemy as primarily a plotting, subversive opponent, who requires counterplots and countersubversion for his defeat.[24] There is also a tendency to regard the enemy as a single force, and to see his advance or retreat across the continent as a concerted movement under a unified command, to be defeated only by a unified counterattack. Ultimately, "total" independence must be achieved not only from the countervailing force of colonialism, but also from its aftereffects: "Rid of foreign domination, we are still dominated by the conditions of colonialism." [25] There is therefore a visible overlap among the arguments of African Socialism, Pan-Africanism, and comprehensive anticolonialism.

In addition to ideological criteria, there are also a number of sentimental criteria for state action. The term *sentimental criteria* applies to those reasons of state that involve neither interests nor ideology (although they may be supported by ideological justification) and have only a tangential bearing on the ideas of national security, no matter how defined. Such sentiments in Western Africa include historic missions of leadership and irredentism. Like ideologies, historical sentiments usually grow out of the struggle for independence; like personal interests, they usually are associated with a particular group of leaders, and may be used to consolidate their efforts at nation-building. Ghanaian concepts of leadership grew out of Nkrumah's London-based efforts at preparing unity and out of Ghana's relatively early achievement of independence. Guinea's concepts of leadership derive from the vanguard action of Touré in showing the rest of AOF that independence was possible and from Guinea's position as a "pilot" state with a policy of African Socialism and Africanization. Algeria's notions of leadership stem from its long struggle for independence, far longer and more bitter than that of most of Western Africa. Irredentist ideas also display a sentimental side and a sense of historical mission. Morocco provides a striking example. As yet, no other state has conceived of its existence in terms of an historic Western African empire, despite the use of historic names as *Ghana, Mali, Dahomey,* and *Mauritania.* Such sentiments lie at the basis of many policy decisions, including Nkrumah's calling of the first Conference of Independent African States in 1958, Guinea's support of independence movements in Entente states and Cameroun during its early years of independence, Algeria's active support and then criticism of the Liberation Coordination Committee, and Morocco's entire policy toward Mauritania. As in other areas of the world, sentimental pretensions are powerful motivating forces and can lead to important policies and actions, many of which may conflict with narrower interests of the state or lead it into areas remote to immediate problems of national security.

THE DEVELOPMENT OF NATIONAL INTEREST

It has been seen that the states of Western Africa adopt their policies for many reasons—reasons often vaguely justified in terms of national interest but usually more understandable in a narrowly partisan or broadly ideological context. Policies may also be formed by personal reasons, whim or accident, or a fortuitous coincidence of events. The absence of precise security threats allows this situation to continue. The lack of national-interest criteria might be explained more positively: there is so much to be done and so few obvious ways of doing it that it is not clear where the interests of the states lie. The new African states have little to defend—but much to acquire in order to achieve the plenitude of existence as a modern state. The irony and the tragedy is that this situation makes it both necessary and difficult to perceive the national interest and to base policies on it. "We have so much to ask and so little to bargain with," Olympio once said.[26]

There are other reasons, more closely connected with the conduct of Western African foreign policy, for the absence of national-interest criteria. The narrowest is the lack of technical intelligence.[27] Although Western African leaders are highly knowledgeable about the politics of their state and its social characteristics, they often have relatively little information on its potential resources, its developmental possibilities, and the ways of meeting its material needs. This is not necessarily a failing of the intelligence machinery of the state; such information frequently does not exist anywhere. Colonial archives, which are frequently filled with rare source material, are either classified in the metropole (for political or diplomatic reasons) or are in disorder in the African state. Economic and statistical studies conducted in Morocco when that state was a protectorate have been discontinued under the independent government for lack of trained personnel, and preprotectorate archives are disorganized. Some of the colonial archives in Guinea have been removed, and the rest are in hopeless disorder. On the other hand, Tunisian, Ghanaian, and Nigerian technical studies and archival services are in reasonably good functioning order. In addition, many of the development techniques needed as a basis for a country's policies are themselves underdeveloped. There is little information—and less agreement—on methods of agricultural improvement, on terrain studies for transportation systems, on the location of raw materials. Yet both information and agreement are necessary for rational cooperation among states and the common exploitation of their resources for national independence, unity, and development.

Basic political and economic information on foreign-policy operations areas is also lacking. Foreign ministries tend to be small, and their desk officers often depend on a thin newspaper-clipping file; because the desk officer is usually responsible for an entire continent rather than a single country, his territory is as vast as his sources of information are meager. The situation is complicated by the political nature of information in many countries. Many of the better foreign newspapers are regarded with suspicion because of their European origins; often there is a party line on the interpretation of events that prevents a large number of varying sources from being fully assimilated. Ghana, with its peculiar relation between press and government, is a striking example: Ghanaian newspapers present a narrowly orthodox image of African events; Ghanaian leaders feel that they speak for the "true" African interpretation of policy, and they end up prisoners of their own misinformation.[28] Policy papers are little used in Western Africa; telephone communication and

personal conversations are preferred to written memoranda. The Senegalese
foreign ministry wrote only one background paper on the entire subject of
the breakup of the Mali Federation[29]; Morocco wrote one policy paper and
two White Papers on the Mauritanian question.[30] Ivory Coast, on the other
hand, engaged a French firm to make an intensive study of the basis of economic cooperation after the formation of the Entente, and Tunisia has published a useful analysis of economic cooperation in the Maghreb, although not
until 1964.[31] The question is always present, too, whether the few studies
that do exist are carefully read by those who need to act on them.

Available technical intelligence is put in a bad operating environment by
the decision-making process common to Western Africa. The penchant of
African heads of state for handling foreign policy personally invites all the
dangers of misinformation on detail that are inherent in summitry. Any observer will perceive and interpret facts in the light of his own experience, but
the high degree of diversity in Western Africa makes this frame of reference
inadequate for the African leader's understanding of many problems peculiar to African states—the myth of African cultural unity notwithstanding.
The impressions of the Guinean delegation visiting Ghana in late 1958, which
included strong reactions to the presence of British experts and to the picture of Queen Elizabeth as head of the Ghanian state, were eloquent testimony to the incomprehension of the British Commonwealth by an ex-mem-
ber of the French Union.[32] Furthermore, summit conferences have too often
been called without adequate technical and political preparation. Of all the
African meetings in which Western African heads of state took part (until the
Addis Ababa conference of 1963), only the Conference of Independent African States in 1958 and several of the Monrovia and Brazzaville conferences
had any serious preparation. Ministers who attended meetings of the Casablanca political committee reported that the meetings were held without any
agenda or planning—"like a Council of Ministers meeting." [33] Government
policies are frequently ad hoc; decisions are made only as problems are posed
and little consideration is given to their future consequences or to the details
of their implementation. Many important suggestions for policy—an African
common market, an African assembly, common Saharan or riverine exploitation, common diplomatic representation, harmonization of legislation and
services, for example—have for the most part remained not only unrealized
but even unstudied. Instead, principles and aspirations are frequently found
to be the only common denominator of agreement and declarations become
substitutes for action.

Finally, criteria of national interest are secondary in determining policy
because of the absence of power in intra-African relations. It is difficult to
attain an end if the means are lacking. In Western Africa, the classical elements of state power are noticeably weak. Area is especially illusory, for the
largest states—Algeria, Niger, Mali, Mauritania—are largely desert, and—
except for spots in the Algerian and Mauritanian Sahara—poor desert at that.
Population figures must be tempered by considerations of illiteracy, hetero-

geneity, underemployment, ruralism, poor integration, and apathy; the 55 million people of Western Africa's largest state, Nigeria, represent both problems and potential—but not power.[34] Military strength is low both in absolute and in relative terms, and is further depleted by domestic preoccupations, inefficiency, and difficult terrain. Economic development is the goal, not the reality, of African politics; the fact that seven states—Senegal, Liberia, Ivory Coast, Ghana, and the Maghreb countries—have a per capita annual income between $150 and $250, while the rest have a per capita annual income between $40 and $100, does not give the richer states enough of an edge to provide durable power. Nor does any Western African state depend on another for food or raw materials, for food is largely home-grown and the predominant trade channels are still Europe-oriented. Of all the classical tangible elements, only the geography of communications has some importance. Coastal states which control inland countries' outlets to the sea, and states which lie astride river, rail, or pipe lines, enjoy a certain position of influence, the advantages and limitations of which can be clearly seen in the histories of the Entente and the Mali Federation. Power and susceptibility to pressure are, however, two sides of the same coin in this respect: inland states (Mali, Upper Volta, Niger) or states with geographically eccentric regions (Tindouf in Algeria, Nzerekore in Guinea) find their national interest in good relations with a maritime neighbor, but port states—Senegal, Guinea, Sierra Leone, Liberia, Ivory Coast, Ghana, Togo, Dahomey—need good relations with a hinterland area for the full commercial use of their port facilities. The greater economic development of certain coastal states does little to tip this balance of needs in their favor, as Mali-Senegalese and Upper Volta-Ivory Coast relations show.

The element of state power that has risen in importance—in the absence of other, more solid bases—is ideological prestige. The importance of ideological criteria for policy, the personal nature of perception and decision in policy-making, and the confusion between slogans and action—all combine to give a position of influence to those states which can appropriate, manipulate, and monopolize slogans. Because slogans, in turn, become the vocabulary of policy and the framework of perception and interpretation, their power in intra-African relations becomes more important than the gap between aspirations and reality might suggest. The power of comprehensive anticolonialism made it politic for strongly liberationist movements to be included in pronouncements by the Monrovia Group, despite the remoteness of the problem to the states involved. Guinea, Ghana, Mali, and Algeria have frequently used slogans to enhance their policies, but the less idealistic and less ideologically oriented states have also been susceptible to their appeal. This type of power, however, is not conducive to a clear consideration of national interests.

The common characteristic of these hinderances to national-interest policies is underdevelopment. In each area of weakness—technical intelligence, the decision-making process, elements of state power—improvement is likely as the states acquire experience in conducting foreign policy and develop economically, socially, and politically. But because operational obstacles to the pursuit of national interest tend to be overcome unevenly, power differentials and differing appreciations of national interest are likely to appear from country to country even over the short run. Differences in the use of intelligence, in the effectiveness of the decision-making process, and in the available resources of power are already evident in Western Africa.

In the end, pursuit of national interest depends on the development of a hierarchy of values and the realistic appraisal of needs, goals, threats, and opportunities. Hence successful national-interest policies depend on the ability to compromise at the proper time.

The national survival of a nation that is conscious not only of its own interest but also of that of other nations must be defined in terms compatible with the latter. In a multinational world this is a requirement of political morality; in an age of total war [and rising expectations] it is also a condition for survival.[35]

It might also be added that in an area where a number of countries are competing for scarce means of development, it is a precondition for success. Western African relations in the 1956-63 period tended to be gloriously free of meaningful compromise, with the result that competing alliances and counteralliances pursued essentially common goals through conflict. Admittedly, where the goals differed, as in the dispute whether independence or unity should come first, competition advanced both goals. But in the lesser issues and rivalries before 1963, compromise was a virtue yet to be learned. Even at Casablanca in 1961, agreement on the hotly debated issue of withdrawal from the United Nations Congo force (ONUC) was superficial and did not last beyond the conference. After 1963, when the situation had changed and the states had become more familiar with the conduct of foreign relations, there were more instances of compromise. The Mali-Mauritanian and Mali-Senegalese agreements of 1963, the Morocco-Mauritanian détente of 1964, and the Algero-Moroccan armistice of 1964 are examples of bilateral compromise. The establishment in 1964-65 of an "evolved" Brazzaville Group is an example of multilateral compromise, and even broader is the compromise reached at Addis Ababa between the Monrovia and Casablanca Groups. Obviously compromise is not always desirable—although such a danger has not yet presented itself—but in the absence of total agreement on goals and absolute coincidence of national interests, some compromise is essential.

The responsible development of national interest also involves a corollary consideration: respect for mutual obligations. Although there is sometimes a tendency—particularly in revolutionary-idealist regimes—to consider international agreements secondary to "revolutionary morality," and national interest equivalent to "class interest," [36] states soon learn that in order to earn respect and extract commitments, they must fulfill their own obligations. As in the case of compromise, this verity takes long to learn. Condemnations and policy commitments signed at Casablanca regarding Mauritania and Israel were not honored by Ghana,[37] nor did Nkrumah's proposal of a committee of seven in the preparations for the Addis Ababa conference result from consultation with his UAS and Casablanca Group partners. Disregard for commitment was particularly evident in the Casablanca Group's African common market proposals, which were accepted and then twice postponed when none of the members ratified the agreement.[38] The obligation to consult is one that plagues many an alliance member. A typical case in Western Africa was the short-lived customs-union agreement between Upper Volta and Ghana, in which the former did not consult the other UAM/OAMCE or West African customs-union members (although Ghana did consult the UAS).

National interest, it has been seen, is a criterion as applicable by the new states of Western Africa as by any other state. But national interest suggests only an approach to foreign relations; the actual content depends on perception and interpretation by the decision-making elite. The process of evolving an appreciation of national interest is as much a part of the developmental process as any other aspect of development, and as such is touched by Western Africa's preoccupation with the achievement of forms applicable to the modern world without alienating the national—and even traditional—content derived from the people and their history. The resultant image of national interest is, and may well continue to be, specifically African, within the classical framework of the concept.

Although the newness of most Western African nations makes it difficult to discern which historical elements are relevant and inalienable, some very general guidelines can be perceived.[39] The cultural clash between Arabs and Black Africans (based on feelings of superiority and memories of slavery) and between Europe and Africa (reflecting a history of subjugation and the imposition of new values) affects the perception of interests. The myth of African unity, subjected to external pressures and influence, creates continuing uncertainty as to whether present African states or larger regional units are the proper frame of reference for national interest; at some point in a future process of unification, the new unit becomes the relevant reference point, just as the inchoate nation now takes precedence over the component traditional nations or tribes. The characteristic search for ideology—a search that encompasses the entire process of wedding old ideas and ideals to the new—means that the general strength of the ideology will doubtless play a more important role in the perception of national interest in the new nations than it does in many established states. Naturally, this new national interest would be divided between the desire to develop a modern indigenous culture and keep out of Europe's wars, and the need for aid and support from the Northern Hemisphere. The welfare function, which was the tribe's paramount *raison d'être*, is important for the modern state because of the desire for rapid, coordinated economic development. All these elements give national

interest a specifically African character which tends to emphasize the ideological and welfare factors at the expense of narrower notions of territorial
security.

DECISION-MAKING AND THE INFLUENCES ON POLICY

There are two ways of examining intra-African foreign-policy-making in
Western Africa. One is functional, based on an analysis of component processes such as socialization or sociation, communication, and the formulation
and execution of policy. The other is institutional, depicting the roles of the
actors and influences in the decision-making and execution process as a whole.
Although the absence of fully formed institutions and the presence of newly
emerging patterns in the area might suggest the greater relevance of the
former approach, the latter permits comparison with other societies—developed and underdeveloped—and brings out the evolving nature of the Western
African scene.

The predominant mode of Western African political leadership is institutionalized charismatic. The importance of charisma as a vehicle for political
institutional transfer has frequently been noted;[40] postcolonial political development has begun the process of institutionalizing the position of the
charismatic leader. The progression in the unit of legitimization from party
to government to state to nation carries the leader to a position of dominance
at the head of all four units. The leader becomes the "original ancestor" of
the new nation, and the fact that this is, of course, a political rather than
geneological concept illustrates at the same time the politization, personaliza-
tion, and popularization of national life.[41]

Decision-making in intra-African politics derives from this situation and
is focused on the president and the presidency. The declarations of the president become the national ideology, consecrated into *-isms* formed on the
leader's name—such as Bourguibism, Nkrumahism, and ben Bellaism. Specific, even minute decisions are made by the president, whose prestige and
experience in dealing with other leaders give him special competence in intra-
African relations. His anger and his ardor, his whims and his convictions
become the mood of his country's policy, and his friendships and acquaint-
ances mark its limits. When the chief is absent—he must attend conferences
and take vacations—or occupied with other problems, the progress of African
relations awaits his return, for there is no alternative person or institution
qualified to handle them. It is therefore necessary to deal with problems
seriatim, so that long-term or sustained action in one field, such as African
relations, is not possible and projects progress slowly. On the other hand, because of the personal nature of decisions, short-term bursts of energy, rapid
action, and equally rapid changes are also possible. Within this pattern of
relations and decisions, the roles and influence of all other groups and institutions work through the presidency and must be seen primarily as modifica-
tions of the rule of centralized personalized power.

The president is surrounded by lieutenants, councils, advisors, and representative groups. His primary lieutenant in intra-African relations is the foreign minister. In Ghana, Morocco, Ivory Coast, Senegal, Dahomey, and Niger, there has also been a ministerial position dealing with African or regional affairs; other states in the area have foreign-ministry desks or sections. The foreign minister is either a political figure brought in the government to balance the political forces in the country (as in Dahomey, and Mauritania) or a close friend, political alter ego, or relative of the president (as in Tunisia, Morocco, Senegal, Mali, Guinea, Liberia, Ghana, Algeria).[42] Although capable men have occupied the post in a number of countries, diplomatic skill or experience is a by-product of selection, not a primary criterion for it. The tenure of Western African foreign ministers has varied widely, from seven years (Grimes of Liberia) to a month (Guillabert of Senegal), although the average is a little more than two years. It is relatively rare that the head of state or government himself occupy the foreign ministry, but his predominant role in the making of policy—and even in its execution—keeps his minister primarily a department head, an advisor, and an administrative assistant. Foreign-ministers' meetings have thus been useful for drawing up agendas, blocking out positions, and defining problems, but not for bargaining, reaching compromises, or conducting negotiations. The most ambitious mission of Western African foreign ministers was the attempt of Barema Bocoum of Mali and Louis Beavogui of Guinea to solve the problems of succession in Algeria in July 1962—a pious attempt which, not surprisingly, ended in failure. However, since 1962 in the UAM and since 1963 in the OAU, foreign ministers have taken on a more direct decision-making role, reserving only the final signing (and the initial mandate) for their presidents.

Cabinet members other than the foreign minister can serve as presidential envoys because their base in local politics and their method of selection is frequently similar to that of their foreign-office colleagues, but their mission often has little to do with their field of competence. In 1961, the foreign minister of Dahomey was chosen to go to Togo to arrange a heads-of-state meeting because he had spent his childhood in Togo, but the Dahomeyan sent to intervene in the Togolese assassination in 1963 was the economics minister, picked because he was a fellow tribesman of the predominantly Cabré army in Togo. The Ivoirien sent to Guinea to arrange a heads-of-state meeting in 1960 was the minister of the interior, chosen because he was a former labor associate of Touré. When ministers serve as negotiators in their special fields, however, their selection for a given mission frequently indicates that the problem under discussion will be treated as a technical matter, not a political issue. Thus negotiations on problems outstanding between Algeria and Tunisia, Mali and Senegal, Mali and Mauritania, involved cabinet members other than the foreign ministers, and the entire approach of the Entente until 1963 was to depoliticize problems by placing them on the level of technical cooperation among competent ministers—and with partial success.

A major problem of ministerial contacts has been that of coordination. The president may neglect to inform his foreign minister; the foreign minister may keep few memoranda of his conversations for use by his staff; and other ministers may deal directly with the president, without consulting with their foreign-office colleagues. In states which have both a foreign ministry and an African Affairs ministry, the lack of coordination usually blooms into rivalry and undercutting, a chronic problem in Morocco and Ghana, where the African Affairs ministry tends to specialize in political warfare while the foreign ministry practices diplomacy.

Two councils are important in the elaboration of intra-African policy: the council of ministers (the cabinet) and the party political bureaus, two governing bodies with overlapping membership and competing functions. Rarely is the cabinet an organ of collegial decision and collective responsibility in intra-African policy-making; its members are lieutenants who act both as department heads and as presidential advisors, but who do not meet together very often as a decision-making council. In some strongly one-party states —such as Guinea, Mali, and Ivory Coast—the cabinet has increased its activity since independence, at the expense of the political bureau; in other states, such as those of the Maghreb, it has tended to break down into ministerial commissions and inner circles grouped about the president's office or the palace. Nigeria, Liberia, Sierra Leone, Dahomey, and Senegal are exceptions to the general pattern of cabinet disuse; initiative for the Monrovia Group came out of a Senegalese council-of-ministers' meeting, which charged Dia to consult other African states about a new conference on Congo. In general, the council of ministers, by its nature, may be expected to be more aware of national capabilities but less attuned to popular desires than the political bureau, and its competence in intra-African relations is likely to be greater in technical areas than in political matters.

More of a paradox is the role of the party political bureau, for it operates within the same atmosphere of personalized and centralized decision-making without being weakened by it, as is the council of ministers. Throughout the area, the political bureau stands between the general ideology of the regime and the specific decisions of the president, and—more than any other organ —is responsible for formulating the principles of policy. It is also the channel for the dissemination of guidelines for discussion and education within party cells and to the public. Furthermore, it serves as a decision-making body for intraparty relations, a cover under which intra-African relations continue to be conducted, although there are few instances of the political bureau being used to make specific decisions complementing intra-African policy. Mention of these three general functions, however, does not imply that all parties stand in the same relation to government or that all political bureaus are equally effective in carrying out their functions. In some states—Guinea, Mali, Ghana, Algeria, Tunisia, Ivory Coast—the single party provides an articulated hierarchy parallel to, and interlocking with, government; in several of these states the party is considered to predominate over the government, which then becomes simply an executory committee of the party bureau. In these states, the three functions of the political bureau are generally filled;

the president predominates in the bureau but it is there that decisions on principles and occasionally details of African relations are made, with the foreign ministry acting as the technical organ of execution. In a number of these states, however—Tunisia, Ivory Coast, Mali—the impact of practice has forced a reversal of the roles; policy and even principles are decided in the president's office or the council of ministers and the party becomes the technical organ for transmitting applicable decisions to the people and carrying back their reactions. In such cases, the political bureau acts only as a department-heads' meeting.

In other states—including Senegal, Togo (before 1963), and Liberia—the party occupies a more ordinary position, that of an electoral machine. The political bureau is little used as an organ either of decision or of execution, although it may still perform its three functions superficially. It issues principles of intra-African policy after hearing a periodic review of foreign relations by the responsible member; it serves as a link between the government and local party organs; and it conducts its own relations with other parties and their bureaus.

In a third group of states, the party-government symbiosis does not exist, and the political bureau of the party—in power or out—serves to elaborate party programs and govern party affairs without any direct governmental role in intra-African affairs. Political bureaus (whatever their local name) in Morocco, Sierra Leone, and Nigeria—all multiparty states—follow this pattern. The three functions in these states concern party activities, but usually do not affect state policy toward other Western African countries; the council of ministers and the presidential or palace councils here predominate over political bureaus. It should not be inferred from these categories that the political bureau is a homogeneous body. There are frequently important differences among the members—in such diverse states as Guinea, Ghana, Senegal, Morocco, Algeria, and Tunisia—showing that party executive bodies are coalitions of several points of view, if not factions and interests.

The test of the importance of the political bureau as a decision-making organ lies not so much in its routine use, when the locus of decisions is often hard to isolate, but in its role in emergencies and in important initiatives. In some states, such decisions are not possible without reference to the political bureau. Before his 1958 trip to Accra, Touré appears to have been given PDG political bureau instructions general enough to allow him to enter into a union with Ghana, and the central committee of the CPP met to approve the proposed union while Touré was still in Accra.[43] In the same year, the executive committee of the Istiqlal formulated plans for a Maghreb unity conference, leading to the Tangier meeting in April. The CPP central committee met again before the Casablanca conference to block out general lines of policy, and before the first Lagos conference of 1962 to decide not to participate without Algeria. The PDG political bureau named and instructed its delegates to the 1959 Monrovia conference, which the council of ministers approved afterward. The following year, the bureau refused to continue steps toward *rapprochement* with Ivory Coast, despite the initiatives of Touré. The Neo-Destour political bureau, not the government, in a meeting in early July 1961, decided on a hard line on Bizerte. More frequently the political bureau in Western Africa sticks to principles and meets only after the fact to ratify decisions made in the presidential circle. Thus the UPS executive committee met the day following the attempted Soudanese *coup* in 1960 and after Dia's bid for power in 1962, when the necessary measures had already been taken; in the latter case, Senghor carefully explained that foreign policy would not change, because it was made by the party, but that it would become more active in the pursuit of goals established by the third party congress, for immobilism had been one of the defects of the previous regime. In matters of initiative, particularly in intra-African policy, the party political bureau tends to confine its activity to enunciating principles of state policy and ratifying decisions made elsewhere. Needless to say, the party congresses served an even more distant and somewhat Scriptural function: the consecration of general policy lines already decided but open to reinterpretation in the light of new events. They have given their stamp of authority to change or to continuity, as the occasion demands, but offer no examples of important decisions in intra-African relations.

A third level of influences on the president in the policy-making process includes groups of advisors. The most important of these, given the nature of decision-making, is the presidential cabinet or staff. Its form varies from country to country. In Accra, Flagstaff House includes a number of advisors to the president, who meet in weekly sessions with other officials of the foreign ministry and the party to discuss African policy. In Abidjan, Bamako, Dakar, Lagos, Rabat, and Algiers, offices of the chief of state or head of government contain advisors who serve as a source of suggestions and information. The functioning of these bodies is little different from that of any other executive staff, and the membership contains, diversely, nationals, Europeans, and exiles from other African countries. The presence of these exiles frequently contributes to distorting the information on which decisions are based and has even provided causes for bad relations between their host countries and home states. Presidential advisors do broaden the base of decision-making, however, and the presidential cabinet is at least as important as the council of ministers and the political bureau as a locus of specific policy-making.

Another group of advisors is the foreign ministry. In all states except Liberia, the foreign ministry was formed in the postwar period after independence, and in a number of states (Morocco, Algeria, Tunisia, the Entente states, Guinea, Nigeria) was not created until after the other ministries had been established. Within a remarkably short time, under the pressure of necessity, the foreign ministries have developed at least a skeletal structure along classical lines, with area and functional desks. Perhaps the most surprising aspect of this evolution has been the relative underdevelopment of the African sections of the ministries. In most cases, one Afro-Asian desk covers the segment of the world that includes the largest number of countries, the greatest population, and the majority of nonaligned states. A number of European countries, the United States, the Carnegie Endowment for International Peace, and the United Nations offer training programs for African foreign ministry personnel, but the graduates, trained in at least the procedures of modern diplomacy, tend to be placed in European, North American, and international organization sections of their foreign ministry.

Desk officers in the foreign ministries tend to take an active part in ministerial deliberations, but the output of these discussions frequently stops at the higher levels of the ministries; the desk man may or may not see his ambassador's reports—when they are written—and he frequently must rely on public information media for technical intelligence. Lack of secretarial assistance, a chronic weakness of African bureaucracies, also hampers intra-ministerial communications and record-keeping. The economic-affairs desk officer frequently deserves special recognition for his activity, perhaps because it is frequently easier to handle economic material—even with the limited statistical material available—than to seize the vagaries of political matters, especially because the latter are so completely and exclusively within the competence of higher authorities.[44] Obviously, however, detailed evaluation of one desk or another depends on the personal competence of the individual who mans it.

The intermediate level in the foreign ministries tends to function best. The secretary-general, permanent secretary, or secretary of state for foreign affairs, as he may be called, is a man who is both at the top of the technical desk heap and the bottom of the political pile. Having access to both groups, he is in the best position to bring technical information to the attention of political figures. Where the foreign minister is a political figure—as in Guinea, Senegal, Ghana, Morocco—it has been the secretary-general who has run the department. When he fails, the link between the political and the technical is broken, and policy—liberated from its informational basis—is free of the constraint of reality.

A third group of advisors to the president is composed of his diplomatic representatives. If their job is properly performed, ambassadors and their staffs serve as a primary source of information, as spokesmen for their country's foreign policy interests, and as guardians over their country's commercial interests and expatriate populations. Unfortunately, in Western Africa, ambassadorial relations are frequently regarded more as a sign of prestige and friendship than as an institution serving a positive function.[45] Very few states maintain embassies for the purpose of gathering information in countries with which relations are not warm (an exception being the Moroccans in Ivory Coast) or for the purpose of advancing a specific foreign policy (again, an exception being the Moroccans in Guinea, who worked hard to keep Guinea from recognizing Mauritania).

Ironically, the criticism has frequently been made that there are too many African ambassadorial posts and that they place a costly burden on the

DIPLOMATIC REPRESENTATION AMONG WESTERN AFRICAN STATES, 1964

From \ To	Maghreb					UAS				Entente						
	Tunisia	Algeria	Morocco	Mauritania	Senegal	Mali	Guinea	Ghana	Liberia	Ivory Coast	Upper Volta	Niger	Dahomey	Sierra Leone	Togo	Nigeria
Tunisia	✕	A	A	A†	A	A†	A†	A								
Algeria	A	✕	A			A	A	A	A	A	A†	A‡	A			
Morocco	A	A	✕			A	A	A	A	A						A
Mauritania	A			✕	PR				A							
Senegal	A	A	A		✕	A	A	A	A					A**		A
Mali	A*	A	A		A	✕	RM##	RM	A	A	A	D		A#		A##
Guinea		A	A†	A		RM##	✕	RM##	A	A##	A‡	A††	A††	A##	A	A
Ghana	A	A	A	A	A	RM	RM	✕	A	A	A	C	A	HC	C	HC
Liberia					A	A	A	A		A				A	A	A
Ivory Coast	A‡				PR‡		A	A		✕				A**		A
Upper Volta					PR		A		A		✕					
Niger							A	A	D			✕	D	A**	D‡‡	A
Dahomey							C						✕			C
Sierra Leone					A##		A	HC	A					✕		HC
Togo							A								✕	C
Nigeria						A	A	A	HC	A	A		C	HC	C	✕

A-Ambassador, HC-High Commissioner (Commonwealth members), RM-Resident Minister (UAS states), C-Chargé d'affairs, D-Delegate, PR-Permanent Representative, *-Resident in Morocco, †-Resident in Senegal, ‡-Resident in Ivory Coast, #-Resident in Guinea, **-Resident in Liberia, ††-Resident in Togo, ‡‡-Resident in Dahomey, ##-Withdrawn in 1964 for reasons of economy.

Sources: *Europe-France-Outremer*, XLI, 409 (March 1964); embassies in Washington, D.C.

finances of the new states. Although this comment may be valid insofar as Western African representation outside the continent is concerned, it is difficult to see its validity in intra-African relations.[46] There is a real need for small, efficient embassies headed by capable and dedicated men who feel that their job of representation and information is as important in Ouagadougou or Nouakchott as it is in Paris or Washington. Such men are hard to find. Until they are available—as they are in some foreign services, most notably in Morocco's and Tunisia's—ambassadors will continue to fall far short of their potential value as presidential advisors.

Instead, intra-African diplomatic representation has shown serious weaknesses. It is undermined by the practice of sending out special envoys when important contacts are necessary, and by the long absences of many of the ambassadors (a habit encouraged by presidential example). Some states' missions are headed by exiled politicians, whose effectiveness as either representatives or informants is seriously limited. Moreover, the language division that plagues Western Africa has found many states with few diplomats trained in the language of the country to which they are accredited. On the other hand, a few embassies have been overzealous to the point of engaging in subversion—Ghanaians have been sent home from Liberia (September 1961 and February 1963) and Ivory Coast (February 1963) and the Nigerian foreign minister has made charges of subversion against the Ghanaian high commissioner's office in Lagos.

Several attempts have been made to deal with problems of representation within Western Africa. One is to pool ambassadors, a solution included in the UAM agreement and adopted by some of the Entente states. Multiple representation poses problems of coordination and dissemination of intelligence, and is effective only when there is a high degree of policy cooperation among the accrediting governments—or little business to be transacted. Another method of simplifying the ambassadorial problem is by multiple accreditations. In a number of cases, a nonresident ambassador is accredited to Togo, Mauritania, and the three lesser Entente members. This solution is one merely of form, for the effectiveness of an absent ambassador is nearly nil. Only rarely is even a skeletal staff left behind in the ambassador's absence. A third approach is the development of special ties, as in the institution of resident ministers in the UAS. The experiment was highly unsuccessful. The ministers were frequently not admitted to the host state's cabinet meetings, to which they were supposed to have access, and were usually barred from the political bureau, where the real decisions were made; neither ministers nor ambassadors, they sometimes received less favorable treatment than other envoys. A fourth solution is quite the opposite: that of nonresident ministers or no ambassador at all. Among the Entente states, there is only one ambassador (the Voltaic envoy to Abidjan) and two "delegates" (Niger's envoys to Abidjan and Cotonou); the rest of the business is handled by frequent meetings of the cabinet ministers concerned. Such an approach is effective for the negotiation of technical problems, but is not geared to handle political problems or matters concerning expatriate nationals—topics left to the attention of the heads of state and frequently beyond their powers of solution.

A last group of advisors, the military, has been limited almost exclusively to a technical role in Western African relations. In Morocco, General ben Hammou Kettani made a controversial statement applauding ONUC's role (and the Moroccan army's actions) in Congo, contrary to the stand of his government and the Casablanca Group, but with no effect on policy.[47] Colonel Haouri Boumedienne also made the clearest statement of Algeria's revolutionary aims in a declaration in Cairo, indicating the crucial role of the former ALN in Algerian politics even before the 1965 military coup.[48] In other countries, however, the army has played an insignificant role in the intra-African policy-making process. Because the army is one of the few well-organized institutions in many Western African countries, the reverse might be expected. Because of its political potential, however, the army has been subjected to strict party control in such countries as Tunisia, Senegal, Mali, Guinea, Liberia, Ivory Coast, and, in a sense, Algeria. In most of these states it is the political qualifications of an officer that determines his appointment and promotion. In a few other states—Ghana, Nigeria, Sierra Leone, Morocco —the army has inherited from its colonial background a spirit of apolitical loyalty that the independent governments have sought to preserve. In internal politics, the army has frequently played a crucial role in supporting the government in times of domestic disturbances (as in Morocco, Algeria, Tunisia, Mali, Nigeria, Guinea, and Liberia) or in expressing dissatisfaction or opposition (as in Togo, Dahomey, Algeria, Niger, and Ivory Coast). In these cases, the issues were domestic and unrelated to intra-African affairs.

The foreign-policy-making process also involves certain representative groups: parliament, national organizations, and political parties. The parliament is used to express national positions and give weight to official stands; its president and commission members are frequently chosen as envoys. Often the parliament is allowed to go through the motions of a debate on African (or other) foreign policy, but without effect. Although a parliament may occasionally serve as the focal point for pressures brought to bear on relations with the non-African world—such as the debates over the Anglo-Nigerian defense pact in 1961 or the Americo-Moroccan base negotiations in 1957— intra-African relations have never aroused a Western African parliament to such a degree.

National organizations—labor unions, youth and women's organizations, even farm and business groups—have a more complex role. Their strength comes from the presence of their leaders on party and government councils, from the mass membership organized behind these leaders in a crucial modern sector, and also from the ability to make their own African policy and carry out their own relations with other states' national organizations if their demands are not heeded by the government. Influence is thus derived from political position (the degree of integration into the party-government hierarchy) and relations (the local strength of the organization).

The most important of these developing pressure groups are the labor unions. In no Western African country is there a labor government, although Guinea comes closest to being the exception. There, the labor movement (National Confederation of Guinean Workers of the General Union of Black African Workers [CNTG-UGTAN]) led and dominated the nationalist movement (PDG-RDA). The party, however, did not become an auxiliary of labor; when labor leaders became party leaders, they left the union in the hands of secondary figures as a party auxiliary. The reverse process has led to somewhat similar results in Ghana, Tunisia, Algeria, Liberia, and Mali; there, the party moved in to control the labor union, usually by means of a deal which granted government support to one group of labor leaders in their effort to unite the unions in exchange for party-government control over the resultant single national union. Because the process was one of exchanging concessions between party and union, the result was a two-way influence pattern, consecrating labor's participation in policy decisions as well as party control over labor activities. In a third pattern, government has controlled the conditions under which labor operates, but has been unable or unwilling to unite the unions, control their politics, or subordinate the union to the party. Such is the situation in Morocco, Nigeria, Senegal, Ivory Coast, and Upper Volta. In these states, labor's role in deciding and executing African policy can be expected to be less direct.

In the formulation of African policy, the labor unions, according to their influence within the party and government, have served to keep radical slogans before state policy-makers; in its execution, they have strengthened one another's positions by participation in African labor conferences and national labor congresses. The activities of UGTAN in French West Africa, of the All-African Trade Union Federation (AATUF), founded in Casablanca in May 1961, and of the African Trade Union Confederation (ATUC), founded in Dakar in January 1962, and of the repeated attempts at coordinating North African labor movements between 1956 and 1962, although ineffective in consolidating the trade unions, did serve to keep policies and slogans alive and raised the prestige of Guinea, Ghana, Mali, Senegal, Algeria, Morocco, and Tunisia. The moderate policies and the modest approach to African unity of the Entente states and Nigeria have been reflected in their unions' greater aloofness from African labor politics.

In these attempts at labor unity, did the unions act as a cause of government action or as a consequence? Or were they the alternative to government inaction? Did they act as autonomous agents or as party-government auxiliaries? The questions are crucial to an understanding of the role of unions, but the answers are inconclusive.[49] Revival of AATUF in October 1963 was clearly the result of Algerian government initiative and Malian governmental support; but this is a lone example. Both AATUF and ATUC appear to be labor echoes of the Casablanca and Monrovia conferences, on the heels of which they followed; but the AATUF meeting had been proposed in December 1958, in preparation since September 1959, and originally called for May 1960—

all before the Casablanca meeting of 1961. The ATUC meeting was a reaction to AATUF, not a result of the Monrovia conference. If the catalepsy of both African international organizations can be termed existence, both have outlasted their political counterparts, the Casablanca and Monrovia Groups; but both have remained outside "the spirit of Addis Ababa," their unification at the end of 1963 having fallen through. Labor unions in the UAS sent representatives to one another's jamborees but never took any concrete steps toward the coordination foreseen in the UAS charter, but then neither did their heads of state. As a tentative conclusion, it may be suggested that unions operated as executory agencies of government policy to the extent that they were effectively controlled by their governments and to the extent that such action coincided with the wishes of union leaders (in Tunisia, UGTT leader Ahmed Tlili was more interested in African labor unity than was Bourguiba). In general, African labor's politics are an emanation of the same African unity myth (strengthened by an equally strong labor myth of proletarian unity) that lies behind government policy.

Other national organizations play a similar role, although limited by their relative weakness within the government. African youth and women's organizations have followed labor unions in their attempts to unite, and Guinea's position has been particularly enhanced in the process, although the influence of youth and women in African policy-making is slight. In a few countries— Ghana, Ivory Coast, Senegal, and the Maghreb states—there are socioeconomic groups such as farmers' unions, industrial and commercial organizations, and cooperative associations. Although such organizations could, by their nature, contribute to the development of a national-interest policy, they are in reality instruments of government control rather than organizations of socioeconomic interests. Some of these groups are members of Pan-African federations (such as the Ghana-led All-African Union of Farmers) but neither the international organizations nor the local groups have a significant role in the making or execution of state policy.[50]

Similar in position, although not usually considered among national organizations, are the Muslim sects, whose mass and transnational characteristics give them great potential influence in intra-African relations. Particularly the Tijaniya and Qadiriya sects—leaders of which are important figures in Senegalese, Malian, and Nigerian politics and in Moroccan and Algerian religious life—could be expected to create a basis for friendly relations among the countries in which their followers are located.[51] Because of their traditional nature and their national orientation, however, these sects have had little actual effect. In a few cases, their leaders have been appointed ambassadors—in some instances, the Muslim countries. On a broader level, the presence of Islam serves to counteract historical Sudanese antipathy to the Arabs of North Africa, but its general influence on African policy is even less important than that of Catholicism or Rotarianism in other parts of the world.

The final representative group in the policy-making process is the political party. Below the level of the political bureau, its role is largely one of recruitment, education, support, and mobilization rather than participation in the making of decision, the articulation of interests, or the formulation of goals. Even officials of the PDG, whose philosophy is one of symbiosis between the elite and the masses in policy-making, admit that their principle does not hold in the making of foreign policy. They do claim, however, that regular Thursday party-cell meetings are used for discussing government policy; "the question of Kashmir and the war in Algeria are fully understood by our people," a Guinean ambassador claimed. The assertion that the identity of the elite and the masses within the party makes for a "people's foreign policy" is procedurally inaccurate; also—given the understandably low level of popular aspirations, expectations, and information in Western Africa—it is a meaningless proposition. Unity and disunity, regional brotherhood and narrow nationhood, sealed borders and open borders—even peace and armed uprisings—have all been justified in the name of "the public's wish." In Western Africa, public opinion still is an instrument of the party, and the party is the means of mobilization.

Basic reasons for this situation are found in the role of public information media and public opinion in intra-African policy. Because of the high rate of illiteracy, the press is an elite—not yet a mass—medium of communication. (The only exception is the Arabic press in North Africa.) A number of daily African newspapers run background articles on other African countries from time to time, and some have regular and reasonably well-informed editorials on African affairs. All issues of the party press throughout the area carry lengthy hortative articles in general sloganistic terms; these are designed to mobilize public support by justifying policy and channeling thought. The small daily press is also supplemented by a number of party weeklies for internal consumption (such as *Al-Istiqlal* in Morocco and *Fraternité* in Ivory Coast), by three weeklies circulated throughout French-speaking Africa (the two excellent reviews from Dakar and Tunis, *Afrique Nouvelle* and *Jeune Afrique*,[52] and their highly ideological competitor from Algiers, *Révolution Africaine*), and by daily and weekly papers from London and Paris. African publications help Africa know itself; at the same time, they encourage perception of African events in nationally accepted terms. With few exceptions—such as Morocco and Nigeria, where the press is not only free but competitive—these terms follow the party-government lead; their role in the policy-making process is therefore to keep the elite on the track it has set out for itself, not to exert influence on specific issues. Only in rare cases— as in Ghana, Algeria, and, to a lesser extent, Tunisia—is the press itself one of the components of the elite; there its position is similar to that of the labor unions: both under the control of, and an influence on the government.

Thus, public opinion regarding African policy in Western Africa is the opinion of the elite. The inertness of the masses is simply a natural corollary —both cause and consequence—of the highly centralized position of the small, decision-making elite. Intermediate groups and figures outside the presidential circle attempt to find personal access to the council chambers of the chief, rather than force their way in by mobilizing support among the masses. Their access to the masses is barred by those who "got there first" and who surround themselves with popular symbols and mobilized crowds. The people in Western Africa are not "in the street," as in the Middle East, but in the courtyard of the presidential palace, where their potential for milling about—both literally and figuratively—is very narrowly limited. How narrow are the limits on the elite within the palace? Probably less restrictive than it may think. Several states have reversed their policy in Western African relations without incurring any repercussions; the reversal is skillfully justified—often in the same broad terms that were used to defend the previous policy. The Morocco-Tunisian rupture (1960) and *rapprochement* (1964), the Senegal-Mali rupture (1960) and *rapprochement* (1963), the Ghana-Togo rupture (1959) and *rapprochement* (1963), the Guinea-Ghana Union (1958) and its dissolution (1963), the Guinea-Ivory Coast rupture (1958) and *rapprochement* (1962), the Casablanca-Monrovia split (1961) and reconciliation (1963)—can all be justified as a change in situations rather than a change in policy. In reality, however, both kinds of change were present, and the changes in policy were made by the elite without any protest from the public. Yet in each case the policy was presented as having been imposed by public opinion. Public opinion, under the impact of a radical independent Algeria, did play a role in the general trend of Tunisian policy. Public opinion also affected Morocco's relations with Mauritania, forcing the king's absence from his seat next to ould Daddah at Addis Ababa under pressure from the irredentist Istiqlal party during the first national elections. But it is doubtful, even in these two cases, that a contrary policy would have aroused public opinion to the point of endangering the governmental position. Public opinion in Africa is not only outside the decision-making process, but it also appears not to care about the details of intra-African relations. The lack of public reaction to policy shifts, and the fact that no specific policy changes have been effected by the pressure of public opinion, provide eloquent testimony. After a concerted letter-writing campaign (of unknown impetus) to Flagstaff House, the Ghanaian policy favoring withdrawal of troops from Congo was reconsidered at the end of 1960 and reversed—an exception that appears to be unique.[53] Public opinion —inchoate though it may be—does have a role in domestic politics and the general stability of Western African governments. As a direct influence on intra-African policy, however, it is still irrelevant.

Nevertheless, the significant point is that, on a more general level, the elite thought otherwise. Western African leaders tend to be prisoners of their own popular and sloganistic manipulations. Having rallied general public support through frequent public appeals and efficient political machines, they consider such support to be real and meaningful in terms of narrower issues as well— including those of intra-African relations. In Europe or America, government leaders justly fear the reactions of public opinion, which are expressed indirectly through the parliaments or directly at the polls. In Western Africa,

HEADS OF STATE AND GOVERNMENT

Liberia July 26, 1847	Morocco March 2, 1956	Tunisia March 20, 1956	Ghana March 6, 1957	Guinea October 2, 1958	Mali (Soudan) September 22, 1960	Senegal August 20, 1960	Togo April 27, 1960
Tubman (president, 1943-)	Mohammed V (king, 1927-61) Hassan II (king, February 26, 1961-)	Bourguiba (premier, April 11, 1956-57; president, July 25, 1957-)	Nkrumah (premier, March 22, 1952-60; president, April 27, 1960-)	Toure (premier, May 14, 1957-58; president, October 2, 1958-)	Keita (premier, April 15, 1959-60; president, September 22, 1960-)	Dia (premier, May 18, 1957-December 18, 1962) Senghor (president, September 5, 1960-)	Olympio (premier, May 16, 1958-61; president, April 9, 1961-January 13, 1963) Grunitzky (president, March 5, 1963-)

FOREIGN MINISTERS

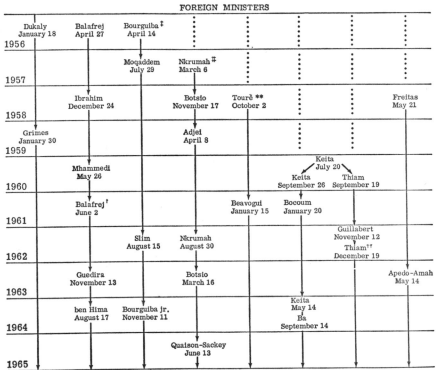

1956 Dukaly January 18	Balafrej April 27	Bourguiba [‡] April 14					
1957		Moqaddem July 29	Nkrumah [#] March 6				
1958	Ibrahim December 24		Botsio November 17	Touré [**] October 2			Freitas May 21
1959 Grimes January 30			Adjei April 8				
1960	Mhammedi May 26				Keita July 20 / Keita September 26 / Thiam September 19		
1961	Balafrej [†] June 2			Beavogui January 15	Bocoum January 20		
1962		Slim August 15	Nkrumah August 30			Guillabert November 12 Thiam [††] December 19	
1963	Guedira November 13		Botsio March 16				Apedo-Amah May 14
1964	ben Hima August 17	Bourguiba jr. November 11			Keita May 14 Ba September 14		
1965			Quaison-Sackey June 13				

* During 1957-58, Africans held only the position of vice-president of the government council (vice-premier) in AOF territories.

† Also Minister for Mauritanian Affairs (ould Omeir: June 2, 1961-August 20, 1964, and ben Driss: January 7, 1965-) and for African Affairs (Khatib: June 2, 1961-November 13, 1963).

‡ Also Secretary of State for Arab Relations (Moqaddem: April 14, 1956-July 29, 1957).

Also African Affairs Bureau (headed successively by Padmore, Baako, Dei-Anang, Barden).

** Secretary of State for Foreign Affairs attached to the Presidency (Fodé Cissé: October 2, 1958-January 15, 1961).

78

Dahomey August 1, 1960	Niger August 3, 1960	Upper Volta August 5, 1960	Ivory Coast August 7, 1960	Nigeria October 1, 1960	Mauritania November 28, 1960	Sierra Leone April 27, 1961	Algeria July 3, 1962
Maga (premier, May 18, 1959-60; president, December 11, 1960- October 27, 1963) Apithy, (premier, May 25, 1957-59; president, January 19, 1964-November 27, 1965)	Diori (premier, December 18, 1958-60; president, November 11, 1960-)	Yameogo (premier, October 21, 1958-1959; president, December 9, 1959-)	Houphouet-Boigny (premier, May 1, 1959-60; president, November 27, 1960-)	Azikiwe (governor-general, November 16, 1960-63; president, October 1, 1963-) Tafawa Balewa (premier, September 2, 1957-)	ould Daddah (premier, May 20, 1957-61; president, August 20, 1961-)	M. Margai (premier, April 27, 1961-64) A. Margai (premier, April 29, 1964-)	Abbas ("premier", September 19, 1958-61) ben Khedda ("premier", 1961-62) ben Bella (premier, September 26, 1962-63; president, September 15, 1963-June 19, 1965) Boumedienne (president, 1965-)

FOREIGN MINISTERS

Assogbe December 30	Diori November 9			Tafawa [ttt] Balewa October 1	ould Daddah November 28	Karefa-Smart May 31	
		Kone January 4	Houphouet- [***] Boigny January 4	Wachuku July 17			
Zinsou [tt] February 12					Laghdaf November 3		Khemisti September 28
Soglo October 28 Mama December 4	Mayaki [##] June 23		Alliali February 16		Deyine July 1		ben Bella April 11 Bouteflika September 18
Lozes January 25						Rogers-Wright May 1	
				Tafawa Balewa January 7	ould Daddah January 18 ould Cheikh July 26		

[tt] Also Minister of State for Special (African) Affairs (Mustafa Cissé: December 19, 1962-December 8, 1963).
[tt] Also Secretary of State for African Affairs (Aplogan: November 15, 1962-October 27, 1963).
[##] Also Minister for African Affairs (Ikhia: June 23, 1963-March 1, 1964).
[***] Also Minister of State for Entente Affairs (Denise: November 22, 1960-61) and Minister for Entente Affairs (Diomandé: January 2, 1961-February 15, 1963).
[ttt] Also Minister of State for Foreign Affairs (Bomalli: October 1, 1960-January 6, 1965).

the effect of public opinion on intra-African relations—as on decision-making itself—is confined to the perceptions of the elite. Decisions and their execution emanate from the presidential palace, within the limits of effective communication, coordination, and political control.

One final ingredient of the decision-making process is important: the external (African) environment. Choices and possibilities in African policies have frequently been severely limited. These limitations have operated less strongly in bilateral relations than in broad attempts at unity, alliance, and counteralliance. In bilateral relation, such as those between Senegal and Mali, Ghana and Togo, Morocco and Algeria, and Morocco and Mauritania, obvious alternatives exist. But, given the unity myth, the steps from Accra in 1958 to Addis Ababa in 1963 were largely a product of unavoidable factors. North African unity was objectively impossible as long as Algeria was not independent. The attainment of independence by Guinea in 1958 made the independence of the rest of AOF possible, if not inevitable, shortly thereafter; the option of the Mali Federation for independence was the direct cause of Houphouet-Boigny's about-face in 1960, and Guinea's choice of independence over unity meant that the Mali Federation was condemned to collapse. Thereafter, when states met at unity conferences, their final resolutions were turned out in terms of the lowest common denominator. There was no exchange of concessions: when the attending members (who brought their policy with them) agreed, the communiqués could be precise; when their points of view differed, the conference remained vague. Thus any universal conference before 1963 was doomed to generalities. At Abidjan and Brazzaville (1960), Casablanca and Monrovia (1961), and Lagos (1962), a certain measure of agreement was reached because the participants already had similar policies. Those who had different policies stayed away. Before 1963, the African states could not meet on a regional basis because the ideological positions within any given region were different; they could not meet on a continental basis because important areas of the continent were not yet independent.[54] After Algeria won independence, the ideological problem and the attendance problem—which were linked—no longer existed. By this time the pressure for universal attendance was greater than the pressure for ideological purity, and the limitations on success that had existed since 1958 were no longer operative at Addis Ababa. The absence of a few states (Morocco and Togo) was no longer an important matter. Again the rule of attendance had its effect: the converging forces which resulted in the conference were so strong that only one result was likely, and even such an outburst as Somali's against Ethiopia did not succeed in disrupting the progress of the meeting. Given the magnitude of the pressures and the insignificance of the obstacles, any universal African conference at that time on any terms would probably have achieved the same result.

By the same token, the effect of the unity slogan (as a factor in the external environment) on the decision-makers meant that potential catalysts in the formation of alliances in 1962-65 did not have the same effect as similar events in 1958-62. The ben Bella-ben Khedda rivalry, the assassination of Olympio, the Niger-Dahomey dispute, and the Morocco-Algerian war were not powerful enough to break the spell of unity. It is perhaps strange to consider that African relations were the result of situational determinism that left the decision-makers little choice. It must be emphasized that the environment referred to contains not only concrete elements such as the nonindependence of Algeria but also the attitudinal atmosphere—that is, not only objectively discernible facts but also the peculiarities of subjective perception by the decision-makers. Given the way things were and the way they saw them, the leaders could frequently act only the way they did.

NOTES

¹ See Arnold Wolfers, *Discord and Collaboration* (Baltimore: Johns Hopkins U.P., 1962), pp. 147-65.

² See James S. Coleman, "The Politics of Sub-Saharan Africa," in Gabriel A. Almond and James S. Coleman (eds.), *The Politics of Developing Nations* (Princeton, N.J.: Princeton U.P., 1960), p. 331; Charles F. Andrain, "Democracy and Socialism: Ideologies of African Leaders," in David E. Apter (ed.), *Ideology and Discontent* (New York: Free Press, 1964), pp. 159-60. See also Sekou Touré, *The International Policy of the Democratic Party of Guinea* (Conakry: PDG, n.d.), p. 6; Sekou Touré, "African Emancipation," in Paul E. Sigmund, Jr. (ed.), *The Ideologies of the Developing Nations* (New York: Praeger, 1963), pp. 158, 168. Note, however, that specific interest may in fact be totally absent—another problem that new nations have to deal with.

³ Annette Baker Fox, *The Power of Small States* (Chicago: U. of Chicago, 1959), p. 182. See also Jean-Louis Quermonne, "Les engagements internationaux des nouveaux États," in J-B Duroselle and J. Meyriat (eds.), *Les nouveaux États dans les relations internationales* (Paris: Colin, 1962), pp. 347-48.

⁴ See, for example, M. J. Field, *Search for Security* (London: Faber, 1960), p. 296; Claude Cheysson, "The Role of the New Elites in the Struggle for Modernization," unpublished paper presented to the Georgetown University Conference on French-Speaking Africa, Washington, D.C., August 1964.

⁵ Cited in Claude Phillips, *The Development of Nigerian Foreign Policy* (Evanston, Ill.: Northwestern U.P., 1964), p. 32.

⁶ Touré speech, AFP-G, December 15, 1958; Kwame Nkrumah, *I Speak of Freedom* (London: Heinemann, 1961), p. 107.

⁷ "Each African country resents the imperialist intervention in Congo as an attack on its unity and sovereignty, but it has also contributed to the reinforcement of African consciousness and of solidarity among the people" (Algerian Foreign Minister Abdelaziz Bouteflika, *Révolution Africaine,* January 3, 1965); "It's a process which, starting from Congo—the heart of Africa—threatens the whole continent, the African countries struggling for their independence as well as those already independent and intent on remaining so" (ben Bella, *Jeune Afrique,* January 10, 1965).

⁸ See discussions by Robert C. Good, "State-Building as a Determinant of Foreign Policy in the New States," in Lawrence W. Martin (ed.), *Neutralism and Nonalignment* (New York: Praeger, 1962), pp. 3-12, and "Changing Patterns of African International Relations," *American Political Science Review,* LVIII, 3 (September 1964), 632-41.

⁹ The argument between conventional (legal) and revolutionary legitimization is one of the major sources of conflict in Africa. Senghor told the UPS National Council, "The

adoption of irrational attitudes by some African countries would have ruined Africa's international prestige if other African states, including Senegal, had not defended the principles which form the basis of morality and consequently of international law" (Radio Dakar, January 3, 1965). Bechir ben Yahmed wrote of Tshombe: "It is not and never has been sufficient to be 'legal' to be sacred. Men in power are never judged on their legality, but on their policy. . . . France had a legal position in Algeria, and the supreme legality is that of Verwoerd in South Africa" (*Jeune Afrique,* December 13, 1964). Or again, of the closing lines of Touré's and Azikiwe's New Year 1965 speeches: "Mankind is marching on. It is advancing toward universal unity and social harmony. Long live the Revolution!" vs. "To those who have contested and lost in the elections, I appeal to them as good combattants to close ranks and join with those who have succeeded in the great task of nation-building. Long live the Federation. Long live the Constitution!" (Radio Conakry, January 1, 1965; Radio Lagos, January 4, 1965.)

[10] For background discussion, see Taylor Cole, "Emergent Federalism in Nigeria," in Taylor Cole and Robert O. Tilman (eds.), *The Nigerian Political Scene* (Durham, N.C.: Duke U.P., 1962), p. 47; James S. Coleman, "The Foreign Policy of Nigeria," in Joseph E. Black and Kenneth W. Thompson (eds.), *Foreign Policies in a World of Change* (New York: Harper and Row, 1963), pp. 390-91.

[11] For representative Communist opinion, see I. I. Potekhin, "On African Socialism: A Soviet View," in William H. Friedland and Carl G. Rosberg, *African Socialism* (Stanford: Stanford U.P., 1964), p. 105; R. Avakov and G. Mirskiy, "Class Structure in the Underdeveloped Countries," in Thomas Perry Thornton (ed.), *The Third World in Soviet Perspective* (Princeton, N.J.: Princeton U.P., 1964), pp. 292, 295-96, 298; N. Numade, *The African Revolution* (New York: New Century, 1963), pp. 6-7, 30-32. A sound discussion of the growing elites as "the new class" is found in Kenneth W. Grundy, "Mali: The Prospects of Planned Socialism," in Friedland and Rosberg (eds.), *op. cit.,* pp. 178-79.

[12] It would be a gross misrepresentation to see the Accra-Abidjan rivalry as a continuation of the Ashanti-Baoule rivalry within the Akan nation, or to consider the breakup of the Mali Federation as a heritage of animosities between the Toukouleur and Mali empires. Moreover, it is hard to see any direct relevance of Abd al-Mumin, Hajj Omar, Samory, and Ousman Dan Fodio, to the modern nations, although of course their indirect relevance as roots and myths in the nation-building process is evident; see Thomas Hodgkin, *Nationalism in Colonial Africa* (London: Muller, 1956), pp. 169-84.

[13] This is well described in Virginia Thompson, "Dahomey," in Gwendolen Carter (ed.), *Five African States* (Ithaca, N.Y.: Cornell U.P., 1963), pp. 224-26, 246-48. By building up even its own interest and by dealing with opposition groups and economic needs realistically, the government elite performs the helpful task of consolidating its own legitimacy and restoring governmental authority that it had undermined when acting as a nationalist movement; see Good, in Martin (ed.), *op. cit.,* pp. 9-10; Coleman, in Almond and Coleman (eds.), *op. cit.,* pp. 333, 335.

[14] Good, in Martin (ed.), *op. cit.,* p. 12.

[15] For a good example, see Thompson, *op. cit.,* pp. 256-57. For a relevant analysis of similar "pseudoevents," see Daniel J. Boorstin, *The Image* (New York: Atheneum, 1962).

[16] On the concept of self-abnegation and self-preservation, see Wolfers, *op. cit.,* pp. 81-102; George Liska, *International Equilibrium* (Cambridge, Mass.: Harvard U.P., 1957), pp. 200-201.

[17] The opposition of ideology to realism may raise questions; however, see Apter, *op. cit.,* p. 20; Joseph J. Spengler, "Theory, Ideology, Noneconomic Values, and Politico-economic Revolution," in James J. Spengler and Ralph Braibanti (eds.), *Tradition, Values, and Socioeconomic Development* (Durham: Duke U.P., 1961), pp. 32-33; Dorothy Nelkin, "Socialist Sources of Pan-African Ideology," in Friedland and Rosberg (eds.), *op. cit.,* p. 73. The difference is expressed in the words of Houphouet-Boigny and Nkrumah: ". . . [At Monrovia, we] chose freely between the dream and the reality. The

dream is the unity of the African continent with a central unitary government. It is a wish we all have, but it is not the reality of today. That reality consists of unity of inspiration toward constructive cooperation in mutual respect and in the affirmation of the personality of each state," Houphouet-Boigny, Radio Brazzaville, September 2, 1961. "I have often been accused of pursuing 'a policy of the impossible.' . . . But that did not stop us from going forward with our efforts, buoyed by the certainty of ultimate victory, and [independence] has come, as I said, much sooner than anticipated. That is how I feel about African unity," Kwame Nkrumah, *Africa Must Unite* (New York: Praeger, 1963), p. 170. Hella Pick has written of the Brazzaville Group: "All twelve believed themselves to be realists and wanted to deal with the Congo and Algeria problems not on the basis of preconceived ideas of what was right or wrong, but on what was possible," "The Brazzaville Twelve," *Africa South in Exile*, V (April-June 1961), 80.

[18] Tunisia, and some parts of the Moroccan political spectrum, are borderline cases; although their experiences have been similar to those of the revolutionary-idealist states, the effect has not been as sharp nor the duration as long. Attitudes reflecting both schools of thought have been the result.

[19] Obviously, ideology is used here in a different—even opposite—sense from that used in Harold D. Lasswell and Abraham Kaplan, *Power and Society* (New Haven: Yale U.P., 1950), p. 123, or Karl Mannheim, *Ideology and Utopic* (New York: Harcourt, 1936). The use here excludes "moderate ideologies," if such exist, because of their pluralism and realism. For some general suggestions of a "moderate ideology," however, see Andrain, in Apter (ed.), *op. cit.*, pp. 167-69; James S. Coleman and Carl G. Rosberg, Jr. (eds.), *Political Parties and National Integration in Tropical Africa* (Berkeley: U. of California Press, 1964), pp. 5 *et passim*. Coleman and Rosberg (*op. cit.*), concentrating on internal politics while this study concentrates on external politics, uses the terms *pragmatic-pluralistic* and *revolutionary-centralizing* where this book uses *conventional-realist* and *revolutionary-idealist*. For more attention to these problems, see I. William Zartman, "National Interest vs. Ideological Determinants," in Vernon McKay (ed.), *African Diplomacy* (New York: Praeger, 1966).

[20] Senghor, Radio Dakar, January 3, 1965.

[21] Aristide R. Zolberg, "The Dakar Colloquium: The Search for a Doctrine," in Friedland and Rosberg (eds.), *op. cit.*, p. 126. See also Nkrumah, *Africa Must Unite, op. cit.*, pp. 165-70. On the accommodation of a socialist foreign policy to international relations, see Barrington Moore, *Soviet Politics—The Dilemma of Power* (Cambridge, Mass.: Harvard U.P., 1951).

[22] See, notably, Nkrumah's letter to Tshombe (*Ghanaian Times*, December 22, 1962), appealing to Tshombe's "African patriotism" and intimating that there was only one way of thinking as a "true" African.

[23] Nkrumah, *Towards African Unity* (Accra: Flagstaff House, 1963), p. 2.

[24] ". . . a newspaper of the calibre of the [London] *Times* never attacks without a motive. . . . We are actually in the thick of a psychological war in which the enemy is the [European] Common Market" (Radio Accra, June 30, 1961).

[25] Touré, *The International Policy of the Democratic Party of Guinea, op. cit.*, p. 19. For an answer, see d'Arboussier, *op. cit.*, pp. 29-30.

[26] Quoted by Vernon McKay in manuscript, "Africa and Disarmament," p. 6; see also Thiam, *op. cit.*, pp. 159-60.

[27] See Joseph Frankel, *The Making of Foreign Policy* (New York: Oxford U.P., 1963), pp. 95-110.

[28] See K. A. B. Jones-Quartey, "The Ghana Press," in *Report on the Press in West Africa* (Dakar: University of Dakar, 1960), mimeographed.

[29] "Note à l'attention de M. le Ministre des Affaires Étrangères," November 1960.

[30] "Les Frontières du Maroc" (Rabat: Interim Commission, 1957); *Livre blanc sur la Mauritanie* (Rabat: Ministry of Foreign Affairs, 1960); *Taqyid ma ishtamal 'alih iqlim Tuat* (Rabat: Royal Palace, 1962).

[31] Campagnie Générale de Recherches pour l'Afrique; *Les Rapports de l'Afrique* (Tunis:

Secretariat of State for Cultural Affairs, 1964). The United Nations Economic Commission for Africa has also provided basic studies; see, for example, *Report of the ECA Industrial Co-ordination Commission to Algeria, Libya, Morocco, and Tunisia* (United Nations doct. E/CN.14/248, February 5, 1964).

[32] See d'Arboussier, *op. cit.*, p. 53; interview with Alioune Drame. Nkrumah attacked the Mali Federation in July 1960 as a "sham"; Keita replied that Ghana was not independent as long as parliament was opened by a representative of Queen Elizabeth. Because Nkrumah was only premier in 1958, most heads of state decided not to attend the Conference on Independent African States; they sent their foreign ministers instead.

[33] Interview with Mehdi Zentar.

[34] This situation has led to criticisms from the Nigerian opposition against Nigerian restraint in foreign policy. A delegate to the All-Nigerian People's conference pointed out that the UAS had a greater role in Pan-Africanism and that South African refugees came to Accra, not to Nigeria; Radio Accra, August 21, 1961. In the parliamentary debate on foreign policy, the opposition said Nigerian policy was undynamic and ran counter to progressive African opinion, and Foreign Minister Wachuku felt obliged to give ten reasons why Nigeria did not show more dynamism in foreign affairs. Nigeria's policy of not throwing its weight around was expressed by Nnamdi Azikiwe, however, even before his nomination as governor-general (and then president): "Nigeria should not seek to impose its leadership on Africa or elsewhere, and it should not attempt to browbeat the rest of Africa or any nation to bend their knees in acknowledgement of the existence of a colossus that it is" (quoted in Coleman, "The Foreign Policy of Nigeria," *op. cit.*, p. 400).

[35] Hans Morgenthau, "What is the National Interest," in Ivo Duchacek and Kenneth Thompson (eds.), *Conflict and Cooperation Among Nations* (New York: Holt, Rinehart & Winston, 1960), p. 274; Fox, *op. cit.*, p. 184.

[36] Ben Bella, *Le Monde,* April 5, 1963; interview with M. A. Bouattoura.

[37] Ghana recognized Mauritania just before the Casablanca meeting and confirmed the recognition just afterward. On the other hand, a Mauritanian delegation to Guinea in February 1961 was unable to shake Guinea's commitment to the Casablanca declaration.

[38] The economic committee in Cairo in March and the political committee in Cairo in June 1962 postponed the original opening date to July 1, 1962 and then January 1, 1963; when Egypt ratified the agreement by decree on April 15, 1963, it was too late, for the Group had collapsed.

[39] This approach is used effectively for the Arab world by Charles D. Cremeans, *The Arabs and the World* (New York: Praeger, 1963), pp. 131-36. See also Zolberg, in Friedland and Rosberg (eds.), *op. cit.*, pp. 120-22; Immanuel Wallerstein, *Africa: The Politics of Independence* (New York: Vintage, 1961), especially Chap. 8.

[40] See particularly David E. Apter, *Ghana in Transition* (New York: Atheneum, 1963), pp. 303, 323.

[41] See Jean Buchmann, *L'Afrique noire indépendante* (Paris: Pichon & Durand-Auzias, 1962), pp. 135-37, 355-58; Leon Carl Brown, "Stages in the Process of Change," in Charles A. Micaud (ed.), *Tunisia: The Politics of Modernization* (New York: Praeger, 1964), pp. 55-62.

[42] The important case of Jaja Wachuku in Nigeria poses a problem of classification. As a faithful representative of Tafawa Balewa's views, he was a lightning rod for the prime minister, not a spokesman for his own party, the NCNC.

[43] References to Ghana and Guinea from interviews with Nathan Welbeck and Camara Daouda.

[44] Material in this and the following paragraph is drawn from contacts in nine of the sixteen Western African countries' foreign ministries during 1962-63.

[45] For example, Dr. K. O. Mbadiwe, the Nigerian prime minister's advisor on African affairs, denied that relations with Ghana were strained, because "there has been no suspension of diplomatic relations between the two countries," Radio Lagos, May 22, 1961. Such

misconception of the ambassador's role also explains Nigeria's severance of diplomatic relations with France over Saharan atomic testing.

[46] For a good discussion of the point, see Jacques Hubert, *Les relations extérieures d'un État nouveau: le Senegal* (Dakar: Faculté de droit, 1963), pp. 225-32.

[47] *Le Monde,* February 19, 1961; *At-Tahrir* (Casablanca), February 21, 1961.

[48] *Le Monde,* May 3, 1962.

[49] This study arrives at answers similar to those presented by Elliot J. Berg and Jeffrey Butler, "Trade Unions," in Coleman and Rosberg, *op. cit.,* pp. 340-81. See also, on this subject, Stephen Low, "African Labor Movements," in E. M. Kassalow (ed.), *National Labor Movements in the Postwar World* (Chicago: Northwestern U.P., 1963). A full study of intra-African labor politics remains to be done; the best treatment to date is found in Jean Meynaud and Anisse Salah-Bey, *Le Syndicalisme africain* (Paris: Payot, 1963), pp. 141-164. For a good treatment of North Africa, see Werner Plum, *Gewerkschaften in Maghreb* (Hannover: Verlag für Literatur und Zeitgeschehen, 1962), especially pp. 85-100.

[50] A notable exception is the role of the chambers of commerce of Bamako and of Abidjan in arranging transshipment of goods to Mali via Ivory Coast after the breakup of the Mali Federation—"a strictly commercial operation in which the Ivory Coast government has no concern," according to the Ivory Coast government (Radio Paris, August 23, 1960, and interviews with J. Krantz Grandmougin of the Bamako chamber of commerce). See *Bulletin mensuel de la chambre de commerce d'Abidjan* for regular details on the operation.

[51] For a detailed discussion of the sects, see J. Spencer Trimingham, *Islam in West Africa* (Oxford: Oxford University Press, 1959), pp. 88-101. Note that the judgment is quite different on internal politics, where the sects often play an important role. Allal al-Fassi, Istiqlal leader and Morocco's leading *sufi* (mystic); Hajj Ibrahim Niassa, a Tijani leader and Senegalese politician of importance, who is related to political figures in Ghana and Nigeria; and Amadou Hampaté Ba, Malian scholar and ambassador as well as Tijani *moqaddem* (official), are important examples of political figures (of three very different types) whose stature is enhanced by their religious position. The effect of their *religious* position on foreign relations is more debatable.

[52] For example, the circulation of *Jeune Afrique* was 14,000 copies in Tunisia, 10,000 copies each in Algeria and Morocco, 2000-3000 each in Mali, Senegal, Guinea, and Ivory Coast, and about 2000 in four other French-speaking African countries combined; *Jeune Afrique: Tarif de publicité* (Tunis: Jeune Afrique, 1963).

[53] Interview with Nathan Welbeck.

[54] It is interesting to note what was "important": Algeria was; but neither Kenya nor Zambia—both active, prestigious states—were necessary to the success of Addis Ababa.

3 INTRA-AFRICAN POLICY AND ITS LIMITS

Foreign relations have been conducted among the states of Western Africa within a limited range of choice: the worst possibilities are subversion, the breaking off of relations, and a flow of vile propaganda (military violence is usually excluded); the best possibility is close alliance and economic cooperation (loss of sovereignty through unification is usually excluded).

THE LIMITS ON VIOLENCE AND INTERVENTION

War is a case of ultimate use of power, "an act of violence designed to oblige the adversary to carry out our will," according to Clausewitz. It is, however, only one end of a spectrum of violent acts designed to impose one state's will over another. Techniques of violence other than conventional war include guerrilla warfare and terrorism. These acts can be divided according to their instrument (regular army, irregular armed force, or terrorist agents) or according to their aim (the weakening, destruction, or replacement of government authority). Even this spectrum, however, is not complete. It shades into other, nonviolent or pre-violent instruments of intervention. This half of the spectrum includes subversion, through the aid and training of foreign political groups; conspiracy, by paradiplomatic support of political exiles; and propaganda, used to further policies shared by the agent government and opposition groups in the target state. These three techniques aim at strengthening alternative personnel, weakening the target government's legitimacy, and weakening the target government's policy support, respectively. The aims are not mutually exclusive, of course; as one moves up the ladder toward conventional warfare, aims and techniques frequently tend to include all lower categories. In one form or another, the opposition movement—especially when in exile from the target state—is the instrument used in most techniques of intervention; even in times of conventional warfare, the opposition movement can serve as a fifth column, if inside the country, or a government-in-exile, if outside, giving political support to the military activities of the state's regular army.

Two aspects of intervention are typically African. One is the extension of the concept to include propaganda. States in other areas in the world consider the use of propaganda—to support a given policy and cast derision on its opponents—as an accepted technique in the conduct of foreign relations. In Western Africa, however, the use of propaganda is viewed as unwarranted interference in the domestic affairs of an independent nation. This attitude derives, in part, from the sensitivity of the states to their newly won independence; it finds even greater justification when the propaganda questions the legitimacy of the target government (because of its "wrong" policies) and

87

Table 1: *Techinques of Foreign-Policy Intervention*[1]

Technique	Instrument		Aim
Conventional warfare	Regular army	**Compulsion**	Replacement of target government authority
Guerrilla warfare	Guerrilla bands		Destruction of target government authority
Terrorism (assassination)	Terrorist agents	**Coercion**	Weakening of target government authority, elimination of personnel
Subversion	Political organizers		Strengthening of alternate personnel
Conspiracy	Political exiles	**Persuasion**	Weakening of target government legitimacy
Propaganda	Public-opinion media		Weakening of target government's policy support

(Violent: Conventional warfare, Guerrilla warfare, Terrorism. Nonviolent: Subversion, Conspiracy, Propaganda.)

advocates alternative political leadership. Of course, complaints against the use of propaganda do not prevent the target state from replying in kind; on the contrary, the fighting of fire with fire is a natural response, and frequently results in the escalation of techniques of intervention. Conversely, when one technique has proven ineffective, alternatives lower in the spectrum of intervention are also used.

The second unusual aspect of intervention is the location of the break in the spectrum. In other areas of the world, it may be possible to make a meaningful distinction between violent and nonviolent techniques. In Western Africa, however, a sharp distinction must be made between conventional warfare (which has rarely been used) and the other elements of the spectrum —violent and nonviolent—which have come to be the commonplace ingredients of intra-African relations.

Only once in Western Africa has conventional warfare been used by one state against another. On October 8, 1963, after sixteen months of gradual military buildup in a no-man's-land that served in lieu of a border, the Moroccan and Algerian armies entered into full-scale hostilities. The immediate background of the month-long war consisted of a number of incidents involving the expulsion of Moroccans from Algerian border villages, a revival of Moroccan pressure on Algeria to honor past promises to negotiate a firm boundary line, and a local revolt in Algeria which was beyond the capabilities of the troops assigned to the sector. An Algero-Moroccan agreement on October 7th provided for the withdrawal of Moroccan soldiers from the border regions in order that Algerian troops might deal with the revolt. The following day, however, Algerian troops occupied two Moroccan border posts in the contested zone, killing ten members of the Moroccan auxiliary forces. The two nations mobilized and rushed reinforcements to the border zones. Within a week, the Moroccan army had recaptured the border posts; by the end of the month it had moved to within a few miles of Tindouf, an Algerian administrative center (claimed by Morocco) 150 miles southwest of the initial combat area. Algerian attempts to cut the Moroccan offensive's supply line were repulsed, but on October 14th the Algerian army opened a new front around Figuig, where the border was not in doubt (although it had never been formally demarcated). Despite a general cease-fire negotiated between the two parties for November 2nd, fighting continued around Figuig until November 5th, ending with Moroccan evacuation of the important oasis. At the end of hostilities, the two border posts in the central zone were in Moroccan hands and Tindouf was under Algerian control. Except for Figuig, which now lay between the lines, the situation was essentially the same as it had been before the hostilities began. On February 20th, 1964, the two parties and the Ethiopian and Malian members of a cease-fire commission agreed on the location of a demilitarized zone in the area of combat; the border posts in the central sector were evacuated, Figuig was returned to Morocco and the dominating heights over the oases demilitarized, and Tindouf was omitted from the agreement. These agreements, although slowly and painfully negotiated, were the result of OAU good offices and of continuing diplomatic contacts which were maintained by both parties—alongside virulent propaganda attacks—throughout the combat. The war involved the use of mortars and artillery, armored vehicles, and airplanes, as well as infantry. Credible estimates of up to 1500 troops per side have been given for a single combat region; casualties were probably less than one hundred dead and several hundred wounded on each side. If, indeed, the war had any purpose and was not merely an escalation of incidents, it represented an attempt by Morocco to bring the border problem to Algeria's attention and defend national territory, and an attempt by Algeria to secure territory and to divert and unite domestic political forces.

In addition to this single instance of conventional war, there have been a few cases in which Western African states feared the use of military force by their neighbors. Ivory Coast was concerned over a possible attack from Ghana in 1959 and 1963, and in 1960 Ghana claimed that Togo was preparing an attack; in both cases, although there was real subversion, evidence of a military venture was slim and the threats never materialized. In early 1958 (after the Sakiet affair) and again in mid-1961 (during the Bizerte crisis) Tunisia faced attacks from France which it was able to withstand only because the French aims were limited in time and scope. Armed infiltration from Senegal and Ivory Coast into Guinea in April and December 1960 was a case (on which details are incomplete) of subversion, not military attack, and the source appears to have been French, not African. The only case of conflict between two Western African armies, other than the Algero-Moroccan border war, was the meeting of Soudanese and Senegalese armed forces in the breakup of the Mali Federation, and this was an internal affair with no blood spilt.

If, with the single exception of the Algero-Moroccan border war, there has

Table 2: *Military Establishments in Western Africa, 1964*

State	Army (in thousands)	Planned Increase	Ratio (per thousand civilians***)	Ratio (per border kilometer)	1963 Budget (per cent GNP†††)	1963 Budget (in $ millions)	1963 Budget (per cent)	Police‡‡ (in thousands)	ONUC force (in thousands)
Morocco*	35	55‡	2.8	1.8	4.3	93	20	12	3.3
Algeria*	60	75‡	6	1	3	66	11	10	0
Tunisia*†	21	—	4.6	1.5	1.5	11.4	5	4.6	3.1
Mauritania†	.6	—	.6	.1	5.3	4	21	.4	0
Senegal*†	2.5	10	.8	1.5	3.5	9	5	4	(see Mali)
Mali	3.1	—	.8	.4	2.1	8.7	8	1.2	.6
Guinea*†	4.8	5	1.4	1.6	3.4	5.8	15	3.3	.7
Sierra Leone	1.8	—	.7	2	1.2	2.2#	5#	2	.1
Liberia*	3.5	—	3.5	3	1.4	2.4	6	20.7**	.5
Ivory Coast*†	4	—	1.1	1.4	2.5	8.7	8	2.3	0
Upper Volta*	1	—	.2	.3	.7	2.8	8	1.3	0
Niger*	1	—	.3	.2	1.2	3.4	12	1.4	0
Dahomey*†	.8	—	.3	.4	.6	1.1	4	1.5	0
Togo*	1##	—	.6	.8	.9	.6#	2#	.3	0
Ghana*	8	—	1.1	4	2.2	35.3	8	21††	2.6
Nigeria	8.3	—	.2	2	.9	28	6	23	1.9

Sources: H. R. Coward, *Military Technology in Developing Countries* (Cambridge, Mass.: Massachusetts Institute of Technology, 1964); *Africa Report* IX, 9 (January 1964), country surveys by George Weeks; where given figures differ from sources, rectifications have been made according to on-the-spot surveys or changes in time.

 * States with civic-action programs.
 † States with universal conscription.
 ‡ Figures during the Algero-Moroccan border war.
 # 1962 figures.
 ## Including 20,000 tribal militia.
 ** Including 12,000 paramilitary Builder Brigaders.
 †† Includes gendarmery, national security forces, and so on.
 ‡‡ Raised from 250 after 1963.
 *** Cf. U.S.: 15; U.K.: 10; average Black Africa: 1; average Middle East: 10; average Latin America: 3.
 ††† Cf. U.S.: 10; India: 5; average Black Africa: 1.7; average Middle East: 7.5; average Latin America: 1.7.

been no state use of military warfare, how can this prudence and restraint be explained? At first glance, it would seem that causes of war are not lacking Western Africa. Conflicting border claims and general territorial aspirations do exist; and historical justification, population pressure, and conveted resources also play their parts. The broader goal of Pan-Africanism, referring either to political unification or to policy alignment, also constitutes a temptation to use military force. If war is "politics carried out by other means," such goals—hitherto unattainable through political devices but apparently susceptible to military techniques—would seem to be major potential causes for war. In general, however, Western African governments have not yet deemed their goals so important or so pressing as to warrant military measures, nor have they considered such measures to be more effective or more economical than alternative means. More specifically, military violence has been excluded from intra-African relations for essentially negative reasons: the means for such a venture are lacking, and Africa's ideological values and Cold War position inhibit the use of military force.

Conventional war—the ultimate use of power—depends first on the possession of instruments of military force.[2] In Western Africa, military strength is low—20,000-60,000 troops in North African states and 300-8000 troops in armies south of the Sahara. In the Maghreb, the ratio of the military to civilian population is about 5:1000; in West Africa (except for Guinea and Liberia) it is about 1:1000 or less. The quality of the troops varies: the armies of Morocco and Algeria have stood up well in combat since independence; those of the other states, although they have, for the most part, effectively maintained internal security, have not yet tested their combat effectiveness under their own officers. With few exceptions—Morocco, Algeria, Niger, Nigeria, Mauritania, Guinea—the 1963 military expenditures of the African states were less than 10 per cent of the total budget; only Morocco, Algeria, Ghana, and Nigeria spent more than $25 million on defense in 1963, and only Morocco, Algeria, Mauritania, Senegal, and Guinea spent more than 2.5 per cent of their gross national product. Admittedly, the size of an army is only a relative factor; under the right conditions it may take as small a force to overthrow a government from without as the Togolese and Dahomeyan experiences of 1963 have shown that it takes from within. Statistically, a few African states do have the military establishment to conduct war. But statistics are only a primary guide; other factors circumscribe the availability of military means.

One limiting factor is location. In their primary role—the maintenance of internal security—most Western African armies are not dispersed throughout the country or along the frontiers, but are concentrated in strategic central control points. Generally the gendarmery, not the army, guards the border. Thus the armies of Morocco, Ghana, Ivory Coast, and Senegal (to name a few) are stationed in their respective countries' populous coastal plains, with the elite troops in the industrial towns. Most states have simply taken over the colonial army camps, which were located for purposes of internal control, not for external defense. Logistics too inhibit the use of armies; it is usually difficult to move heavy military equipment—if such equipment were needed—for any distance inside Western African states, and it is nearly impossible to cross international borders anywhere but on a few main roads. In a full-scale military attack, occupation of the capital would probably be the necessary and sufficient goal of military action, even though there would doubtless also be prolonged diversion by border infiltration, guerrilla counter-attack, tribal resistance, and small military forays[3]; however, with few exceptions, respectable distances protect Western African capitals from potentially hostile borders.

Probably the most important limiting factor is the nation-building process itself—especially the effort to make the organizational unit (government) coincide with the popular unit in control and allegiance.[4] The army has an integral role to play in the rapid modernization that Western African governments desire. It is not a role of compulsion, as used by modernizing authoritarian regimes in other areas and at other times; rather, it is a role of constraint. The army is engaged above all in maintaining internal security, backing up the police forces when their power to deal with the problem is exceeded. Thus, the army is called on to overcome tribal resistance to social change, as in Morocco against the Riffis (1958-59), in Algeria against the Kabyles (1963), and in Mali and Niger against the Tuareg (1963-64); to quell urban dissatisfaction over unemployment and dislocation, as in Algeria (1963-64), Morocco (1965), and Ghana (1961); and to put down opposition uprisings, as in Dahomey (1964) and Morocco (1960 and 1963). In Togo, Dahomey, Liberia, Senegal, Niger, and Algeria, the army or parts of it took part in the divisions among modernizers by siding with the opposition. Finally, the Western African armies are often occupied with civic-action programs, which keep the troops cultivating bananas, planting trees, or distributing milk—jobs that hardly enhance soldier-like qualities.

Obviously, the argument that the army is too busy waging peace to wage war would, by itself, be inconclusive. It is quite true that an external campaign often unites the nation and decreases the need for internal-security measures; Morocco and Algeria have both experienced this effect, which in some circumstances could even become a reason *for* war. An unsuccessful military venture, however, no matter how justified, can be counterproductive, as Bourguiba found in the 1961 Bizerte crisis when he threw volunteers against French paratroopers, with heavy losses in personnel and prestige. It is clear, therefore, that certain broader inhibitions also operate on the Western African use of violence.

One limitation is Africa's own ideology, combining the values of independence and unity. The legitimacy of independence and territorial integrity has been confirmed in the declarations issued by numerous conferences, from the first Conference of Independent African States to the second summit session of the OAU.[5] Peaceful settlement of disputes and noninterference in the internal affairs of another state have also been frequently asserted as principles.[6]

As a result, there has been a tendency to consider the use of violence to force one state's will on another as "un-African." Morocco's use of guerrillas against Mauritania between 1957 and 1962 aroused mixed reactions only because it was justified in terms of anticolonialism and antineocolonialism—higher values in the name of which external violence has been condoned; Morocco's and Algeria's use of violence in 1963, on the other hand, had no justification and was therefore publicly deplored throughout Western Africa. The only acceptable justification for warfare so far has been anticolonialism; in the future, the use of violence to spread an African revolutionary system of government could be rationalized if revolution were deemed a higher value than independence, although this shift in values has not yet occurred in Western Africa.[7]

Furthermore, there is a subtle sort of word equation that leads to a condemnation of violence in the name of African unity. Because the prominent tactic of colonialism was "Divide and conquer," all division is frequently identified with colonialism and all unity equated with anticolonialism and "Africanism."[8] Division aggravated by violence weakens the united front that Western African states feel required to present against colonialism, and opens the way to neocolonial incursions. The classic use of the external enemy to foster internal unity finds a special application in Western Africa. Hence political tensions are under strong pressure to remain political or to be resolved in the name of African unity before they reach the stage of open conflict (unless, of course, one of the parties feels compelled to resort to violence in the name of a higher value). Although the predominance of independence and unity over other ideological concepts in Western Africa has worked against the external use of violence, the relationship between these two leading values has also been important. Just as it is possible to conceive of a war to spread revolution, so aggression might also be rationalized through the use of African unity slogans, whatever the "real" reason might be. The predominance of independence over unity has prevented this, so far.

The second factor inhibiting warfare in Western Africa is the relation of the African subsystem of international relations to other, external systems. The African states, although sovereign members of the family of nations, are quite weak; with the withdrawal of the European presence, this weakness could represent a power vacuum in a Cold War world unless the major powers agreed to neutralize the continent, regarding it as a buffer area that each would be satisfied not to control as long as the other did not control it, or unless one of the major powers established a predominant, pre-emptive presence on the continent to prevent the power vacuum from forming. In a broad sense, Europe continues to maintain such a presence throughout the area, with perhaps a few states—Guinea, Algeria—as incipient exceptions. One evidence of this is the large amount of British, French, and Common Market aid to Western Africa. Another is the continuing possibility of European intervention, as shown elsewhere in the continent—Gabon, Congo, Tanganyika, Kenya, Uganda. A third is the system of military agreements that

France has concluded with Senegal, Mauritania, Togo, and the Regional Defense Council of the Entente states (Ivory Coast, Niger, and Dahomey), as well as those maintained by the United States with Liberia and by the United Kingdom with Nigeria until January 1962.

The special Euro-African relation works positively and negatively to impede war in Western Africa. On one hand, the potential role of European military forces as an intervening police unit has strengthened otherwise weak African military establishments and has kept political conflict from taking a military form. This element has deterred Ghana from moving against Togo (if it ever intended to) and on several occasions in West Africa, French control over ammunition supplies was reportedly the factor that prevented hostilities. On the other hand, Western African states are loath to engage—on any side—in a conflict that might mean the return of colonial forces. An aggressor would have to bear heavy criticism for any action that would have such a result. The relation of the African system of international relations to that of the Cold War also acts in a less certain and more indirect way to inhibit war in Western Africa. African nonalignment is generally designed to make the continent a buffer area between the United States and the Soviet Union. The United States has preferred to leave to Europe the major burden of assistance to Africa; it has limited its own aid, and has not intervened directly on the continent unless Communist powers have threatened to do so. This qualified joint nonintervention could break down if there were to be a Western African war that African or European attention could not handle and that might therefore attract active Communist participation. Western African leaders have shown a desire to avoid all situations that might escalate into international war.[9] This desire, accompanied by the other factors already discussed, has kept war unlikely in Western Africa.

With war excluded, the states of Western Africa have resorted to other violent and nonviolent means of intervention in the policy-making processes of their neighbors: propaganda, conspiracy, subversion, terrorism, and guerrilla warfare.

The party-governments of Western Africa have let loose a tremendous barrage of propaganda on African events, but it rarely reaches beyond the boundaries of the state. Newspapers and television (where it exists) are usually controlled by the party or government, carrying the official message to the literate or urban population and, through it (by word of mouth), to other segments of the society. Information ministries, schools, markets, party cells, and party auxiliaries are also used to disseminate propaganda, but none of these sources reaches an external audience of any significant size: language differences and—more important—party-government control of its own and imported media provide an effective barrier. Only in a few countries, such as Nigeria and Morocco, does an opposition press reprint slogans of foreign propaganda.

There are a few other exceptions. African embassies usually carry their national newspapers, although these are read mainly by expatriates. Many states transmit radio programs into neighboring countries, where they find a sizable audience. Guinea, Ghana, Mali, Senegal, Ivory Coast, Morocco, and Algeria broadcast short- and medium-wave programs in several European and African languages; these can be heard throughout Western Africa, and the widespread use of transistor radios—even in such far-flung areas as the Mauritanian Sahara—increases the number of listeners.[10] The cessation of hostile broadcasts from Morocco and Mauritania after the second OAU summit meeting was a significant step in easing tensions between the two states. Ghana's Freedom Fighters' programs and Guinean broadcasts into Portuguese Guinea are other cases of the use of radio propaganda along with other instruments of national policy. International organizations, such as labor unions and women's and youth movements, carry the messages of their dominant members, although the failure of the two largest groups—the All-African Trade Union Federation and the African Trade Union Confederation—to publish and distribute a regular periodical indicates that the effectiveness of this channel is at best sporadic. Conference speeches and declarations are also designed for use as propaganda, but the extent to which they penetrate the target state depends on the accuracy and completeness with which they are reported in the local media of that state. The decision-making elite and the small literate circle that surrounds it are the targets of this propaganda, and it is aimed—sometimes rather broadly—at their personal susceptibilities and attitudes.

Although Western Africa follows most of the rules of credibility laid down for effective propaganda, it frequently ignores "the first lesson . . . that propaganda [is] . . . worthless in isolation; it [has] . . . to be used in conjunction with military, diplomatic, and economic moves." [11] In Western Africa, military and economic moves are blocked by the absence of will and of means, and diplomatic moves are often reduced to the dissemination of propaganda. The absence of real carrots and sticks as alternative means of exercising pressure tends to reduce the power of propaganda. Slogans become an alternative, instead of a support, for action.

What is left as a field for effective propaganda is that area where general ideological values are already commonly held by the individual national elites, largely on the basis of their own common historical experiences with colonialism and their common underdevelopment. (Thus Algerian or Ghanaian propaganda tends to be effective in Mali because its values and symbols are similar.) When even these features vary—as they do in Senegal's and Algeria's experience with colonialism, for example—or when a similar condition evokes divergent policy responses—as do Mali's and Niger's common poverty—the effectiveness of foreign propaganda is severely limited by local attitudinal barriers and countervalues, and by divergent interests. Whatever power remains in the slogans is relegated to a high level of abstraction. The most eloquent testimony to the limitations of slogans is the fate of Nkrumah's Pan-Africanism. In spite of its persistence, consistency, and volume, and its general appeal throughout the area, it has not been an effective weapon of

Ghanaian policy. External resistance and Ghana's inability to realize even limited concrete successes with such attempts as the UAS or the Casablanca Group have been the main causes of its ineffectiveness. Guinea's propaganda in favor of independence, on the other hand, was successful because of the sympathetic attitude of the Mali Federation and because Guinea's own independence did not collapse under adverse conditions. UAM propaganda in support of Mauritanian independence won out over Morocco's counterefforts because the UAM had substantial means—United Nations votes and French backing—to give support to its words.

Because the government controls the information media and countervalues are firmly entrenched in the official elite, frequently the only way for propaganda to reach into a Western African state is through an opposition group. The group may already be predisposed to the message, for its opposition to the government is usually viewed in ideological as well as policy or personal terms, and its embattled position within the state tends to make it welcome foreign assistance. Because the concept of nation is not fully developed in Western Africa, the opposition group may find no incompatibility between its position as a national party seeking power and its acceptance of alien support. In fact, it may even define its objectives in non-national terms, calling itself "an African party" or a branch of an African Socialist movement: it can then justify support in the name of the international ideology, instead of being forced to rely on purely local sympathies. It also claims an unverifiably large element of support among the "true" patriots of its country, and justifies foreign assistance as necessary to meet the government party's authoritarian control over national politics. In its international outlook on domestic politics, the opposition party enjoys the sanction both of history and of the ruling party's example. There is scarcely a political party in AOF or the Maghreb that did not belong to a regional party alliance, enjoy outside support, and even include nationals from neighboring states as important members. After independence, the party-government symbiosis in most states meant that governmental relations could be solidified by interparty contacts and alliances. States that give aid to opposition movements also justify their action in ideological terms: such aid is merely a "continuation" of their efforts at African liberation, for the opposing governments are (in their eyes, at least) too neocolonialist or not "African" enough.

Propagandistic support finds its way into the target country through opposition (often clandestine) press and tracts, and through radio broadcasts. Since it won independence, Ghana has given such support to the Sawaba in Niger, the Action Group in Nigeria, the Sanwi movement in Ivory Coast, and the Togolese opposition groups; Morocco encouraged the Nahda party in Mauritania. Tunisia and Algeria have provided platforms for Moroccan UNFP spokesmen, as Morocco did for the ephemeral National Tunisian Democratic Front. Mali gave asylum and assistance to Senegalese opposition figures and to leaders of the Sawaba; and Guinea absorbed Dahomeyans and Malians opposed to their countries' policies and supported UGTAN labor unions in other countries in their opposition to their home governments. In addition to these cases, some of which involve financial as well as verbal support, Guinea and Ghana have given money to the People's National Party and the All People's Congress in Sierra Leone, while Nigerian businessmen contributed to the United Party in Ghana. In the preindependence period, Ivory Coast's contribution to RDA parties, in power or out, was one of the major factors in maintaining the party alliance. In none of these cases has outside support—moral or financial—been the decisive factor in keeping opposition movements alive; real local support is necessary. Where such support exists, however—as in Morocco, Nigeria, Togo, and perhaps Niger—the opposition can be an effective channel for foreign propaganda.

Support for opposition movements may lead to subversion and violence, the purpose of which is to weaken the target government—not merely its policies. The same historic and political reasons that sanction support for an opposition group in another state can also be used to explain continuing attempts at coercion in Western Africa. The agencies that channel assistance to subversion and violence in other states are many, varying from official branches of the government through party organizations to private supporters. Morocco has had a full ministry of state for African affairs, headed by Abdulkrim Khatib, which served as a clearing-house for aid to liberation movements throughout the continent; alongside it was a ministry of state for Mauritanian affairs, which acted as an official front for the Mauritanian liberation movement in addition to distributing social services to Saharan refugees. The African ministry was founded in June 1961, after the formation of the Casablanca Group, in an effort to provide an official base for the co-ordination of aid to the FLN. The Mauritanian ministry was originally formed as a Saharan section within the interior ministry in late 1957, and became a separate ministry in June 1961. Ghana's Bureau of African Affairs is a half-government, half-party organism; its finances are administered by the government through the African Affairs Secretariat, which is an autonomous section of the foreign ministry, but its programs are under party control, for its contacts are with foreign nationalist movements, not with other governments.[12] The bureau was originally established by George Padmore in early 1958 as the planning secretariat for the All-African People's conference; on Padmore's death, it took a radical turn and fell into the hands of A. K. Barden. Associate organisms are the African Affairs Center, which lodges visiting freedom fighters, and the Kwame Nkrumah Ideological Institute of the party at Winneba, which indoctrinates them. Algerian contacts with insurgent movements appear to have been channeled through the Africa, Asia, and Latin America desk in the foreign ministry, in liaison with the president's office and the army. In other cases, such as Togo or Nigeria, contacts appear to be purely personal and subversion is not a regularly conducted government business. In all cases, subversion—whether government-inspired or privately initiated—coincides with current relations between the host and target states.

According to the government brief in the treason trial which ended on

March 14, 1964, two groups associated with the UNFP and the Moroccan Army of Liberation established revolutionary cells throughout Morocco in 1962-63 in order to overthrow the monarchy, using a base of operations in Algeria.[13] In July of the same year, a Moroccan military tribunal condemned a band of Moroccans who had been captured the previous month crossing the border from Algeria, where they had been trained and armed; Algeria denied the charge. Similar bands were also captured in 1965. On the other hand, Algeria had charged that Morocco was encouraging the 1963 Kabyle revolt by infiltrating agents and by massing troops along the border, which Morocco in turn denied. At the end of 1962, ben Bella gave asylum to Tunisians involved in the assassination plot against Bourguiba, although Algeria did not appear to have been implicated in the plot itself.

Ghana has been involved in subversion against two Entente states. In Ivory Coast, Ghanaian subversion took the form of arms aid, infiltration, intimidation, extortion, sanctuary, and use of Ghanaian facilities for propagandizing the Sanwi's stand. In 1963, after the assassination of Olympio (which Houphouet-Boigny believed to be the work of Ghana), the Ivory Coast government discovered plans for a *coup d'état* involving several ministers; several Ghanaian expatriates were in touch with the plotters and were believed to be involved in arms traffic across the border, although there is no proof that any official Ghanaian agency had a hand in the affair. The National Committee for the Liberation of Ivory Coast, led by Camille Adam, which advocated a *Non* vote in the 1958 referendum, was given asylum and propaganda support by Guinea in 1959. Adam wandered from Guinea to Nigeria to Ghana before being persuaded to return home just when Ivory Coast won its independence, but neither Nigeria nor Ghana gave him any concrete support. It is interesting to note that in early 1961, several thousand Ashantis fled from Ghana to Ivory Coast, where they asked asylum from persecution and support for the overthrow of Nkrumah; Houphouet-Boigny granted them asylum, on condition that they pay their own way, but specifically denied support, and turned down another request by a United Party leader to see him the same year.[14] Ghana has an equally long history of intervention in Niger. A badly managed offer of Ghanaian financial and moral support for the Sawaba in the 1958 referendum was made, but came to nothing. After the banning of the Sawaba the following year, dissident leaders sought refuge in Mali as members of the PFA alliance and then gravitated to Accra, where a large Niger colony gave them a natural base. Financial support came from the Afro-Asian People's Solidarity Fund, the All-African People's Organization (located in Accra), the Ghanaian African Affairs Bureau, and—to a much lesser extent—from Mali. Malian facilities for propaganda and political action dried up after *rapprochement* between Bamako and the government of Niger. A new opportunity for the Sawaba was opened when the Dahomeyan government was overthrown and relations with Niger soured; Sawaba leaders moved to Porto Novo, where they had direct access to the Niger border. In early October 1964, Sawaba armed bands attacked several points in southeast and southwest Niger without success; their arms appeared to have come from Ghana and Dahomey. Six months later, in mid-April, an assassination attempt against President Diori by a Sawaba member failed, although one bystander was killed and five injured. The would-be assassin had been trained in Ghana and Algeria.

Ghana, Togo, and Nigeria have also acted as bases for attempts at mutual subversion. Ironically, the one case of a successful *coup*—in Togo—appears to have been almost entirely an internal affair. In December 1961, Togo anounced discovery of a plot against Olympio and subsequently accused Ghana of providing direct assistance to the plotters. The following month, the two opposition groups were banned and their leaders took refuge in Ghana. One of them, Antoine Meatchi, was given the support of the African Affairs Bureau and made several trips into Togo to contact opposition groups during 1962. At one point, rumors of a Christmas Eve *coup* in Togo were so persistent that the Dahomeyan foreign minister went to Ghana to investigate and head off the event. When the assassination finally came (on January 13, 1963), Olympio had already been warned at least twice of attempts to overthrow his government; despite Ghanaian army movements in southwest Ghana the day before the *coup*, there is no proof of Ghanaian implication in this particular plot or even of any direct participation by Meatchi in its planning, although he returned to Togo to join the government, at the call of a faction of the plotters.[15]

Togo also served as a base for anti-Ghanaian activities prior to the assassination. Nkrumah too had been the subject of three assassination attempts in 1962 and 1963, and a number of terrorist bombings had also taken place.[16] In a declaration of June 9, 1962, and notes of December 7, 1962, and January 6, 1963, Ghana protested the presence of former Finance Minister K. A. Gbedemah among the five thousand Ghanaian refugees in Togo, charging him with leadership of the terrorist activities. Other Ghanaian political figures—including former Foreign Minister Adjei and Information Minister Tawia Adamafio—were arrested in 1963 and sentenced to death in February 1965 for "agreeing . . . in Accra, Lomé, Abidjan, and Lagos to commit . . . treason." Ghana, in turn, was implicated in the conspiracy of Obafemi Awolowo discovered in late 1962. Awolowo, leader of the Nigerian opposition Action Group in parliament, was convicted in September 1963 for accepting Ghanaian aid in training guerrilla groups and for receiving arms and financial assistance from Ghana. Nigeria also was a refuge for members of Olympio's government who fled the 1963 *coup*. In April, a conspiracy was discovered and in November former Interior Minister Theophile Mally was condemned *in absentia*, along with others. He denied complicity in the plot, as he did again from Nigeria in July 1964 when the Togoloese government announced discovery of a stock of explosives and a new plot. The interplay of plots and counterplots along the Benin Coast in 1962-63 is a striking example of conspiracy, subversion, and assassination in Western Africa. In all cases, the host state granted asylum and support to opposition groups who left their home country to continue resistance to the regime. As a weapon of foreign policy subversion in the Benin area has been only counterproductive, resulting in worse, not closer, relations.

Another incident was an aftermath of the breakup of the Mali Federation. A plot by pro-Mali elements in Senegal—including a spy ring, a Malian training camp, and Moroccan expatriates' involvement—was discovered and in April 1962, Doudou Gueye, a former minister of the Mali Federation, was convicted *in absentia*. (He was residing in Bamako, where he was presidential advisor on African affairs.) Senegal granted him partial amnesty in December 1963 and full pardon in July 1964, as part of the Senegal-Mali reconciliation, although in 1964-65, Mali-based subversion against Senegal continued. As elsewhere, the subversion was part of continuing difficulties between states, and has served no purpose except further to envenom relations.

Although in some of these cases conspiracy and subversion have also expanded into assassination and terrorism, there has been no instance of the use of guerrilla warfare against an independent Western African government. In a number of cases—Algeria, Portuguese Guinea, and (on a smaller scale) Morocco and Tunisia—guerrilla warfare has been a major ingredient in the struggle for independence, with support from neighboring countries. In only one instance—the Moroccan attacks against Mauritania—was guerrilla warfare used by one state against the emerging national elite of a neighbor; even then, however, the guerrilla attacks were on a small scale and, after Mauritania gained independence, they turned to terrorism and then disappeared. The nature of these attacks owed much to the desert terrain, the nomadic way of life, and the tribal patterns of raids and vendettas that characterize the western Sahara.[17] In mid-1956, remnants of the Moroccan Army of Liberation from the Rif and Atlas mountains traveled south to the edge of the desert and joined forces with tribal bands in western Algeria, northern Mauritania, and Spanish Sahara to form the Saharan Army of Liberation. The guerrilla force had political leadership (parts of the Istiqlal party) and a distinguishable strategy: to create a zone of insecurity in the western Sahara that would aid both the Algerian and the Morocco-irredentist cause. Early attacks (beginning in June 1956) were directed against French outposts in western Algeria, but soon spread into Mauritania; in early 1957, two-hundred-man bands were making raids on major towns and outposts in northern Mauritania and by the end of the year had forced Spanish troops to withdraw from the interior of Spanish Sahara and regroup in the territory's three administrative centers. In November 1957, a large-scale guerrilla attack captured most of Ifni territory from the Spanish. In response to the growing effectiveness of the Army of Liberation in creating insecurity in the region, and in preparation for the transfer of the southern Spanish protectorate (Tarfaya) to Moroccan control, the French and Spanish armies joined forces in February 1958 to end the guerrilla war. The joint Operation Swab was successful in sweeping the Army of Liberation northward into Tarfaya[18]; some of the major marauding tribes, such as sections of the Reqeibat, rallied to the French and Mauritanians as a result of the operation, while the guerrillas in Moroccan territory were subjected to increasing Moroccan government control and finally integrated into the regular army in 1960.

Although some groups in Morocco sought to bring the guerrillas under control, others sought to extend violence into Mauritania as the new state moved toward sovereignty. The National Council of the Mauritanian Liberation, headed by Mauritania's original exile to Morocco, Horma ould Babana, and working with Morocco's ministry of state for Mauritanian affairs (also manned by refugees), installed terrorist bands in Malian territory and in 1961 and 1962 carried out a number of isolated bombings in Mauritania. The return of many of the refugees (but not ould Babana) to Mauritania and the reconciliation between Mauritania and Mali in 1963 put an end to these raids; soon after, however, Mauritania arrested the refugees on evidence that they were merely acting as a fifth column for subversive agents sent from Morocco. Between 1957 and 1963, through use of the French army, the increasing political control and popularity of its new government, and the diplomatic support of the UAM, Mauritania was able to defeat the Moroccan use of violence. After the disruption of the guerrilla campaign, Morocco's shift to terrorism and subversion was an admission of weakness, particularly inasmuch as ould Babana's National Council, operating from Morocco, could arouse no widespread support from the Mauritanians themselves.

The common characteristic of the various instruments of intervention in Western Africa has been their ineffectiveness. Propaganda has been limited in its effect because it is divorced from supporting instruments of policy and because any given state in the area lacks concrete elements of power over another. It is also limited by its inability to penetrate individual states in specific issues and by the absence of a broad base of public opinion. Conspiracy, subversion, terrorism, and guerrilla warfare have also been tried, but have been unable to shake the growing consolidation of the state; their effects on policy have been largely counterproductive, for they increase antipathy rather than seriously weaken national parties and governments. Nevertheless, these techniques have been important enough to impel states to take measures to increase their military security and to coordinate their efforts against subversion. Perhaps paradoxically, however, these attempts at cooperation have also born little fruit. Military coordination has failed because there was little to pool in the way of military forces; antisubversive efforts have failed because of the very nature of the threat, which is scarcely susceptible to defeat by outward-directed cooperation.

The Casablanca Group, the Brazzaville Group, and the Entente all included common defense agreements.[19] The Joint African High Command grew out of Nkrumah's proposal of an all-African force to operate in Congo and similar situations.[20] Not until the June 1962 meeting of heads of state in Cairo was the High Command officially constituted (with headquarters in Accra) under the military command of an Egyptian general, Mohammed Fawzi, and under the political command of the Group's secretary-general on advice of the political committee (the heads of state). An elaborate network of branches, field commands, and general staff was foreseen, but there were no troops. Some members, such as Guinea and Mali, considered even the earmarking of units to be too much of a burden on their small forces, while others did not want their assigned units stationed outside the national territory. Even hopes of "paper planning" in Accra, followed by symbolic exercises by a composite unit, were never realized. Nevertheless Nkrumah, the only leader who appears to be interested, has continued to call for a working all-African military body.

The Brazzaville Defense Union (UAMD) was set up with headquarters in Ouagadougou after the conclusion of a defense treaty in Tananarive in September 1961. The collective defense agreement among states "conscious of their weakness if they remain isolated and resolved to unite their efforts for the maintenance of peace and security" provided for consultation to meet threats to security. A supreme council of defense ministers met annually (at Ouagadougou in mid-February 1962 and early March 1963 and at Niamey in early December 1963) and once in special session in Douala in late August 1962. Not until early 1963 was any concrete planning done. In February, Albert Balima, UAMD secretary-general, called for the formation of a composite battalion to act in the treaty area as an intervening force against subversion and military crises. At the same time, he announced that the UAMD general staff, under Senegalese Colonel Mademba Sy, had been working on standardization of weapons and regulations in member armies.[21] At the March meeting, "concrete measures" were taken to constitute "intervention units" against subversion and to coordinate military intelligence. After the meeting, however, Balima resigned in a dispute over the secretary-general's powers; Colonel Sy followed him in July. The spirit and institutions of Addis Ababa undercut any impetus toward military unification within the Brazzaville Group, and in March 1964 in Dakar, the UAMD was neither integrated in the UAMCE nor specifically dissolved, but simply ignored. The UAMD members wanted amalgamation even less than the Casablanca Group did, and the events in Togo in January 1963, which came close to ending in an intra-African military confrontation between Ghana and Dahomey, convinced them that tight military agreements might be dangerous rather than necessary.[22]

The states that were particularly impressed by the Togolese events were the members of the Entente. Ivory Coast, Niger, and Dahomey, along with France, are members of the Regional Defense Council, which meets annually as a result of defense agreements signed in April 1961. After the assassination of Olympio and the discovery of a plot against Houphouet-Boigny, the Entente met in February 1963 to discuss antisubversion measures. In July, Togo signed its defense agreement with France and sent observers to the Regional Defense Council (beginning with the meeting of September 1964 in Abidjan). Houphouet-Boigny also sought to include Keita and Touré, along with Yameogo, and Diori, in his campaign against subversion in April 1964 at Bouake; no announcement was made of any measures to be taken. In November, Yameogo and Diori met to plan action against Ghanaian subversion, and the following month they consulted with Houphouet-Boigny. The final result was diplomatic pressure—only temporarily successful—on Ghana to expel subversive groups in Accra, notably leaders of the Sawaba movement. In February and May 1965, the charge was carried to a larger forum, the OCAM, which adopted an antisubversive resolution specifically naming Ghana, and threatened not to attend the 1965 meeting of the OAU in Accra; at the same time, Upper Volta also sent troops to Niger. The difficulty in meeting subversion with military agreements or even with coordinated policy action is that subversion, by its nature, circumvents armies and can only be met by effective policing and politics at home.

Another policy adopted in Western Africa to deal with the problem of intervention is the severance of relations. Severance takes various forms. Ghana and Togo, Senegal and Mali, Ghana and Ivory Coast, Ghana and Nigeria, and Morocco, Tunisia, and Algeria have all practiced different forms of diplomatic rupture, ranging from a complete break to the temporary recall of ambassadors. The effects have been inconclusive. The target state suffers little, while the state taking the action loses a source of information and representation of its policy views. As retaliation for intervention, severance of relations has usually only hardened the lines of animosity. In the Moroccan and Tunisian breaks with Algeria, and the periodic Togolese-Ghanaian ruptures, withdrawal of ambassadors also brought an end to negotiations in progress and agreements already in effect, thus bringing hardship on economic or regional segments of the populations involved. (It is interesting that the Senegalo-Mali break did not interrupt the laborious negotiations over the assets of the Mali Federation, which were carried on without publicity between 1961 and 1963.) An even sterner measure involved exclusion of a state from political groups in existence or in formation. Tunisia was excluded from the short-lived Algero-Moroccan Interministerial Council of the Arab Maghreb in 1962, and Dahomey was apparently never invited to Entente meetings during 1964, after it had denounced the Dahomey-Niger Common Organization (OCDN) agreement of 1959. Again, the result has been the weakening of the alliance, not the effective punishment of the excluded state.

Expulsion of expatriates has also been used. Dahomeyans, Togolese, and Ghanaians were expelled from Ivory Coast in October 1958, though by local mobs rather than by official action. The official reactions of Dahomey and Ivory Coast—then in the process of forming the Entente—were remarkably restrained. Niger, on the other hand, began expelling its Dahomeyan residents in order to increase its pressure against the government of Colonel Soglo; but the move was quite ineffective, because Dahomey was able to retaliate by cutting off Niger's access to the sea. Moroccans were expelled from Algeria and Algerians from Morocco in the mounting tensions between the two neighbors in 1963, but the tensions escalated into a border war rather than bringing about a change of policy. Ghana expelled Nigerians and Voltaics in the process of national consolidation soon after independence—with little effect, for neither of the two target states had control of its foreign affairs. In no case has the expulsion of expatriates been an effective weapon of influence. Instead, Ivory Coast and Dahomey, Morocco and Algeria, and Niger and Dahomey set up special commissions of reinstatement and indemnification after relations grew better, and Togo helped settle half its Ghanaian refugees.

It is worth noting that the large expatriate groups found in nearly every Western African country have been little used as instruments of their home states' policies—which is probably why expulsion has been so little used or so ineffective. Algerians in the Moroccan government services carried out espionage for the FLN before and after Algeria won independence, but this case is a rare exception.[23] In fact, the reverse situation was more common: Dahomeyans in Guinea, Senegalese in Mali, Nigerois and Togolese in Ghana, and Mauritanians in Morocco have all been used from time to time to pressure their home governments in favor of the policies of their host states. Their effect has been significant, even if not crucial, in a number of cases.

The most extreme example of rupture is the closing of a border. Since Algeria won independence, its borders with both Morocco and Tunisia have—on occasion—been closed. The Ghana-Togo border was closed for long periods both before and after the Togolese *coup* of 1963,[24] and in 1963 Ghana closed its border with Upper Volta. Although the Senegal-Mali border was never officially closed, traffic between the two states was abandoned. Dahomey closed its border with Niger in late 1963. The aim of Morocco, Tunisia, Ghana, Mali, and Dahomey was to punish neighboring states with which they had policy disagreements, by imposing deprivation on their national economy or on border populations. Only in the last two cases was compromise forthcoming as a result of the border closing—although not until a change of regime had taken place in Senegal and Dahomey; only in the Dahomey-Niger dispute was the border closing effective enough to make the compromise rapid. In all other cases, the action merely hardened antipathies without forcing accommodation. One particularly ineffective case that backfired was Nigeria's severance of relations with France in 1961 because of the French nuclear tests in the Sahara. This resulted in cessation of all French trans-shipments through the port of Lagos to Dahomey and Niger. Within ten days, envoys from its two French-speaking neighbors were in Nigeria, pleading with the government to reopen the trade routes. During the Monrovia conference, Nigeria finally acceded to their request. The political effect of the move was dissipated, however, for cessation of French trade hurt Nigerians seeking replacement parts for French items more than it hurt France, and the chance of pressuring France through Niger and Dahomey (although predictably fruitless) was lost.

For the most part, the ineffectiveness of most attempts to close borders results from a combination of factors. Public opinion and regional considerations, as has been noted, have little effect on national policy. In some cases, trade between the countries involved is so unimportant that closing the border is no serious deprivation. In all cases, the border is so permeable to traditional, pedestrian traffic that it can never be completely closed. To a great extent, the ineffectiveness of such classical methods of pressure as the severance of political and economic relations goes far to explain the high incidence of propaganda and financial and military support of opposition groups. The latter techniques, in turn, are usually only effective enough to nurture unfriendly relations and divert the attention of both sides from common problems and positive programs.

THE POLITICS OF BOUNDARIES

Problems created by boundaries are among the more frequent causes of war, and Western Africa has some of the strangest boundary problems in the world. Unlike some national borders in other parts of the world, few boundaries in Western Africa follow the walls and moats of history, those natural

Table 3: *Western African Land Boundaries**
(All distances in kilometers)

State	Total	Geometric	River	Others		Scale of Map Used	
						Maximum	Minimum
Tunisia	1402	362	53			2,000,000	1,000,000
(Claims)	1514	462	53				
Algeria	5970	4000	800	142†	75+	2,000,000	200,000
Morocco	1938	1020	762			2,000,000	1,000,000
(Claims‡)	1890	1340	390				
Spanish Sahara	1992	1942				2,000,000	
Mauritania	4760	3800	930	10†		2,000,000	500,000
Senegal #	1700	192	1046			2,000,000	500,000
Gambia	750	750				1,000,000	
Port. Guinea	715	206	80			500,000	
Mali	7030	3713	1600	10†	75+	2,000,000	500,000
Guinea	2923	153	1132		138+	2,000,000	250,000
Sierra Leone	895	105	395		130+	1,000,000	250,000
Liberia	1310	30	872			800,000	250,000
Ivory Coast	2930	125	1750		8+	800,000	500,000
Ghana	1994	428	963	9†		500,000	
Upper Volta	3105	1028	1390			2,000,000	250,000
Togo	1507	438	536	9†		2,000,000	500,000
Dahomey	1792	286	686			2,000,000	1,000,000
Nigeria	3732	60	320	210†	140+	2,000,000	1,000,000
Niger	4253	2717	622			2,000,000	1,000,000
Totals**	28597	13364	7344	370†	353+		

* Distances have been measured on maps by means of a measuring instrument designed to follow irregular lines. The scale of the largest and smallest maps used for measurement is given. Measurements will err by underestimation; breakdowns for geometric, river, and other components are minimum figures.

† Roads, + watershed.

‡ Boundary estimated along a straight line that follows the escarpment south of the Dra, leaving the *confins* in Morocco and Tindouf in Algeria. No line has been suggested for putting Tindouf in Morocco.

Senegal figures exclude Gambian boundary.

** Totals do not add up because shared boundaries are not counted twice.

defense lines that mark the military conflicts and diplomatic compromises of the national past. These boundary lines therefore have none of the legitimacy conferred by national history. This has its advantages and disadvantages: the might of conquest and the right of diplomacy have not sanctified the borders, but the Schleswigs and the Alsace-Lorraines are not present either.

All boundaries in Western Africa are recent, colonial creations. Some were a result of the Berlin conference of 1884-85, which declared that European states could claim the territories they effectively occupied; most were merely administrative divisions within French North and West Africa. Usually, the borders were established without any precise knowledge of the terrain and traditional nations (tribes) involved. Thus, half of the boundaries are geometrical, mainly straight lines. Over a quarter of the boundaries, however, are physical. For the most part, these follow small riverbeds, although two major rivers—the Senegal River between Senegal and Mauritania, and the Niger River between Niger and Dahomey—are also used. Gambia combines the two criteria: it is bounded by straight lines and arcs drawn on either side of the Gambia River. Crestline and watershed boundaries are rare in Western Africa (less than four hundred kilometers, or 2 per cent), for there are few mountains; those that exist were placed, by the colonial divisions, inside one country or another.

The most serious problem—and most frequent reproach—concerning the unnaturalness of Western African boundaries relates to human geography. This complicated question requires much clarification. All boundaries between the Atlas on the north, and the Senegal and Niger rivers and the sixteenth parallel on the south, run through regions with a population of less than one person per square mile. Moreover, all boundaries through the Poor Middle Belt of West Africa (running roughly parallel to the coast from the Futa Jallon in Guinea to the Jos Plateau in Nigeria) cross regions with populations of less than twenty-five persons per square mile. The only borders that cross regions with populations of over one hundred persons per square mile are those along a hundred-mile-deep coastal strip (excluding the borders of Mauritanian, Spanish Sahara, and Ghana-Ivory Coast) and those of northern Ghana and Nigeria. From the point of view of population density, therefore, there are encouraging factors of stability. Unfortunately, statistical considerations—like considerations of physical geography—must bow to other, more important human factors if the permanence of a frontier is to be ascertained.

Because boundaries separate nations, their stability depends on the willingness with which a citizen accepts the order to turn his back on a particular neighbor, or the willingness with which a national leader accepts the fact that people in certain areas are turning their backs on him and his leadership. Nation-building is essentially a back-turning process, for the organizational unit seeks to establish and inculcate coincidence between the popular and the territorial units. All boundaries are artificial in the sense that it is not natural to draw lines separating neighbors from contact with each other; but, as nations and states develop, people learn to live with boundaries—a learn-

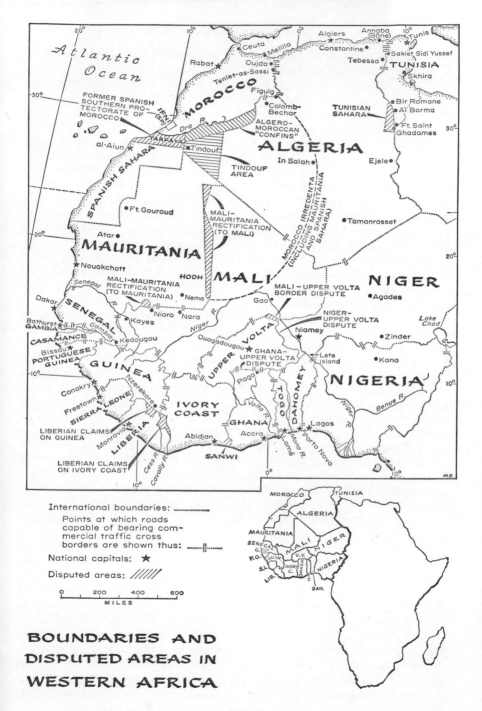

International boundaries: ....
Points at which roads
capable of bearing com-
mercial traffic cross
borders are shown thus: ...||....
National capitals: ★
Disputed areas: //////

0   200   400   600
      MILES

BOUNDARIES AND
DISPUTED AREAS IN
WESTERN AFRICA

ing process imposed by the exigencies of government and of conducting international relations among territorial states.

The much-repeated charge of artificiality directed against African boundaries refers specifically to their disregard of tribal geography. In these terms, there is nothing but truth in the charge; only in a few spots do Western African boundaries coincide with tribal limits.[25] More important: Is such coincidence possible or relevant? Few are the spots in the area where tribes themselves observe fine territorial distinctions; they intermingle, intermarry, and migrate. Even the great empires of the Sudan and the Maghreb were not territorial states. In modern times, the tribe may have a sense of community and a seat of authority, but it does not have fixed territorial limits. It is a human, not a geographical, unit. Thus, any line that cuts between some tribes will cut through others, and it would be difficult to draw any boundary in Western Africa that would coincide with tribal geography.

The basic question concerns the relevance of tribal geography to modern states. In the mid-twentieth century, the Western African tribe is no longer an organizational unit comparable to the government or the party, any more than it was a territorial unit. Although it is still the predominant national group in much of Western Africa—the primary focus of allegiance and identification throughout the area between the Gulf of Guinea and the Atlas Mountains—until replaced by the modern state, it has had little importance as a unit of political action. Border conflicts involving the Reqeibat and neighboring tribes in Morocco, Algeria, and Mauritania (1958-60); the Tuareg of Mali, Niger, and Algeria (1963-64); the Manjaks of Senegal and Portuguese Guinea (1961, 1963); the Ntribus and Ewes of Togo and Ghana; the Assini of Ivory Coast and Ghana (1960); and the Fulani and Bariba of Niger and Dahomey (1963-64) are relatively rare exceptions when it is realized that the frontiers of one country such as Ghana cut through seventeen major tribes. Even more important is the fact that only in the case of the Tuareg was the tribal action carried out autonomously, without instigation or assistance from a party or government.[26] Had it been a political unit as well as a social group, as it was in the past, the tribe would have posed such a threat to the modern government that it would have been either destroyed outright or adopted as the basis of government. But government and party have replaced the tribe's political functions, and state services and the nation are slowly replacing many of its social functions, leaving the traditional nation with little relevance as a basis for boundary determination.

True as this may be for the sociopolitical aspects of the Western African tribe, the situation is slightly different for tribal socioeconomic life, which is still vigorous. In many of the above cases—Reqeibat, Tuareg, Assinis, Fulanis-Baribas, Ewes—political unrest was caused by economic troubles. Trade, migration, and marriage are all part of contemporary tribal life, even when the tribe is split by borders. Given the permeability of Western African boundaries and the laxity of border control between most states, these divisions usually pose few problems. When an attempt is made to close the border, however, hardships are imposed on traditional ways of life. But the fact is that the whole process of modernization imposes hardships on traditionalism, of which the clash between nation-building and tribal life is only one example. Nationalism means closer ties within and looser ties without; it means the construction of a coincident nation-state-government and the centralization of allegiance on the new entity, just as it means the redirection of economic and social patterns within the new unit. There is no reason why the construction of the new nation should be based on criteria of traditionalism in boundary-making any more than in any other sector, although of course there is no reason not to expect tribal-based problems along the borders from time to time.

In sum, tribal criteria for borders in Western Africa are neither possible nor relevant. In Western Africa, it is not the boundary but the nation that is artificial. The coincidence of popular, territorial, and organizational units has not yet been achieved; boundary lines are still imprecise in human and political terms. As the nation consolidates, borders begin to find their *raison d'être*. In the process, the tribes will slowly lose their present importance, although both new irredentist claims and minor rectifications may be expected to arise.

Other than unification, few alternatives to the present Western African boundaries have ever been proposed. The greatest deterrent to territorial revisionism has been the fear of opening a Pandora's box. If any one boundary is seriously questioned, why not all the boundaries in Western Africa? And, then, what is "natural"? One alternative is to redraw the borders on the basis of physical features, but the absence of sharp geographic divisions in the area would be as troublesome to territorial revisionists as it was to the colonial boundary-makers; the one case of a long geographic border—the Senegal River—has cut up a natural demographic and agricultural region, and made development of the river basins dependent on international cooperation. In an age of boats and bridges, it is no more logical to set a boundary in a river than it is to set it on a road or railroad, which serve the same purpose. Another alternative is to reconstitute states on the basis of natural geographic regions. Treatises on artificiality have also shown how Western African borders cut across the area's latitudinal vegetation belts, but (wisely) no one has taken up the implied suggestion that the states be rearranged to fit these zones. The colonial practice of carving out territories from harbor to hinterland—Senegal, Guinea, Ivory Coast, Ghana, Togo, Dahomey, Nigeria, and the Maghreb—gives the advantage of diversity; the more homogeneous states —Liberia, Sierra Leone, Mali, Niger—have more limited development possibilities. (If Congo had been confined to a geographically homogeneous region, it would never have had an outlet to the sea.) Two other alternatives are left: regional unity and tribally based irredentism. The first pools the resources of several states and increases possibilities of development; the second, reviving memories of historic empires, poses problems of international conflict.

On the basis of this general appreciation of the boundary situation in Western Africa, it is possible to examine specific border disputes and attempts at rectification. The case of the southern Moroccan boundary is certainly the most complex. It includes two inextricably related problems: the actual border problem with Algeria between Teniet as-Sassi and the western Tarfaya boundary ($9°40''W$), and the border problem of Morocco Irredenta.[27] The narrow boundary problem results from a Franco-Moroccan judgment in the 1845 Treaty of Lalla Maghnia that no border was necessary because "a country which is found without water is uninhabitable and a delimitation thereof would be superfluous," and from a Moroccan decision after 1956 to await the independence of Algeria before finally drawing a border which, in this century, has appeared quite necessary. Between 1956 and 1960, a bilateral commission accepted in principle by both Morocco and France met rarely and never agreed on a settlement of the southern border. In May 1958, an incident involving Moroccan and French troops in the contested territory resulted in an agreement to constitute a no-man's-land in the Algero-Moroccan *confins*. Morocco's hope that an independent Algerian government would prove more understanding than the French appears to have had no more concrete a basis than a too-literal interpretation of mutual professions of North African brotherhood, until 1960, 1961, and 1962, when GPRA Premier Ferhat Abbas and then his successor, Benyussef ben Khedda, gave assurances that the problem would be negotiated after independence.[28] Similar assurances were refused by Ahmed ben Bella, however, during his visit to Morocco in 1962, and when independence came and Moroccan troops moved in to occupy the *confins*, they found Algerian troops already there. The new situation was worse than the old, for Algeria refused to discuss the border and both sides began occupying the no-man's land, with not even a presumed border running through it. When Moroccan and Algerian troops met over contested positions during 1963, a number of incidents finally led to the Algero-Moroccan border war in October.

In addition to the previous Franco-Moroccan agreement not to draw a border and the Moroccan decision to await Algerian independence before solving the problem, another element hindered a boundary solution: Morocco Irredenta. The Moroccan thesis was that the nineteenth-century Sherifian Empire had been dismembered by French and Spanish colonial conquest since the early 1900s. Under foreign rule, say the Moroccans, the people continued to consider themselves subjects of the sultan and members of the Muslim community he headed. In 1956, the core area, made up of the French and Spanish protectorates and Tangier, was restored to complete sovereignty, and two years later the southern Spanish protectorate (Tarfaya) rejoined the kingdom. According to the Moroccan thesis, "unredeemed" parts of the empire still lie under colonial (Spanish), neocolonial (Mauritanian), or simply neighbor's (Algerian) rule. The attempt to secure the return of these lands is really a microcosm of Western African relations, for it involved the use of warfare, subversion, severance of relations, propaganda, alliances, and mediation, as well as continuing diplomacy, and it concerned basic elements of security, ideology, identity, sentiment, and national interest.[29]

Sentimental attachment to irredentism was Morocco's major *leitmotiv* in its African relations between February 1958 (when the cause was formally espoused by Mohammed V), and May 1963 (when Hassan II refused to sit next to ould Daddah at the African summit at Addis Ababa); since then, the problem has primarily affected its relations with Algeria, although as late as October 1964 Hassan stayed away from the Maghreb reconciliation meeting at Tunis in order to avoid the president of Mauritania. The propagandist and diplomatic phase of the policy began unofficially soon after Morocco gained independence; it was first reflected in official Moroccan diplomacy with the protests that began in August 1956 over French exploitation of the Sahara, and continued along with the various steps by which Mauritania acceded to full sovereignty. The diplomatic offensive, however, was ineffective and even counterproductive. It ruptured diplomatic relations with Tunisia, Senegal, and Algeria; provoked Moroccan boycott of meetings of the United Nations Economic Commission for Africa, the African National Radio and Television Union, the Inter-African and Malagasy Organization (Monrovia Group), the Organization for African Unity, and Maghreb cooperation; and ended in Morocco's isolation in Western Africa after the collapse of the Casablanca Group. Indeed, the only positive contribution of Moroccan irredentism to the Western African diplomatic scene was its role in the formation of the Casablanca Group, its importance in holding together the Brazzaville Group, and its place among the local issues that kept the two apart while the pressure for a single African unity organization could mature. Certainly none of these effects was one of Morocco's original goals. The case of Moroccan irredentism is only one example of the primacy of national independence as a goal (perceived and defined by the national policy-makers) over other, conflicting values of African unity and development.

The case of the Togo-Ghana border involves an entire state rather than a boundary.[30] Ghana came into being in 1957 with an eastern border that followed tribal lines for 170 of its 498 miles. The unification of British Togoland and the Gold Coast through the May 1956 plebiscite placed many formerly split tribes totally within Ghana, but it left nearly 100,000 Ewes (along with lesser tribal groups) divided between Ghana and Togo. (There is no better illustration of the fact that, in Africa, a line which unites some tribes will divide others.)

The legislative elections of April 1958 in the French trusteeship territory of Togo brought to power a government headed by the Ewe leader, Olympio, whose policy had—until 1952—paralleled that of Ewe unificationists under British rule but had thereafter changed to champion an independent union of the two Togos. Although Ghana supported Olympio's movement as one working toward independence from colonial rule, the permeable nature of the border and the uncertain allegiance of the Ewes posed problems in the Ghanaian policy of national integration. Late in 1958, a number of Ghanaian

Ewes (including two members of parliament) were imprisoned in Ghana, and others who had moved freely across the border were threatened with arrest for showing Togolese sympathies. A year later, as Togo moved toward independence, Nkrumah predicted that it would become the seventh region of Ghana. Relations again took a turn for the worse. In the spring of 1960, the Ghanaian army held its annual exercises ten miles from the border. In reply to rumors of an imminent Ghanaian attack on Togo, Olympio merely questioned Ghana's ability to execute such an action militarily and defend it diplomatically. Rumors of a Togolese plot to unite the Ewes by force (despite the inexistence of a Togolese army) provoked more arrests in Ghana and on March 10, 1960, a Ghanaian note to France charged that the Togolese constitution (in fact, still unwritten) contained irredentist clauses. In July, three months after Togo won independence, however, Nkrumah was in Lomé on a state visit, discussing plans for renewed economic cooperation between the two states. By September, relations had become bitter again, and Ghana—charging Olympio had failed to produce the promised plans for cooperation—closed its eastern border. Togolese elections in April 1961 were the next occasion for worsening relations, as opposition groups charged repression by Togo and fled to Ghana. In September, Togo's national assembly unanimously adopted a resolution favoring reunification of the two Togos and, in early December, it announced the discovery of a plot allegedly supported by Ghana against Olympio. The situation improved (as might have been expected) when Olympio was assassinated in January 1963 and Antoine Meatchi, a Togolese refugee in Ghana, became the vice-president of the new regime. Ghanaian newspapers proclaimed, "Ghana and Togo are one," and after several weeks' hesitation Ghana reopened its border. The new Togolese government, however, did not move to join Ghana; it continued to act as an independent regime aware of the delicacy of its position. As might also have been expected, the border was closed once more (in mid-July 1963, after a series of border incidents). Several incursions by Ghanaian police into Togo, in January and February 1965, resulted in the death of a Togolese border guard. The problem of the Ewes and the border has been left far behind in the exchange of charges and countercharges since 1958; it remains unsolved, although growing awareness of Ghanaian and Togolese nationality may very slowly begin to spread along the border regions. The situation has served as an instrument for both sides in their efforts to consolidate their regimes and divert dissatisfaction over internal conditions to external problems, and has brought Togo into closer cooperation and alliance with its French-speaking neighbors. A "soft" policy, opening the border and also schools in the frontier region to Togolese, and offering common services, would doubtless have served Ghana's purposes better than its offensive "hard" line.

The dispute between Ivory Coast and Ghana over the "Sanwi state" is a tribal matter, exacerbated by uneven patterns of modernization and Ghanaian interference. The southeastern corner of Ivory Coast had lain "outside the mainstream of African organizational life" since the beginning of

Houphouet-Boigny's nationalist movement.[31] In the elections of 1957, 1959, and 1960, it either supported opposition candidates or had a high rate of abstention. Economically, too, it was alien; although the region was rich in coffee and cocoa, the farmers were immigrants from other parts of the country or were tribesmen the Assinis had long considered vassals. In early 1959, the Fraternal Society of the Sanwi sent a delegation to de Gaulle to request autonomy under a treaty signed in 1834; in early May, after obtaining no satisfaction from France, it set up a Sanwi independence movement under Chief Amon Ndouffou III. Some of its leaders fled to neighboring independent Ghana, where they received arms and aid in subversion. Others, charged with violating the external security of the state, were arrested and tried in Abidjan in early 1960, and imprisoned for several months. The coming of independence to Ivory Coast, and the consolidation of its regime, reduced the importance of the Sanwi movement. Dissidents petitioned Houphouet-Boigny and were granted a reprieve in December 1961; they returned to Ivory Coast in April, under a general amnesty. Nevertheless a number of Sanwi leaders remained in contact with the African Affairs Bureau in Accra and a small Sanwi colony settled on the eastern side of the border among fellow tribesmen in Ghana. In September 1962, those who stayed in Ghana joined a Freedom Fighters' Front, and in June reissued their "constitution" and program. In 1960, Ghana openly claimed the area in the name of tribal unity, the 40,000 Sanwis being related to Nkrumah's native Nzima tribe, but Accra has denied both aid and claims since then.

The southern Algero-Tunisian border was left undelimited at the time Tunisia gained its independence, with the treaties of 1910 and 1955-56 providing grounds for questioning the usual map version.[32] A mixed inspection commission sought to trace the frontier in April 1957; after an initial rebuff, Tunisia succeeded in gaining recognition of its sovereignty over Fort Saint only by linking the matter with current negotiations on state property with France and, in a subsequent note to Paris, reserved its rights over the uninhabited desert south of the line between Fort Saint (Marker 220) and Bir Romane. In one of his weekly talks in 1959, Bourguiba specifically raised the question of the Tunisian Sahara, suggesting either a "natural prolongation" of Tunisian territory south from Bir Romane to about $30°N$ (the parallel near Marker 233, south of Ghadames) "just as parts of Libya, Algeria, Morocco, or Senegal [*sic*] will be their prolongation," or a common agreement that beyond a certain limit "the door opens on an area undivided and shared by all, where communications, water points, pasturage, and underground wealth are at the disposal of all." [33]

This view was subsequently reiterated in negotiations with France and then in Tuniso-Malian and Tuniso-Moroccan communiqués of June 1961, when the Franco-Algerian negotiations at Evian turned on the Saharan question; the three parties wished to emphasize the non-French nature of the Sahara, but the declaration also stated Tunisia's claim to part of the desert. Resultant ruffled feelings between the GPRA and Tunis over the subject were temporarily smoothed over as Tunisian policy took a militant turn during the Bizerte crisis of July and a detachment of volunteers was sent to Marker 233 to make clear Tunisia's determination. The volunteers were annihilated; de Gaulle recognized Algeria's territorial integrity; and the matter was dropped on the Tunisian side. Broad negotiations between Tunisia and independent Algeria finally ended in a number of agreements in September and November 1963; the November accord provided for their joint use of Saharan oil and gas, but left details undecided and the border unsettled. Bourguiba's entire policy appears to have been directed toward the affirmation of Tunisia's right to share raw materials from the "North African desert," rather than toward the acquisition of the uninhabited 15,000-square-mile triangle of the Great Eastern Erg between Bir Romane and Ghadames. Out of this problem has come Bourguiba's theory of *dépassement*, according to which border problems can be left behind as solutions are found on a higher level of cooperation. A rich oil strike at al-Borma right on the contested border in mid-1964, however, showed the necessity for a specific border settlement; in line with Bourguiba's theories, it is conceived in the novel form of joint Tunisian-Algerian sovereignty over the contested oil area.

Another unresolved boundary problem concerns the insignificant island of Lete in the Niger River between Dahomey and Niger. In this case the boundary was merely a symptom of deeper troubles between the two states. In late October 1963, the PDU (RDA) government of Hubert Maga in Dahomey was overthrown by a military *coup* led by Colonel Christophe Soglo, who installed a provisional unity government. In early December, however, Maga and some of his supporters from northern Dahomey were arrested on charges of plotting to restore the former regime; in the process, citizens of Niger were killed or arrested and Niger was accused of supporting the plot of its former RDA ally. Later in the month, Niger announced that it would expel all Dahomeyans (variously estimated at 15,000-50,000) living on the northern side of the Niger River. Dahomey closed the border and announced the dissolution of the two states' joint commercial organization. Both sides mobilized, Niger charging that Dahomey was preparing to seize the five-mile-long island of Lete in the Niger River. In January, elections were held under the new Dahomeyan constitution, and Soglo's regime gave way to a new civilian government under Apithy and Ahomadegbe, who combined their forces in a new, single Dahomeyan Democratic Party (PDD). With the passing of the provisional government, the crisis temporarily subsided. At the March conference of the UAM at Dakar, Presidents Diori and Apithy signed a reconciliation agreement. A meeting of the two parties at Dosso in early June restored commercial cooperation between the states and scheduled new negotiations in Cotonou to solve the expatriate and border problems. Nevertheless, the Cotonou meeting at the end of the month brought no decision on either partition or ownership of the island of Lete. The matter was of reduced importance as long as the general relations between the two countries improved, but when the internal stability of both regimes weakened in late 1964, the problem was

revived in the bitter terms of the preceding year. A renewed attempt at negotiations by the Entente brought a settlement in January 1965 on a Tunisian-
type formula: inhabitants of Lete, along with the rest of the Entente populations, were to enjoy dual citizenship.

There have also been a number of smaller claims and conflicts that have
neither turned into major disputes nor been solved. One series concerns the
undemarcated borders of Upper Volta, which caused bitterness in relations
with Ghana in 1964 and with Mali in 1963. Another problem has concerned
Dahomey, which the Nigerian Action Group proposed incorporating as the
fourth region of Nigeria in 1960; the claims were implicitly disavowed by
Nigerian Premier Tafawa Balewa, and the matter blew over. These, and
new problems of the same type, can be expected to reappear from time to
time as the new nations try to fit comfortably into their territorial frame.
They usually involve technical problems of demarcation, aggravated by political differences between regimes.

Other conflicts have already been settled, often with a show of maturity.
The Mali-Mauritanian frontier underwent the first rectification ever to be
made between two independent African states.[34] The problem arose from the
mixture of nomadic and seminomadic populations along the desert and
savannah border region. An attempt was made by the French colonial government to stabilize the administration of the region in July 1944, when the
Hodh district was transferred from Soudan to Mauritania, but demarcation
of the border was unclear. Administrative means of dealing with the nomads
were worked out in meetings between the two autonomous territories between
1958 and early 1960; however, attempts by a commission of experts to settle
the border itself at the same time ran into continual deadlock, each side but-
tressing its position with sound legal, geographic, and sociological evidence.
In the fall of 1960, just as both states became independent, a number of
tribal incidents along the disputed frontier embittered Mali—already sensitive
over the breakup of its federation with Senegal—and led to two years of bad
relations between the two neighbors, marked by raids by pro-Moroccan bands
on Mauritania from Malian territory. Realization of the fruitlessness of the
quarrel led to futile attempts at *rapprochement* in late 1962. The negotiators
did manage to arrange a meeting between Keita and ould Daddah, and in
mid-February 1963 the two heads of state met at Kayes to begin negotiations
all over again. In the settlement, Mali gained a rectified straight-line frontier
across the Saharan region (respecting traditional rights to certain wells); in
exchange, Mauritania won recognition of a southerly line in the savannah
region near Kayes. In the absence of natural social or geographical lines, the
determination of the border was political.

Three other frontier problems were solved easily and peaceably. Liberia,
which had defended its independence against its colonial neighbors during
the past century only at the price of slices and slivers of territory, made a
serious attempt to regain a portion of the lost areas during negotiations with
France in early 1958. The territory in question was the Mount Nimba re-

gion of Guinea and the land between the Cavally and the Cess rivers in Ivory Coast. After Guinean independence, Tubman used the occasion of Touré's visit in mid-November 1958 to renounce all claims to the Guinean region.[35] Since then there have been negotiations on Guinean use of the new Liberian railroad from Buchanan to the mountains to ship out iron ore, resulting in a yet-unimplemented agreement signed in January 1962. Liberia's border with Ivory Coast was stabilized with equal grace. During a state visit by Houphouet-Boigny to Tubman in mid-November 1961, the two presidents agreed to accept present borders, ending Liberia's claim to land west of the upper Cavally River. They also recognized the river boundary lines on the right (west) bank, thus perpetuating the classic error of a Liberian diplomat who unwittingly had given up control over the entire river. But the boundary rivers were opened to citizens of both states, for the first time making it legal for Liberian rubber plantations to ship their goods down Ivory Coast's river.[36] Similarly, a protocol signed by Niger and Upper Volta in June 1964 settled border problems between the two Entente allies; delimitation of boundaries, movement of populations, coordination of administrative and security, and provision for a census to facilitate tax collection were the points involved in the agreement.[37]

One final aspect of Western African boundaries remains to be noted. Throughout the area, the precolonial concept of boundaries was one of frontier marches, not border lines. The classical West African empires were composed of one or more centers of power; control and allegiance was conceived of in terms of people rather than land, concentrated about the centers, and diminished with distance. The Fula Empire was where the Fulas lived and maintained control; they could move long distances and keep the empire intact as long as they preserved a cohesive society and independent political control. In a nomadic society, such as that from which the Muslim legal ideas of North Africa sprung, it was the people—the community of believers—that determined the geographic scope of the state, not the territorial limit of the state or its effective control that determined the allegiance of the people. Morocco was traditionally divided into *bled al-makhzen* ("government region") and *bled as-siba* ("dissident region"); both considered themselves part of the Sherifian Empire and owed religious allegiance to the sultan as *imam* ("religious leader") but only the *bled al-makhzen* owed political allegiance to the sultanate. In the Maghreb, the Sudan, and the Guinea coast, the nation was a social unit and determined the state. Today, the state and its boundaries are the framework for the nation-building process, and the state is a territorial unit. At present, however, the "state" is a state of becoming, not a state of being. As a result, although boundary lines are drawn on a map and customs posts are (sometimes) located along these lines, effective government control is not yet coterminous with the territorial limits of the state. The state still tends to be bounded by frontier marches.

This situation goes far to explain the relative infrequency of border wars and border claims. It also reinforces the suggestion that such disputes may become more frequent in the future, as the frontier zones narrow to boundary lines and the authority of one state meets that of another. At present, nearly every Western African state has a buffer zone between itself and its immediate neighbors, a quasi-no-man's-land of incomplete government control and much human intercourse across the formal boundary. The general nature of West African geography reinforces this fact, for the area is made up of vast zones across which no natural boundary is visible. It is hard to draw a meaningful line through the Sahara, although the desert itself forms a huge, natural boundary-in-depth.[38] The forest zone of West Africa performed the same function during the time of the classical empires, as did the Poor Middle Belt between the Sudan and the forest. Thus the intertribal frontier march, the natural zone, and the buffer area are three distinct concepts that reinforce one another.

There is a specific application of this characteristic in the international relations of Western Africa. In a number of cases, entire states constitute boundaries-in-depth and have seized on this position to adopt a buffer policy. It should be emphasized that the "buffer state" is a misleading concept, for it implies that the position of the state is determinative and that there is no choice of policies open.[39] On the contrary, the buffer policy is only one of several alternatives available to a state, and its selection depends on the policy choice of state leaders as well as the policies of the neighbors being "buffed." A buffer policy may be one of strict neutrality, depending on the mutual tolerance of both neighbors, or it may be combined with a policy of protectionism, whereby the middle state serves as a glacis for one neighbor. Even in the latter case, however, the "buffing" state maintains a certain amount of neutrality toward its protector, for fear that too close a relationship might upset the balance that keeps it alive; hence, it may be expected that a state playing the role of a buffer will try to better its relations with both neighbors when it betters its relations with one. "Buffing" may be a historic policy open to a country with certain geographical relations, but it need not be a permanent condition.

Togo, the sliver that separates former French West Africa from former British Gold Coast, had been prepared by its colonial history as well as its geography to adopt a buffer policy between Ghana and the Entente states. Its Ewe problem with Ghana puts it in a weaker position toward its western neighbor; hence it is with its eastern neighbor, Dahomey, that Togo should be expected to develop special ties. This expectation is strengthened by the need of Dahomey, itself a sliver, for support; if Togo were to disappear, Dahomey would be in danger itself of becoming either the battleground or the buffer between Ghana and Nigeria. On the other hand, it would be expected that Togo would avoid too close a relation with its eastern neighbor, because of its buffer policy; rather, it would seek to overcome inherent differences between former British and former French territories. Togo's trilingual colonial background, and its ties with both AOF and British Togoland, suited it to this task. The result was that Olympio was wary of the conferences he attended and the commitments he made between 1958 and 1963. It was only in the Monrovia meeting, which Olympio encouraged when faced with the existence of the rival Casablanca and Monrovia alliances, that Togo found a group ecumenical enough to join. Dahomeyan Foreign Minister Zinsou's hurried visit to Accra after the assassination of Olympio was essentially made to ascertain if Nkrumah would continue to allow the existence of an independent Togolese buffer, or whether Ghana's intention to move in would make it imperative for Dahomey to move first. The new Togolese government improved its relations with Ghana, and then, in July and November, joined the UAM (UAMCE) and the West African Monetary Union. Under the pressure of increasing signs of hostility from Ghana in 1964 and 1965, however, it has increasingly looked to the UAM and the Entente for protection. The buffer policy maintained by Togo, the similar role adopted by Dahomey from time to time, and the checkerboard pattern of relations along the Benin Coast have all helped prevent the oft-proposed Benin Union from coming into being.

Mauritania is a buffer state between North and West Africa, its intermediate position reflected by its ethnic mixture of Arabs and Negroes.[40] Because of its Arab population and its historical relation to Morocco, it is in a weaker position toward its northern neighbor, against whom it needs protection. Its Arab majority, however, prevents too close a relationship with Black Africa. Its southern neighbor, Senegal, is not eager to have Morocco for a neighbor; at one time when it appeared possible that Mauritania (like Poland) might be divided among its three neighbors, Senegal had some aspirations to the Negro-inhabited right bank of the Senegal River. As the danger faded, Senegal became more interested in the maintenance of a buffer state between itself and Morocco. Thus Mauritania remained aloof toward the RDA, turned to a special relationship with the PFA and the Mali Federation, and then joined the UAM, where it gained allies and active support for its independence but maintained total freedom of decision on all political matters relating to its Arab nature (such as the Palestine question). Mutual security discussions were held with Senegal in November 1962. Because of its special relations with Mauritania, on the other hand, Senegal has frequently tried to mediate the Morocco-Mauritania conflict. With its independence assured since 1963, Mauritania has been bettering relations with Algeria, moving from a protected to a balanced buffer position in Western Africa. Its withdrawal from OCAM in July 1965, when the alliance was no longer needed to protect Mauritanian policy, is a further step in reaffirming a buffer policy.

Upper Volta opted for a buffer policy in 1961, when it was receiving no satisfaction from Ivory Coast over financial and customs arrangements. Its location at the crossroads of the Entente and the UAS places it in an ideal position to follow such a policy, but the delicate balance that is necessary would make such a role difficult, tiring, and perhaps costly. When satisfaction was achieved in new negotiations with Abidjan, Upper Volta returned to the fold.

Two colonial territories are also well-positioned for a buffer policy, although the response of their neighbors (the territories do not make their own policy) has varied widely. Spanish Sahara is a little Mauritania, and it separates the object of Morocco's irredentism from its source. Morocco's relations with Spain are complicated and delicate, but Morocco has refrained from pressing Spain openly on the subject of Spanish Sahara. Mauritania has excellent relations with Spain, both in commercial matters and through military co-operation, and has also been discreet on the question of Spanish Sahara. Both are satisfied with the status quo,[41] because neither of the two would like to have a common frontier and neither is sure who would get Spanish Sahara if the Spanish left. The situation is aided by the absence of a nationalist movement in the territory. In Portuguese Guinea, there are several nationalist movements, the one supported by Guinea being more active than the one supported by Senegal. The nationalists are fighting for an independent state, but both the Guineans and the Sengalese would probably be pleased to accept the geographic and tribal division of the territory into two annexable sectors. Neither neighbor, however, voices its claims;[42] because they already have a common border farther north and are not hostile to each other, a buffer policy by an independent Portuguese Guinea may not be possible or necessary.

African leaders have come to realize that the consolidation of their states poses boundary problems. They have sought to reconcile the fact of national existence and control of a given territory with the equally obvious fact of traditional and continuing human activity across its frontiers. The result has been a search for solutions that recall their conflicting attempts to achieve both independence and unity. Specialists have suggested ways around this dilemma: such measure as bilateral agreements on simplified border regulations, regional agreements to the same end, or multilateral associations to harmonize economic and social matters while leaving political control and sovereignty unaffected.[43] The modern African expression of the same idea comes most explicitly from Bourguiba in his theory of *dépassement*. Apithy has echoed the same argument in regard to Niger, and Senghor has repeatedly invoked it as a solution to the Mauritanian problem. Houphouet-Boigny has offered the idea of dual citizenship. Senegal maintains functioning boundary commissions with Guinea and Mauritania to keep minor administrative conflicts from becoming major political issues. Another solution is to engage in technical discussions during times of lessened political tensions in order to delineate and demarcate imprecise borders. There is little to be gained by postponing such discussions on the pretext that harmonious relations should be left disturbed or that they obviate the need for boundaries, for inevitably the imprecise boundary will become an additional bone of contention if relations turn sour. The technical decisions must be ratified by the political authorities of the state, to give official sanction to the border. Because knowledge and mapping technology were inaccurate at the time the colonial boundaries were established, a more precise determination of Western African boundaries is clearly in order.

THE LIMITS ON UNITY AND COOPERATION

On the question of unity, Western African foreign policy faces a dilemma. On one hand, as has been seen, the slogan of unity carries a powerful ideological value. The idea that in unity lies strength, in a context in which power is illusive, combined with a certain me-tooism in the face of worldwide attempts at regional unification, has provided impetus to the unity drive. The notion that "Africa Must Unite" is reinforced by the myth of geographic unity implicit in the island-continent, and is further aided by the cultural myth which holds that colonialism, underdevelopment, and new nationhood give the states of the continent a common basis upon which the geographic suggestion can be made a political possibility. On the other hand, the ideological value of independence has run counter to that of unification—in fact, if not entirely in theory. Every Western African state has a different independence date, a distinct ruling elite, separate national institutions, a growing sense of nationhood, and a *situation acquise* and a going concern to defend. Their experiences were not nearly as similar as those of the Thirteen Colonies or the Canadian Provinces, and were much closer in many ways to the situation in nineteenth-century Latin America. Despite the hopes placed by the Pan-Africanists in the unitary wave of the future, in the short run the loss of individual sovereignty that union would bring has been an unacceptable alternative.

But the slogan remains. The dialectics of the dilemma have led to three outcomes: outward-directed attempts to combine similarities of external policy into a foreign-policy pressure group, inward-directed cooperation in subcontinental areas where there are common characteristics and a possibility of common internal policies, and a search for a satisfying institutional definition of *unity* that would reconcile the dilemma.[44] International relations in Western Africa are filled with examples of each outcome: no case typifies one response alone; each combines elements of all three. The movement toward the OAU is a continental example, even though it grew out of a Western African core area. The other cases are regional (sub-area) examples, frequently involving both inward- and outward-directed aspects within varying institutional forms, and always built about a new approach to the problem of achieving a satisfactory unity. Not one has lasted in its original form, and many have completely disappeared. Yet each has had great experimental value, as Western Africa continues to seek a solution to its ideological dilemma and its real needs.

The federal approach to unity was seen in its worst light in the Mali Federation, the creation of which was the result of the strong federalist wave that remained in French West Africa (AOF) after the dislocation of the federation by the *loi cadre* of 1956 and the referendum of 1958. In the period of maneuvering and negotiation after the referendum, all the autonomous territories of AOF fell away except Soudan and Senegal. These two territories were held together by their common attachment to the idea of unity and by their common dependence on the Dakar-Niger railway. There is little question that a federation with a larger membership—as originally planned—would have had a far better chance of lasting. The federal institutions were designed for a two-member federation, but they were neither supple nor strong enough to keep Soudan and Senegal together in the face of deep ideological differences over internal and foreign policy. Even the common ideal of unity was not viewed in the same terms by the two partners; although they agreed that unity had priority over independence, there was great divergence between Senegal's pluralistic ideas and Soudan's centralistic conception of unity.

The federal constitution of Mali, drawn up in Dakar in January 1959, provided for a federal government, assembly, judiciary, and army, capping similar institutions in each of the two member states. In March, a federal political organization, the African Federalist Party (PFA), was created out of the two component parties (UPS and US [RDA]) and their allies in other territories. When plans were being made for independence, a new constitutional convention to provide for a federal presidency was held in Dakar in mid-April and early May 1960 and in Bamako in late May. The head of state was to have limited powers but was to act as arbiter among the other institutions, replacing the much stronger figure of the French president. It was this post, crucial despite its weakness, that was the stumbling block over which, in August, the Mali Federation fell.

The institutions of the Federation never functioned as governing bodies. The two states exchanged ministerial delegations as if they were merely friendly neighbors. Each sent to other territories missions composed only of its own representatives. The two territorial sections of the party were national organizations with no effective coordination; they met in congress as opponents in bilateral negotiations, not as sections of a single party. Up to and during the final *coup* there were continuing attempts by the Soudanese in the federal government to exercise functions and nominate personnel lying within the competence of the territorial governments. The only place the federal army functioned as a unit was in Congo, and even there there were rivalries and riots. The Mali Federation only lasted two months as an independent state, during which time little federal government action was taken on internal or external policy. There is no basis for judging either the Senegalese or the Soudanese approach to unity as the "right" one. The loose federal concept or the unitarian concept could have worked if both sides had subscribed to it. The two concepts might even have been able to coexist if the federal government had been constituted as an effective neutral arbiter. Instead, it was a battleground.

A working federation in Western Africa has existed in Nigeria, and there are also three unitary states with regions of different colonial heritages: Nigeria, Morocco, and Ghana.[45] Nigerian independence saw the preservation of the British colonial unity with a federal system of three regions, redivided in 1964 into four, with the former German and then British territory of the Northern Cameroons governed as an integral part of the Northern Region.

Morocco integrated the northern Spanish protectorate and the international zone of Tangier as provinces in the newly independent kingdom in 1956, and added the southern Spanish protectorate as Tarfaya province in April 1958. Ghana achieved its independence in 1957 with Togoland, the former German colony and then British trusteeship territory, already integrated into the state as the fifth region. In the case of the Nigerian Federation, the distribution of power among more than two units has maintained internal unity, despite some difference in their views on federalism. In the three cases of integration, smaller, weaker regions have been incorporated in larger, centrally governed units. The one approach illustrates the Senegalese thesis; the other, the Soudanese. But the basic conditions of success in Nigeria (three or four counterbalancing units) or in the three integrationist cases (a larger unit absorbing a smaller one) were not present to help the Malian experiment. In the absence of a clear consensus or one or another form of unity, the Mali Federation collapsed.

The Maghreb unity move, which reached its most concrete attempt at realization during 1958, failed because—in the simplest terms—there was nothing to unite.[46] Unity could not be unification because, before 1962, only two of the three Maghreb states were independent. The Algerian party did not have control over a territorial state, and was too busy fighting for independence and developing popular feelings of Algerian nationalism—as its two neighbors were preoccupied with their own going state concerns and nationalism—to be interested in or capable of fusion with Tunisia and Morocco. In fact, the formation of the Algerian provisional government (GPRA) in September 1958 marked the demise of the institutions of Maghreb unity; a month after the GPRA was founded, the permanent secretariat of the Arab Maghreb, the only institution of the 1958 "union," met for the third and last time to decide on the creation of a Maghreb consultative assembly (which was never appointed) and to schedule a fourth meeting in mid-December in Tunis (which was never held). Two years later, Bourguiba revived the idea by proposing an "organic political union" between Algeria and Tunisia, although again it was not clear which Algeria—provisional government or not-yet-independent nation—he was discussing.[47] Indeed, the only case of "condominium" was the ALN-occupied border region of Tunisia, which was a constant source of irritation to Tunis, not merely because it was an invitation to French invasion but also because it was an infringement of Tunisian sovereignty and control over its own territory.

Nor could Maghreb unity mean amalgamation of parties. The revolutionary option in Moroccan and Tunisian foreign policy, present as an alternative among Istiqlal and ALM leaders and within the Tunisian opposition in 1956, had been discarded within a few months after independence in favor of priority attention to nation-building. Even the continuing struggle of Morocco and Tunisia for complete independence—centered on evacuation of French bases, and lasting until 1961 in Morocco and 1963 in the case of Bizerte— was carried out within the national framework and did not spur a movement for North African "world revolution." Furthermore, by the end of 1958, the Istiqlal had lost control of the Moroccan government and had split into two factions; by the end of 1960, it had entered into a period of bad relations with the Neo-Destour government of Tunisia over the Mauritanian question. There was no ideological or organizational basis for party amalgamation.

Nor, finally, was Maghreb unity possible on a minimal basis of external policy coordination. Divisive issues were more important to the leaders of the three states than the goal of unity, to the paradoxical point that after 1958 "unity" was used to strengthen sides on the issues. Thus the interministerial council of the Arab Maghreb that was established in January 1962 was only a bilateral arrangement, arising from a Moroccan attempt to consolidate relations with ben Khedda of the GPRA before Algeria attained independence and reflecting the Moroccan pique at Tunisia for having recognized Mauritania. The interministerial council met only once; ben Khedda was out of power within eight months, and his friendship for the Moroccan regime was not shared by his successor, ben Bella. Thereafter, North African political meetings remained bilateral but shifted membership to Algeria and Tunisia, as Morocco was kept away by border and irridentist problems. It is hard—and perhaps fruitless—to seek to discover where specific issues ended and ideological divergences began, for the two were mutually supporting. In an era and an area where conflicts rapidly assume ideological overtones, Morocco's businessmen's monarchy and Algeria's revolutionary republic provided handy—if not always relevant—terms in which political differences could be expressed. The two exceptions were largely situational. From March to July 1961, the coronation of Hassan II and the Bizerte crisis provided two occasions for tripartite meetings in Rabat and Bizerte. Tunisian claims on Algerian territory, the Casablanca-Monrovia split, and the Mauritanian issue quickly re-established bilaterality as the form of North African cooperation. In mid-February 1963, the three foreign ministers met in Rabat "to insist on the necessity of avoiding whatever may cause deterioration in friendly relations," and to discuss foreign-policy views, and economic and technical cooperation. A second meeting, scheduled for mid-April, was never held, first because of the assassination of Algerian Foreign Minister Khemisti and then because of mounting tension between Morocco and Algeria.

Thus, until 1964, North African unity was impossible because other goals of the states and the state-in-formation took precedence over any type of unity, the slogans notwithstanding. None of the proposed institutions could bridge this gap. In this situation, the problem of a monarchy among republics, so often cited as a major barrier to unification, was a secondary matter, entering into consideration mainly as a footnote to ideological disputes.[48] Although there were sufficient units of diffused power in the Maghreb to overcome Mali-type problems, there was no desire for a supranational body of arbitration and control.

The Entente—Ivory Coast, Upper Volta, Niger, and Dahomey—was created to meet a temporary and permanent need. The long-term basis of the grouping was threefold: the twin trade routes which departed from Abidjan and Cotonou by rail and ended in Niamey by road; the Ivory Coast program of aid termed the Solidarity Fund; and the RDA party alliance which united the heads of government behind Houphouet-Boigny through common experiences and similar policy options.[49] Each of these long-term factors had a temporary corollary which gave the Entente its initial impetus as a reaction against the Mali Federation: Abidjan's traditional rivalry with Dakar for trade and development; opposition to the federalist idea that richer states should subsidize poorer territories; and competition with the PRA and then PFA party alliance. The formation of the group marked a partial concession (the establishment of a Solidarity Fund) on the second point, but it held the line on opposition to political union or any supranational aspects. At this small price, Ivory Coast consolidated its position and eliminated its temporary isolation following the *renversement des alliances* in AOF in 1958-59. The realistic basis of the grouping—reflecting political affinities, partial geographic contiguity, and commercial patterns—accounts in large measure for its durability as both an inward-directed and outward-directed alliance.

The Entente was not a year old when it was confronted with a series of major issues on which the members could maximize their power through a common stand. First was the evolution of the Franco-African Community after the Malian and Malagasy demand for independence in late 1959. Negotiations were also carried out at this time among the four states on implementation of their "total customs union." Thereafter came the Entente members' own request for independence and withdrawal from the Community. After independence, attained on alternate days beginning on August 1, 1960, agreements with France remained to be negotiated, over the following ten months, as in the matter of independence, Houphouet-Boigny was mandated to present the common case in Paris, before negotiations were completed in Africa. Solidarity was broken only by Upper Volta's refusal to enter into a defense agreement with France, all evidence on which indicates that the Entente members supported—although they disagreed with—their African partner. During the same time, identical constitutions were drafted for all four states. In 1961 and 1962, the Entente states met to coordinate their position within the Brazzaville and Monrovia Groups, of which they were the initiators and core members. After 1963, the new topic of common interest was subversion; a commission of the Entente states plus Nigeria was appointed by the Monrovia Group to investigate the Togolese situation, but it failed—partly because of an Entente split: Ivory Coast and Upper Volta refused to attend the first meeting where the three others were present. Policy differences over the future of the UAM also contributed to the lessened cohesion. In a meeting in early July 1964, however, the three heads of state decided to continue periodic discussions among themselves even without Dahomey, and in Houphouet-Boigny's conferences with Keita and Touré in April, with Senghor in September, and with ould Daddah in December, his two Entente partners were sitting with him. In January 1965, under the pressure of subversion from Ghana, the three states brought Dahomey back to the fold, and moved to include Togo as well.

The Entente thus went through two times of troubles, each involving one of its members. Such difficulties, however, did not destroy policy coordination among the remaining members, whose continued solidarity, in turn, put pressure on the recalcitrant member to return to the fold. In 1961 and into early 1962, the weak link was Upper Volta, whose dispute over social legislation, tariff rebates, and aid repartition caused it to turn to Ghana for alternative benefits. In addition to revealing the interdependence of the members, the dispute reflected another weakness of the grouping: the unequal development of its members, whose different stages of economic advancement and social modernization posed problems to inward-directed cooperation. The Voltaic grievances were met and the group tightened its cooperation in late 1962 and early 1963, until the Maga government was overthrown in Dahomey in October 1963. Neither identical constitutions nor similar legislation nor even Houphouet-Boigny's arbitration and control could prevent extralegal political change, particularly because the *coup* resulted from social pains of economic development that were acute in Dahomey, as much as from Dahomeyan personal politics. The annually rotating presidency came to rest on Houphouet-Boigny's shoulders in 1963 and meetings at a level below the heads of state have become infrequent. Faltering for over a year during the Dahomeyan crisis because it actively sided with one member, the Entente has been revived and strengthened since early 1965, first by persistent attempts to mediate the Dahomey-Niger dispute, and then by new measures toward greater integration.

In an area where meetings are a positive sign, the vitality of the Entente has been shown by its regular schedule of conferences among heads of state and ministers. Official correspondence among heads of state, with the annual presiding head of state serving as a focal point, was frequent and detailed on a host of problems, small and large.[50] An Ivory Coast memorandum at the time of the first Entente meeting stipulated that there shall be "neither Federal Assembly nor federal government, but meetings of the responsible political figures and executive and legislative delegations of the four countries,"[51] a formula which excluded any formal institutions (except a rotating administrative secretariat). The Entente customs union has never been fully effective, because of variations by all the members. The Solidarity Fund, on the other hand, has functioned. In principle, it was to take in a tenth of each member's budgetary income, and pay out 21 per cent of the total to each of the three poorer members, two thirds of the remaining 30 per cent to be set aside for a reserve and the rest to be used for expenses of the Entente presidency. In fact, the process differed but the result was the same;[52] only Ivory Coast made its payments, which were then divided directly among the other three states; no funds were set aside for a reserve. The maximum sum involved for one year was about $5.6 million.

The Entente has had a successful record of operations, and may eventually lead—beyond the professed wishes of Houphouet-Boigny—to a single confederation of its members. Both inward- and outward-directed, its two facets of cooperation have been mutually reinforcing. The dominant figure of Houphouet-Boigny served as an institution of control and arbitration, supported by the greater development of Ivory Coast, but the importance, location, and number of the other members gave them power within the alliance and provided the conditions for successful bargaining, within the limits of their common views on African affairs.

It would be begging the question—although true—to say that the UAS failed because it never was tried. More important, it was never tried because the founding agreement was negotiated in detail only after it had been signed (the reverse of the usual practice), at which time the component members could not agree on what they were proposing. The absence of contiguity and the differences between British and French colonial heritages—the causes usually cited for the stillbirth of the UAS, dividing Guinea and Mali from Ghana—were only secondary causes. The most striking indication of this fact was the absence of integration between the two ex-French neighbors, Guinea and Mali. The governing structures of both were similar; their parties were both former sections of the interterritorial RDA alliance; their ideologies closely resembled each other. Mali needed an outlet to the sea that Guinea's road, rail, and port facilities (with a good deal of extension, enlargement, and foreign aid) might have provided. An attempt to coordinate parties and internal policies was made at a meeting of Touré and Keita in Kankan in mid-April 1962; Malian and Guinean labor, women's and youth organizations belonged to the same internationals; Mali, on Guinean urging, demanded evacuation of French troops; and the Malian educational reform of 1962 owed much to a study of the new Guinean system. But no effective inward-directed coordination on any level—state, party, party auxiliary, or policy—was ever achieved, except for the common declaration of policy stands which had already been arrived at independently. The explanation lies largely in the fact that the two regimes, despite their Pan-African statements, were among the most successful in creating nationally oriented political institutions, and the leaders were not prepared to give up their separate institutions and identity for those of a new "Guineo-Soudanese" nation.[53] In fact, despite the parallels between the Guinean evolution and events in Mali about two years later, a good deal of resentment was aroused in Mali by unsolicited Guinean advice (notably against rupture with France and monetary reform) and in Guinea by Mali's frequent failure to solicit—or follow—the suggestions.

Guinea in 1958 and Mali in 1960 were looking for allies and foreign aid to overcome their momentary isolation in West Africa; the Guinea-Ghana Union and the UAS were welcome responses to their needs. Ghana was looking for a means to try out its policy of unification and to extend its direct influence in West Africa; the temporary needs of Guinea and Mali were opportunities to be seized, and Ghana proposed a permanent solution. The two unions were thus based on an inherent contradiction: in neither case was there any concrete idea of the obstacles the union would encounter or the means by which it would be implemented, and the initial announcements were the occasion for the wildest of statements on the part of Nkrumah.[54] When the implementation of details came up for negotiation, the distant ideals of the unions were clouded over by real difficulties and mutual incomprehension.

The most persistent negotiations concerned fiscal arrangements, including the repeatedly declared intention to set up a common bank of issue. In October and December 1958, in March and April 1959, and again as late as May and July 1960, Ghanaian and Guinean delegations discussed the problem. In negotiation they gained experience with reality, especially with the complexities and incompatibilities of the franc zone (until February 1960, when Guinea withdrew) and the sterling zone. The common bank was mentioned in the UAS declaration of December 1960, but was finally dropped in the UAS charter of July 1961. Ghana's $28 million loan to Guinea was granted in December 1958, the first foreign aid by a Western African state. A tenth of the loan was granted immediately and three tenths the following year, to be repaid at 2 per cent interest in biennial installments between 1964 and 1970, with annual moratoria on repayment to be accorded if requested. (No repayment was made in 1964.) The remaining six tenths were to be granted in two equal payments in 1960 and 1961 if needed. Instead, because no request was made, Ghana granted Mali $11.2 million out of the remainder in December 1959, under similar terms; one payment was made in 1961. The proposed economic committee of the UAS was never constituted; a customs union was never negotiated; and provisions for union citizenship and a common visa area were never implemented.

But the greatest weakness lay in the field of policy coordination. No meetings of heads of state were foreseen in the Guinea-Ghana Union, but the leaders met once a year between 1958 and 1960 (although without registering any institutional or policy advances). After a flurry of meetings in late 1960 and early 1961, the presidents met two more times in mid-1961 and then never again.[55] Even outside the framework of the union, Nkrumah never once saw Keita or Touré after June 1961 until the Addis Ababa summit two years later. After late 1962, the three states were usually represented in one another's capitals by relative nonentities as resident ministers. Under such circumstances, it is hard to speak seriously of any policy coordination, beyond a pre-existing similarity of views.

One initiative on the part of the UAS was the attempt to establish contiguity by bringing in Upper Volta through the economic door. Politically, it broke down with the refusal of Touré and Keita to undercut their former RDA ally, Houphouet-Boigny, by attending the Ghana-Volta customs-union ceremonies at Paga. Economically, then, the project was largely a Ghanaian matter, creating a rather unorthodox situation in which Upper Volta was a member of two customs unions at the same time.[56] A series of agreements signed in late June 1961 established a customs union, most-favored-nation status, and a 90 per cent rebate on transshipped items between Ghana and Upper Volta. Smuggling (except of re-exports) was defined out of existence. But because Ghanaian customs were equal to or higher than Ivory Coast customs on traded items, and because rail connections from Abidjan were cheaper and quicker than road connections from Accra or Sekendi-Takoradi, the agreement had little effect except to win local popularity in the border region. When Upper Volta returned to close cooperation with the Entente in 1962, the attempt to bridge the Volta gap in the UAS quickly fell through. It was hard to integrate Upper Volta into a union which did not exist.

The UAS experiment, more than almost any other attempt at regional unity, gave its members experience in the matter of detailed negotiations. Unfortunately, the experience never reached the point of successfully resolving differences of policy and approach, or of overcoming the obstacles of the situation. Only Ghana was truly looking for unity—with a certain amount of counterproductive disdain for its partners' capabilities—and it was outnumbered within its own alliance. The other members and potential members were only looking for temporary diplomatic support.

The Casablanca Group was, at best, an alliance for mutual support on external policies, adorned with a charter and protocol on African unity; it failed because the members lost interest in one another's issues or because the issues disappeared, and because the final definition of *unity* took place at Addis Ababa outside the Group. The dynamism of the leaders of Guinea, Ghana, Mali, Morocco, the Provisional Government of Algeria, and Egypt created rivalries on both the personal and the political level, but these personality differences also reflected differences in the nature and interests of the states themselves. Common policies existed, on the recognition of the GPRA and Lumumba's "government," and on concerted opposition to neocolonialism, but common interests were few.[57] Algeria sought support for its claim to independence; Morocco, for its claim to Mauritania; Egypt, for its claim to Israel. But, whatever their sympathies, other members had no direct interest in any of these policies. The UAS states had an interest in West African regional unity, which was not shared by the Arab states, and a sentimental attachment to continental unity, which was not directly advanced by the formation of the alliance. Certainly not all the states had "monolithic regimes," "disciplined, militant, and massively organized single party rule," policies supporting "union through mergers within centralized unitary states or through functional arrangements that stress ideological conformity," or "expansionist" governments "prepared to subvert regimes that oppose their formula for unity"; nor, even if some of these characteristics fit one member or another, were these the only states in Western Africa that could be so described.[58] The Casablanca Group, far from being an alliance with a common goal, was merely a group of states with a few similarities, each seeking support from the others on issues important to its own foreign policy. This mutual "horse-trading" made it important for the members to present a united front but, at the same time, it made the alliance an international pressure group of uncertain cohesion.

The Casablanca Group was also the first of the escalating alliances of Western Africa that sought universalist unity. From their initial meeting, the members specifically excluded the possibility of unification, limiting their efforts to the consolidation of "our identity of views and unity of action" and "the creation of an effective form of cooperation." [59] Within this limitation, their actions were part of the Western African search for an acceptable definition of *unity*. The institution of closest cooperation, an African consultative assembly, quite realistically was neither constituted nor even mentioned after the initial meeting. The Economic Committee (composed of economic ministers) held three meetings, at which a customs and payments union was proposed and then twice delayed. Although this committee's work was important to the search for a definition of *unity*, the original Moroccan proposals, if quite detailed, were made in the abstract, without much preparatory study; only after the project had been accepted was attention given to the problems of uniting the commerce of states which traded very little with one another. The agreement was important, however, because it gave international sanction to the idea of an African common market that had been current in Africa since the first Conference of Independent African States. Because the Casablanca Group was neither regional nor continental, economic cooperation never had a realistic basis. The cultural committee had even less to work on, for the members made a virtue of their cultural diversity—English, French, and Arabic; Black African and White African; Muslim, Christian, and animist.

The political committee met only twice after Casablanca, and not all heads of state were present at either meeting. For the most part, the committee reiterated former stands, largely confined to tightly negotiated details of establishing the group's institutions. It did meet, at the heads-of-state or foreign-ministers level, to coordinate external policy in February 1961 after Lumumba's death, in August before the conference of nonaligned states at Belgrad, in January 1962 before the Lagos conference, and in September before the XVII session of the United Nations.[60] No outstanding problems or effective common stands below the level of generalities were resolved at any but the January 1962 meeting, and the decision in this case was purely negative: not to accept the invitation of the Monrovia Group to Lagos. By the time the fourth meeting of the political committee was to be held, in Marrakesh (mid-October, postponed to mid-December 1962 and then to early May 1963), members of the Casablanca Group had drifted so far apart that national politics and differences on superficial issues (Yemen, Togo) prevented the meeting. Except for Morocco, the Casablanca members preferred to go to Addis Ababa as individual states instead of as a group. The one institution of the Group that did function—the secretariat—was, in a sense, a testimony to the ineffectiveness of the other bodies: during 1962-63, the second secretary-general, Thami Wezzani, was active in attempts to keep the Group alive. In the end he was ineffective and disillusioned, but the member states' conflicting interests and the absence of a real base for unity were conditions far beyond the control of a single man, no matter how dedicated. The absence of a power base for the secretary-general meant that the Group did not even have an institution of arbitration and control as effective as that of the Entente.

The Casablanca Group did accomplish one thing: it was a necessary part of the conjunction of forces that brought about the Addis Ababa meeting. Having failed to attain policy unity, the Group turned to seek universality and, at Cairo in June 1962, in the political committee charged Touré with the task of preparing a Pan-African summit. Guinea regarded the Group as a natural outgrowth of the Guinea-Ghana (and then Mali) Union, to be created not for its intrinsic value but as a stepping-stone to a truly continental definition of *unity*.[61] Such a concept implied a complete dismantling of the Group once a higher framework for unity had been established. Viewed in such terms, the Casablanca Group was wholly successful.

The African and Malagasy Union (UAM) has been the most durable of the broad attempts at unity, largely because its members agreed from the start on outer-directed cooperation, under which policy coordination was permitted by certain common interests, and they buttressed this cooperation with separate institutions for inward-directed harmonization. Although it is far-fetched to speak of many real similarities between such states as Mauritania and Madagascar, their common French background and their moderate approach to the subject of postcolonial ties with the metropole prepared them for cooperation in foreign policy to maintain "solidarity, security, development, and peace." Policy was established at any UAM meeting "by simple majority. Discipline is obligatory in problems of *decolonization*." The United Nations representatives of the members also met "obligatorily to consult together before all important decisions." [62] As a limited concert of states, the UAM had no institutions except a general-secretariat, a budget, a United Nations caucus, and periodic meetings of foreign ministers and heads of state. By its regular activity and its attention to specific policy topics on which pre-existing agreement was coordinated into action, the UAM lived up to its charter.

Western Africa's three major external issues—Algeria, Congo, and Mauritania—played an important part in the founding meetings of the Group.[63] Coordinated policy on these points led to concerted action in the United Nations, in direct support and recognition of the constituted governments of the last two, and in missions to Paris, Tunis, and Leopoldville to express the Group's point of view. The solid support for Mauritania resulted in its admission to the United Nations in 1961, as the UAM states threw their weight behind a deal on new admissions in order to eliminate the Soviet veto. UAM support for Kasavubu and for United Nations operations in Congo was crucial to the continued existence of the moderate Congolese government. Less successful was the demand for negotiations in Algeria and an end to the war in 1961, events that took place in due time but not as a result of UAM influence. At the same time, beginning in mid-1961 before the Group was even formally constituted, its members began a series of persistent attempts to bring all Africa together under their restrained definition of *unity*. Houphouet-Boigny and Senghor were prime movers of the Monrovia conference; the UAM states caucussed and acted discreetly as the dominant bloc at the Lagos conferences of January and June 1962; during the same year the Monrovia charter was edited by the UAM at Bangui and Libreville before being accepted by the Monrovia Group at Lagos; and the UAM caucussed again at Ouagadougou just before Addis Ababa to insure the passage of a Monrovia-like charter on the continental level. The UAM members could go to Addis Ababa strengthened by their own agreement and by the knowledge that they already had a viable alternative on which to fall back if the universal summit failed.

The major inward-directed auxiliary of the UAM was its Economic Cooperation Organization (OAMCE), with which were also affiliated an organization for postal and telecommunications, a banking association, an industrial property office, and a joint airline. The OAMCE was proposed at the Brazzaville conference of December 1960, studied by experts at Dakar in early February 1961, and signed at Yaounde on March 28, 1961. At Tananarive in September 1961, protocols were signed establishing committees to study harmonization of development plans, customs regimes, fiscal regulations, and scientific and technical information; conventions were adopted covering judicial cooperation and extradition, rights and status of expatriates, and telecommunications and postal coordination; and a permanent secretariat at Yaounde headed by Jules Razafinbahiny of Madagascar was created. Committees on transportation and on maritime cooperation were later added, as well as ad hoc meetings of member ministers of education, civil service, and information. The planning committee, with the most far-reaching potential, has not succeeded in its difficult task. The customs study group in mid-January 1963 arrived at an agreement on a common external tariff legislation, but neither external alignment nor internal elimination of tariffs has been totally achieved. A proposed price stabilization fund also was unrealized. Yet within the group there is greater harmonization in practice than among any other Western African states. The conventions have generally been observed, and the OAMCE met regularly to keep up attempts at harmonization. Its task has been facilitated by the fact that the main concern of the OAMCE has been to maintain common services and similar regulations in force under the French West African and French Equatorial African federations, and to extend them to Togo, Cameroun, and Rwanda, rather than attempt to create harmony for the first time among systems of disparate backgrounds. In the external field, the OAMCE has also made advances; it joined the International Labor Office and the International Coffee Agreement as a body, with the members' votes cast on certain matters as a bloc by the OAMCE: it also played an important role in negotiating the convention of association with the European Economic Community.

The success of the Addis Ababa meeting, resulting in the formation of an African unity organization of essentially the same type as the UAM, brought out a basic question within the views of the Brazzaville Group members: Was the UAM created to be a prefederation, a presummit, an anti-Casablanca Group, or a pluralistic institution of control over the Group's technical auxiliaries such as the OAMCE? If it were merely an arrangements committee for a universal summit or a counterweight to the defunct radical alliance, the UAM could disappear after Addis Ababa. Such was the opinion of the minimalist school of thought, notably Houphouet-Boigny. The maximalists, including Dahomeyans such as Foreign Minister Zinsou and the active UAM Secretary-General Albert Tevoedjre, saw the group as a step back to federation among the former French African territories, a position it had already developed through its economic and common service institutions and through its replacement of the organisms of the Franco-African Community. An intermediate school, represented by Senghor, had already won a point with the support of the minimalists in the Libreville and Dakar conferences of September and November 1962, where the general secretariat was qualified as purely administrative and was relieved of any control over the UAM auxiliaries' secretariat. In Ouagadougou in March 1963, the maximalists lost their best-placed spokesman when Tevoedjre resigned as secretary-general, to be succeeded by three Dahomeyans who were politically less dynamic. When many of the UAM-OAMCE ideas were taken up at Addis Ababa and included in the OAU charter, states outside the organization—Guinea most vehemently, but also Ghana and Nigeria—questioned the need for a subgroup of dubious regionality based on colonial affinities. An intermediate thesis—strong during 1964—proposed to dissolve the political UAM and regroup the economic and technical auxiliaries into a new union, which would continue harmonization. But it was not until February 1965, as the OAU began to disappoint even the moderates, that a final decision was made, transforming the Brazzaville organizations into a single inward- and outward-directed OCAM, with political and economic purposes and a Senegalese, Diakha Dieng, as secretary-general. The transformation was made possible by a shift of opinion by the minimalists, notably Houphouet-Boigny, to support a strong political alliance of moderates.

Other attempts to find a satisfactory definition for *unity* have not yet worked their way out of the planning stage, despite serious efforts by their proponents. Like the Entente, the proposed Senegal River Union grew out of a position of isolation—that of Senegal, after its independence and the breakup of the Mali Federation. The major theme of Senegal's African policy after independence has been the re-establishment of good relations with its neighbors through patient diplomacy, while countering economic and political isolation through membership in the UAM and its affiliate organizations. After the breakup of the Mali Federation, the tenor of relations between Senegal and Guinea was shown by two Guinean actions: accusations against Senegal of a plot to overthrow Touré, and sponsorship of Mali's entry into the UAS. Nevertheless, commercial payments, and fiscal agreements were negotiated by a Senegalese economic mission in Conakry in January 1961, and the first two were signed when ambassadors were exchanged in June. On the political level, *rapprochement* was sealed by the voyage of Senghor and Dia to Labé in May 1962 to meet Touré and set up a Senegalo-Guinean Cooperation Commission for handling minor problems between the two states. The previous month, Mali asked for United Nations study and assistance in order to improve the Senegal River basin; in July in Conakry delegates from Senegal and Mali met for the first time since the breakup of the Mali Federation, along with Mauritanians and Guineans, and planned the common development of the Senegal River valley. Further steps in the Senegalese *rapprochement* with Mali were spread out over 1963, beginning with settlement of the finances of the Mali federation in February and ending with the signature of commercial, payment, customs, rail, and port agreements and a meeting of Senghor and Keita at Kidira during June.

Mauritania had also had two years of cold relations with Mali, beginning with its independence in late 1960, but it had remained politically friendly and economically associated with Senegal since colonial times. After independence, Senegal and Mauritania formed a joint commission for dealing with bilateral conflicts and a joint Mission for the Development of the Senegal (MAS) that could serve as a model for a quadrilateral cooperative arrangement.

When Senghor began speaking of a Senegal River Union, the original implication was political as well as simply economic.[64] The *rapprochement* with Mali opened the way for continued negotiations, which in July 1963 in Bamako ended with the creation of an Interstate Committee for the Development of the Senegal, the group's only institution. Subsequent meetings have been devoted to drafting a Senegal River convention and planning cooperation among the four riverine states on irrigation, transportation, and—above all—financing. In the process, Senegal River cooperation has lost its overtones of political unification; different fiscal systems and continuing differences in domestic political systems and external policies—all reminiscent of problems which split the Mali Federation—keep the members farther apart than the banks of their common river.

Other Western African states have attempted limited inward-directed groupings on the basis of natural groupings or man-made communications lanes. Within the Entente itself is the Nigero-Dahomeyan Common Organization (OCDN), established in July 1959 to regulate transportation and commerce between the two neighbors. It was based, like the Entente, on the port of Cotonou, the railroad to Parakou, and the road from there to Niamey; in 1963, OCDN and European exports studied the possibility of extending the railroad to Dosso or Niamey to handle more efficiently the peanut exports and European imports of Niger. There was an administrative council but no political consultation; political relations were handled ad hoc or through the Entente. When the government changed in Dahomey in October 1963, the OCDN agreement was denounced, despite its obvious economic value to both states, and its restitution remained incomplete for over a year because of continuing friction between the two members.

West Africa's rivers and natural trade routes have also served as stimuli to inward-directed groupings. Niger has been particularly interested in such approaches, for its poverty imposes on it the necessity of inventing new bases of development. In the west of the country, the Niger River offers opportunity for cooperation in transportation and irrigation. After an initial contact by a Niger mission to Nigeria in August 1960 and a further charge by the UAM to Niger in 1961 to pursue the matter, two more meetings were held in Niamey—in February and October 1963—before the nine countries sharing the Niger-Benue River system could agree on a new Niger River convention to replace the Berlin agreement of 1885 and the statute of St. Germain-en-Laye of 1919. The Entente states, Guinea, Mali, Nigeria, Chad, and Cameroun finally negotiated a statute covering navigation, cooperative exploitation, and development, and an intergovernmental commission was created at the third Niamey meeting, in November 1964. At the other end of Niger, the Lake Chad basin also offers an opportunity for development, particularly through irrigation projects to expand the agricultural area of littoral states. After initial conferences in late October and December 1962 in Fort Lamy, a second meeting of Diori and Tafawa Balewa with the presidents of Chad and Cameroun in the Chadian capital resulted in the creation of a Chad basin commission in May 1964. A convention, covering a ten-year period, governs development, transportation, and research; it is nonpolitical in nature, and its major problems are in finding internal agreement on cooperation and external sources of finance. To the north of Niger, the Sahara has for years attracted as much attention from Diori as it has from Bourguiba. Under French rule and after independence, Niger was one of the most wholehearted supporters of the Common Organization of the Saharan Region (OCRS)—a major point dividing Diori from Djibo and the Sawaba opposition.[65] When the independence of Algeria brought an end to the OCRS, Diori continued to call for a conference of sovereign Saharan states to plan cooperation. Such a conference did take place in late May 1964 in Algiers, where representatives of Tunisia, Algeria, Morocco, Mauritania, Mali, Upper Volta, Niger, Nigeria, and Cameroun, Chad, and Egypt met with experts from the United Nations Economic Commission for Africa to lay plans for a trans-Saharan road from Algiers through Tamanrasset to Gao and Agades; Algeria, Tunisia, Mali, Niger met in December as a committee to investigate the financing of the project.

None of these attempts at inward-directed cooperation involves any permanent political institutions or any broad coordination of policy. In fact, policy coordination on common use of the Sahara, the Niger, the Chad, and even (since 1963) the Dahomeyan railroad and the port of Cotonou, remains to be put into practice. In Western Africa, mutually useful cooperation of this type has had difficulty in reaching the planning stage—as the years, invitations, and reinvitations invested in these meetings testify; but even more difficult is the application of the plans. The already-noted tendency to mistake plans for reality, the difficulty of finding large sums of "pump-priming" investment, and the inevitable political slights and squabbles that are still able to disrupt the badly needed pooling of resources have contributed to keeping such projects matters for the future.

The final attempt at inward-directed unity in Western Africa was the Benin Union.[66] More frequently proposed than negotiated, it has not yet come into being because of conflicts in national interests and differences in the regional distribution of power, and because its proponents have never had a clear idea of which definition of *unity* they were proposing. The proposal—involving Nigeria, Dahomey, Togo, and Ghana—derives from cultural similarities, overlap of historic kingdoms and present populations, and—above all—interdependent trade (including lateral commerce and common use of the region's few ports). Tema and Lagos are only two hundred miles apart and both tap the local hinterland; between them, Lomé and Cotonou (seventy-five miles apart) have appealed for French aid to develop their own port facilities and liberate Togo and Dahomey from dependence on Ghana and Nigeria, even though neither of the two former French territories has a volume of trade large enough to justify a separate port. Accent on separate national points of view has also been evident throughout each round of discussions on the proposed union, and has been exacerbated by domestic politics, frequent trivial incidents, and conflicting colonial heritages. Better than any other attempt at regional unity, the Benin Union illustrates the inherent conflict between different interpretations of national interest, and between national prestige and regional cooperation.

The problems of union, however, were further deepened by the inequalities of the states involved. Nigeria's size and federal system gave rise to Dahomeyan fears of absorption into its populous neighbor. Togo's problem with the irridentism of its dynamic neighbor, Ghana, has already been analyzed. "Dahomey sees an entente with Togo as the means for the two countries to resist the territorial appetites of Ghana and Nigeria," said Maga just prior to Togolese and Dahomeyan independence.[67] Hence, the fortunes of the Benin Union depended on the political relations of the four neighbors; because these relations were never constant, there was never enough regional stability to develop lasting cooperation—nor, however, was the threat of any one neighbor or peripheral state ever so great as to serve as the stimulus for unity.

The idea of a Benin Union of Dahomey, Togo, and Niger—as a counterweight to the Mali Federation—was launched by Apithy in early 1959.[68] Dahomey's immediate need to protect its economic interests was satisfied by the formation of the Entente, which Togo refused to join, and the idea passed from the scene with the replacement of Apithy by Maga as premier. For Dahomey and Togo, 1960 was a year of strained relations with their respective

English-speaking neighbors, but it was not until late in the following year that the two French-speaking states were able to get together on negotiations even on a customs union. An interministerial meeting in late August 1961 was followed by meetings of Olympio and Maga in October and December, with a bilateral conference of experts, between the two meetings, in early December. A customs agreement, but not a customs union, resulted. In early February 1962, after discovering evidence of Ghanaian subversion in Togo, Olympio proposed the formation of a "regional unit" of Togo, Dahomey, and Nigeria—a proposal that Maga and Nigerian Foreign Minister Jaja Wachuku immediately echoed with approval. Maga had already visited Accra in June 1961, signed a trade agreement with Ghana in July, and met again with Nkrumah the following January and February to smooth over the Togo-Ghana dispute; he now proposed that Ghana be included in the Benin Union, and he brought together the foreign ministers of Ghana, Togo, and Dahomey in Cotonou in February 1962 with hopes of establishing cooperation in the region and bridging the Casablanca-Monrovia gap at the same time. But plans for a triple heads-of-state meeting, the necessary second step to *rapprochement,* collapsed. Nkrumah insisted that Olympio return his 1960 visit with a trip to Accra, and Olympio continued to "think that Ghana spends most of its time interfering in the affairs of other countries." [69] Togo and Dahomey, however, continued to advance their own customs relations with meetings of experts in October and meetings of heads of state and finance ministers in December 1962.

At the same time, Maga sought to pursue economic cooperation with Nigeria. In late February 1962, he initiated customs negotiations at Lagos, and a bilateral agreement was finally signed in late August in the presence of the foreign ministers of Togo, Dahomey, and Nigeria, who met in Cotonou to plan further economic coordination. The conference was to be followed by a meeting of experts who would submit technical recommendations to the three states, but the experts never met. Instead, Olympio was assassinated in January 1963 and Maga was overthrown in October. Despite Dahomey's role in placing Grunitzky at the head of the Togolese government, Dahomey did not recognize the new regime until late May; despite the closing of the Togolese border by Ghana in June and the request by Togo to join the UAM in July, Togo-Dahomeyan conversations on closer cooperation did not begin until September, when Maga visited Lomé, and October, when common use of energy resources was discussed in Cotonou. In January, Maga offered to mediate between Grunitzky and Nkrumah, as he had previously tried with Olympio, and in December Grunitzky offered his good offices between Dahomey and Niger, as did Nigeria. Neither offer was taken up.

The return of Grunitzky and of Apithy to governmental leadership altered the situation, removing the stubborn isolationism of Olympio from Lomé and bringing the "Pan-Beninist" thinking of Apithy to Cotonou (although the activity of Maga is difficult to surpass). In March 1964, an agreement was signed between Dahomey and Togo for cooperative development of the Mono

River between the two states—a project which had been under sporadic study since 1957. In June, Apithy revived the idea of a Benin Union and appointed a Dahomeyan commission to study the technical details of such a project. Deep changes in thinking, however, are necessary to bring about a political union, if indeed such is the goal; problems of trade stagnation, unemployment, and other aspects of underdevelopment may be open to solution within a larger political unit, but in the process some states would have to forego the advantages of separate attention that their present existence as small sovereign units now affords them. Conscious self-abnegation of this sort is unlikely. More evident to date has been emphasis on "individual personalities" and the cohesion of national politics within each state.

All the attempts to find a definition of *unity* advertised themselves as the core of a new, larger grouping of which they were to be the preliminary example. Only the Entente and the UAM served this purpose. The rest could not hold together long enough to bear fruit. These attempts range widely in their search for a formula, from federation to "group" (a new type of organism hitherto unrecognized in international law) to entente; somewhere in between, "unions" such as those of Benin and of Guinea, Ghana, and Mali, never did find an institutional framework with which to experiment. In most cases, the states tried to save their elusive "unity" by falling back on mere policy harmonization, but these common stands that were reached were usually the result of pre-existing policy positions, not the effect of organizational coordination. Even if the states of the area had not been searching for a formula, they would have found—as have other areas in the world—that an alliance is an inherently unstable stage between independent state action and unification. If an alliance does not continually prove itself to be a satisfactory instrument for the achievement of the major aspirations of its members— or, worse, if it instead becomes a hinderance to their achievement—it falls apart. Put another way, there is a dynamic relation between the common and conflicting interests of states in alliances; when the existence of the alliance itself becomes one of the conflicting interests, the group dies. In this situation, institutions can only show how an international organization works, when it does work; only rarely do they show why.

In the absence of an external threat requiring collaboration with others for defense, sovereign governments aware of their prime responsibilities toward their own people usually do not dare to relinquish their freedom of action; on their continuing freedom in policy-making rests their ability to safeguard the national interest. Only in the case of genuine federation in which sovereignties are merged does this obstacle disappear; then the national interest becomes the federal interest, and the responsibility is shifted to the supranational or federal government.[70]

This is a stage reached by none of the groupings discussed above, as yet. Instead, the cases examined reveal the limits imposed on unity by the desire of Western African states for freedom of action.

NOTES

[1] Similar analyses are found in Thomas Perry Thornton, "Terror as a Weapon of Political Agitation," and Andrew C. Janos, "Authority and Violence," in Harry Eckstein (ed.), *International War* (New York: Crowell-Collier, 1964), pp. 92, 139; George Modelski, "The International Relations of Internal War," and James Rosenau, "Internal War as an International Event," in James Rosenau (ed.), *International Aspects of Civil Strife* (Princeton, N.J.: Princeton U.P., 1964), pp. 38, 65; Samuel P. Huntington, "Patterns of Violence in World Politics," in Samuel P. Huntington (ed.), *Changing Patterns of Military Politics* (New York: Crowell-Collier, 1961), pp. 31, 40-44; Harold D. Lasswell and Abraham Kaplan, *Power and Society* (New Haven: Yale U.P., 1950), pp. 87, 97, 252, 265; Victor T. LeVine, "The Course of Political Violence in Africa," in William H. Lewis (ed.) *French-Speaking Africa: The Search for Identity* (New York: Walker, 1965). Note that the aim of conventional warfare may be temporary or permanent, and may cover all or part of the target state's territory, depending on the type of war.

[2] For some specific studies of Western African armies, see John J. Johnson (ed.), *The Role of the Military in Underdeveloped Countries* (Princeton, N.J.: Princeton U.P., 1962); William Gutteridge, *Armed Forces in New States* (London: Oxford U.P., 1962); I. William Zartman, *Morocco: Problems of New Power* (New York: Atherton, 1964); and *Area Handbooks* for selected African countries (Special Operations Research Organization, American University, Washington, D.C.). For some African accounts, see *Mauritanie Nouvelle,* October 2, 1963; *Essor,* October 22, 1962, August 26, 1963, October 8, 1963, February 24, 1964, September 7 and 14, 1964, February 22, 1965.

[3] There have been few cases of arming a local militia for external defense (although Ghana, Guinea, Mali, Algeria, and Liberia have irregular state or party militias for internal security). Morocco planned to arm volunteers against feared French expansion from Algeria in 1958, but never did. Senghor called for a party militia against Soudan in the breakup of the Mali Federation, without effect, but Mali did form a party militia which was reported to be particularly active in watching traffic along the Senegalese border in 1961. Algeria hastily armed volunteers against Morocco in 1963, but many of them fled in battle. Ivory Coast announced plans for a party militia in late 1963, but with no visible results. More realistically, National Assembly President Philippe Yacé explained reasons for dropping an earlier Ivory Coast plan to arm veterans farming along the border by saying, "The farmers would start shooting each other" (*New York Times,* April 3, 1960). In Mauritania, however, local populations have been very successfully used by the army as intelligence sources and even primary police forces who detain any stranger for questioning.

[4] Nkrumah told parliament on January 12, 1965, "The most important role of our armed forces is to assist in the execution of projects of national development." For a list of the growing literature on the military in development, see *The Role of the Military in the Less Developed Countries: A Selected Bibliography,* State Department External Research Paper No. 147, March 1964.

[5] See Colin Legum, *Pan-Africanism: A Short Political Guide,* 2nd ed. (New York: Praeger, 1965), pp. 158, 159, 161, 202, 205, for African pronouncements on these values.

[6] See *ibid.,* pp. 158, 159, 181, 198, 216, 219. Doudou Thiam even speaks of "an embryo-system of international law" (cf. the notion of inter-American law), in *The Foreign Policy of African States* (New York: Praeger, 1965), p. 44.

[7] The Congo revolt in 1964-65 threatened to change this situation, althoug'. even here other African states refrained from direct military intervention.

[8] See Legum, *op. cit.,* pp. 255-57, 263, 265, 275. Retorting to a British press observa-

tion that "there is no love lost between Mr. Houphouet-Boigny and Dr. Nkrumah," the Accra radio on June 3, 1961 said (somewhat unidiomatically): "Is there any power that can in a single sentence [so?] sow the seeds of discord in a family that has been so sorely tried by the colonialists—a family which is determined at all costs to achieve unity and shape its own destiny?"

[9] See, for example, Thiam, *op. cit.*, p. 45; Claude S. Phillips, *The Development of Nigerian Foreign Policy* (Evanston, Ill.: Northwestern U.P., 1964), p. 41, citing Tafewa Balawa.

[10] See Francis Bebey, *La Radiodiffusion en Afrique noire* (Paris: St-Paul, 1963).

[11] Terence H. Qualter, *Propaganda and Psychological Warfare* (New York: Random House, 1962), p. 110. Conditions of credibility, making propaganda believable in a particular social context, are examined in Lindley Frazer, *Propaganda* (London: Oxford U.P., 1957), Chap. 12; Davis McLellan, William Olson, and Fred Sondermann, *The Theory and Practice of International Relations* (Englewood Cliffs, N.J.: Prentice-Hall, 1960), Chap. 12.

[12] Interviews with James Markham, K. B. Asante, Otto Makonnen.

[13] For a review of the plot and trial, see "Le Procès du complot au Maroc," *Confluent* (Paris), XI, 41 (May 1964), 470-510.

[14] Interview with Ivory Coast Ambassador Koreki Mian in Accra.

[15] There are many responsible supporters—including Houphouet-Boigny and Zinsou—for the contrary view, which is best put forth and supported by Russell W. Howe, *Light on the Togo Case* (London: Forum Service, 1963). The facts of the situation appear to be that there were active plots based in Ghana going on at the same time, but that the one that actually ended in Olympio's assassination was a local product.

[16] Assassination and terrorist attempts took place in Kulungugu on August 1, 1962, and in Accra on September 9 and 20, 1962, January 8, 1963, and January 2, 1964.

[17] ". . . [T]he nomadic tribes have repeatedly proved themselves a threat to the integrity of the new national states by fighting for autonomy or entering into alliances with foreign powers." Manfred Halpern, *The Politics of Social Change in the Middle East and North Africa* (Princeton, N.J.: Princeton U.P., 1963), p. 84.

[18] See Christine Garnier, *Desert fertile: Un nouvel État: La Mauritanie* (Paris: Hachette, 1960), pp. 191-203; Paul Mousset, *Ce Sahara qui voit le jour* (Paris: Cité, 1959), pp. 199-207; George Chaffard, *Les Carnets secrets de la décolonisation* (Paris: Calmann-Lévy, 1965), pp. 251-94.

[19] Two other less formal agreements exist. Dia and ould Daddah exchanged assurances of mutual security in Nouakchott in November 1962 (*Le Monde,* November 22, 1962). The communiqué from the Togo-Dahomey-Nigeria foreign-ministers' meeting on August 26, 1962, at Cotonou cited agreement on the necessity of a "mutual guarantee of security"; Wachuku commented: "All I can tell you is that if one of the partners is threatened, the two others will consider themselves threatened" (Radio Cotonou, August 26, 1962). Olympio had already proposed a mutual defense pact of AOF, Togo, Nigeria, and Cameroun, without results (*New York Times,* March 12, 1960).

[20] Nkrumah's initial proposal included the eight participants in the 1958 Conference of Independent African States, plus Guinea and Mali; *West African Pilot* (Lagos), November 29, 1960. Nigeria was not invited because of its defense pact with England; Phillips, *op. cit.*, p. 48.

[21] It is unlikely that much standardization was necessary, because most arms are supplied by France. A résumé of the treaty is given in *International Organization,* XVI, 2 (Spring 1962), 436. The Balima interview was reported by Radio Lagos, February 10, 1963.

[22] Interview with Emile Zinsou.

[23] Algerians in Morocco were organized into FLN cells and Ghanaians in Ivory Coast were grouped into CPP cells with a tribal distribution of membership and officers. Many Africans who live abroad in former French territories have joined national expatriate associations (notably in Guinea and Ivory Coast) similar to those organized on provincial

lines among French expatriates; in most cases, the purpose of these organizations is social rather than political.

[24] Ghana used its border closings as a direct diplomatic weapon—in 1960, to apply pressure for economic cooperation with Togo and, in 1964, to apply pressure for banking and commercial concessions in Togo and a common currency. In both cases, the pressure was counterproductive; see speech by Togolese Foreign Minister Apedo-Amah, Radio Lomé, January 26, 1965. Wartime closing of borders between British and French territories actually accelerated interterritorial migrations; see Jean Rouch, "Migration au Ghana," *Journal de la Société des Africanistes* (Paris), XXXVI, 1 (1956), 1-95.

[25] As in parts of the Tunisia-Algeria, Nigeria-Dahomey, Togo-Ghana, and Mali-Mauritania borders. The best sources for such information, unfortunately incomplete, are *Cartes ethno-démographiques de l'Afrique occidentale* (Dakar: Institut français de l'Afrique noire, 1952, 1954, 1960, 1964), *feuilles* 1-5. See K. M. Barbour, "A Geographical Analysis of Boundaries in Intertropical Africa," in K. M. Barbour and R. M. Prothro (eds.), *Essays on African Population* (New York: Praeger, 1962), pp. 314-15.

[26] Mali, however, claimed that the Tuareg were incited by French mercenaries; *Le Monde*, September 15, 1964; *Essor*, May 11 and September 28, 1964.

[27] On the border, see Anthony S. Reyner, "Morocco's International Boundaries," *Journal of Modern African Studies*, I, 3 (September 1963), 313-26; Geographer, Department of State, *International Boundary Study*, No. 9, September 1961 (Morocco-Spanish Sahara). On the irredentism, see I. William Zartman, *The Sahara: Bridge or Barrier?* (New York: Carnegie Endowment for International Peace, 1963 [International Conciliation Series No. 541]); Allal Al-Fassi, *Livre rouge et documentaires* (Tangier: Peretti, n.d.) and *Livre blanc sur la Mauritanie* (Rabat: Ministry of Foreign Affairs, 1960) from the Moroccan side; *Le République islamique de Mauritanie et le Royaume du Maroc* (Nouakchott: Presidency, n.d. [1961]), from the Mauritanian side.

[28] Abbas meeting with Mohammed V in late May 1960, and with Hassan II at Dar as-Salaam (Rabat) on March 2, 1961, and at Rabat on July 7, 1961; ben Khedda meeting with Hassan II at Mohammedia on January 17, 1962.

[29] The intervention phase is examined in the preceding section.

[30] See James S. Coleman, *Togoland* (New York: Carnegie Endowment for International Peace, 1956 [International Conciliation Series No. 509]); Robert Cornevin, *Histoire du Togo* (Paris: Beiger-Levrault, 1962); *Carte ethno-démographique, feuille* 2, *loc. cit.*

[31] Zolberg, *One-Party Government in the Ivory Coast* (Princeton: Princeton U.P., 1964), p. 67 *et passim*, an excellent treatment of the bases of the movement. Information has also come from interviews with Koreki Mian, and from *Mouvement de liberation du Sanwi: Statuts et programme* (Kringobo, Ivory Coast, May 10, 1958 [*sic*, actually 1959], reissued at Winneba, Ghana, June 5, 1962).

[32] See Geographer, Department of State, *International Boundary Study*, No. 1, April 1961 (Algeria-Libya).

[33] Speech of February 5, 1959, quoted in *Le Sahara* (Tunis: Secretariat of State for Information, 1959), p. 62; other relevant speeches, published by the Secretariat of State for Information, were given on May 7 and July 17, 1961.

[34] See I. William Zartman, "A Disputed Frontier Is Settled," *Africa Report*, VIII, 8 (August 1963), 13-14, and correction, *Africa Report*, IX, 3 (March 1964), 31; Geographer, Department of State, *International Boundary Study*, No. 23, November 1963 (Mali-Mauritania).

[35] AFP-G, November 22 and December 9, 1958, reaffirmed in Tubman's visit to Conakry, AFP-CI, May 31, 1960.

[36] *Fraternité*, December 1, 1961.

[37] *Africa Report*, IX, 8 (August 1964), 20.

[38] The Algero-Moroccan border war shows the collapse of the frontier-march concept as a satisfying substitute for a boundary between states in the process of consolidation.

[39] The relation of position to choice is well expressed by Maga: "The fact that ours is

a link nation and our desire not to compromise our development lead us naturally to adopt formulas of compromise and synthesis" (Radio Cotonou, July 1, 1962).

[40] See Thomas Hodgkin, "The New West Africa State System," *University of Toronto Quarterly,* XXXI, 1 (October 1961), 76.

[41] When pressed, however, both sides have let it be known that their claim over the area still stands—to be revived when the Spanish leave. Thus, on December 4, 1963, in the United Nations, Morocco demanded the return of Spanish North African territories to Morocco, and on July 2, 1964, Mauritania renewed its claim on Spanish Sahara. In 1958, Morocco rejected a Spanish offer to return Spanish Sahara if Morocco would recognize Spanish sovereignty over the Mediterranean coastal enclaves (Ceuta, Melilla, and islands).

[42] Touré's broadcasts in October 1959 said that Portuguese Guinea would be part of (former French) Guinea by 1962. The Senegalese, as is typical, have been more discreet.

[43] See S. Whittemore Boggs, *International Boundaries* (New York: Columbia U.P., 1940), pp. 201-202, and "The Peaceful Solution of Boundary Problems," in H. W. Weigert and Vilhjalmus Stefansson (eds.), *Compass of the World* (New York: Macmillan, 1944), pp. 61-73; Robert D. Hodgson and Elvyn A. Stoneman, *The Changing Map of Africa* (New York: Van Nostrand, 1963), pp. 64-66.

[44] For a further discussion of "inward-directed" and "outward-directed" alliances, see Arnold Wolfers, *Discord and Collaboration* (Baltimore: Johns Hopkins U.P., 1962), pp. 25-35. For other discussions of several of the groups treated below, see William J. Foltz, *From French West Africa to the Mali Federation* (New Haven: Yale U.P., 1965); *Pan-Africanism* (UAS, UAM, Casablanca Group); Claude E. Welch, *Dream of Unity: Pan-Africanism and Political Unification in West Africa* (Ithaca, N.Y.: Cornell U.P., 1966) (UAS); D-G Lavroff, "Les Aspects actuels de l'unification de l'Afrique noire francophone," in *Annales africaines* (Dakar: Faculté de Droit et des Sciences Économiques, 1961), pp. 1-27 (UAM); Zartman, *The Sahara . . . , op. cit.* (Maghreb, Casablanca Group).

[45] Other relevant African cases outside the area are Cameroun, Somalia, and Ethiopia. Similar questions are also posed by the Senegal-Gambia negotiations. Another likely prospect, which has never left the ground, is a federation of Liberia and Sierra Leone, suggested by the speaker of the Sierra Leone House of Representatives in February 1963.

[46] In addition to sources already cited on Maghreb unity, see also George Liska, *The Greater Maghreb: From Independence to Unity?* (Washington, D.C.: Washington Center for Foreign Policy Research, 1963).

[47] A situation that recalls the similar failure of Churchill's wartime offer of common citizenship to the Free French.

[48] There are monarchies among republics within the European functional communities, and such African states as Nigeria, Uganda, and Upper Volta contain local "monarchies."

[49] In the XV and XVI session of the United Nations, Entente members voted identically on 74 per cent of the votes and divided on 7 per cent, a rather high degree of solidarity; Thomas Hovet, *Africa in the United Nations* (Evanston, Ill.: Northwestern University Press, 1963), pp. 139-43.

[50] I am grateful to Loua Diomandé for permission to see the Entente dossiers from 1959 through 1961.

[51] Ivory Coast note of May 28, 1959. The Entente is similar in many ways to the Nordic Council.

[52] I am grateful to the Ivory Coast Finance Ministry for figures on Entente finances through 1963. The maximum sum figure given is for 1961.

[53] Mali was also wary of integration after its experience with the Federation. The closest cooperation between Mali and Guinea was outlined after the dissolution of the UAS, at a meeting of Guinean Development Minister Ismael Touré and Malian Justice Minister Madeira Keita on February 14, 1965, following a meeting of heads of state on December 22, 1964; see *Essor,* February 22, 1965.

[54] "We first thought of a United States of West Africa but events have moved so fast

that we now think of the unity of all Africa," and "Ghana and Mali will have a common parliament" (Le Monde, May 3, 1959 and November 29, 1960).

[55] On the ministerial level, Guinea and Mali did consult before the Senghor-Touré meeting at Labé in May 1962, and ministers of the three states met before the Monrovia meeting of May 1961. In the XVI session of the United Nations, the UAS states voted identically on 87 per cent of the votes and never divided, the highest degree of solidarity in African groups (Hovet, op. cit., pp. 139-43).

[56] For an analysis, see Bulletin mensuel de la chambre de commerce d'Abidjan, September 1961. There was also discussion of a fifteen-year $5.6 million loan from Ghana to Upper Volta, but negotiations were never completed. Despite the elaborate plans, a meeting of Yameogo and Nkrumah in Tenkodogo in August 1962 ended with the admission that neither political nor economic barriers had actually been lowered.

[57] In the XVI session of the United Nations, Casablanca Group members voted identically 81 per cent of the time and divided on only 1 per cent of the votes. But in the entire period between the XIII and XVI sessions, identity existed on 70 per cent of the votes and division on only 5 per cent, suggesting that the high degree of solidarity owed little to the formation of the Group (Hovet, op. cit., pp. 134-43).

[58] John Marcum, "How Wide Is The Gap Between Casablanca and Monrovia?" Africa Report, VII, 1 (January 1962), 3. Despite too-frequent analyses to the contrary, there was nothing about the Casablanca Group (except the hopes of one member: Ghana) that permits classifying it as a Group favoring close political integration and unification.

[59] Casablanca charter, cited in Legum, Pan-Africanism . . . , op. cit., p. 205.

[60] The Casablanca states' ambassadors in Moscow were also very active in winning Soviet support for Tunisia in the Bizerte crisis.

[61] Interviews with Alpha Amadou Diallo and Alpha Abdoulaye Diallo in Guinea.

[62] Quotations from Articles 2, 4, and 5 of the UAM charter; italics in the text. In the XV and XVI sessions of the United Nations, UAM members voted identically half the time and divided 11 per cent of the time; on African issues, identical voting rose to 60 per cent and division remained the same, a rather low degree of solidarity (Hovet, op. cit., pp. 131-43).

[63] In matters partially outside the area, the UAM was also active in attempting to mediate the Franco-Tunisian crisis over Bizerte during August 1961, and was successful in mediating differences among Gabon, Congo (Brazzaville) and Dahomey (all UAM members) over expulsion of populations in October 1962.

[64] Senghor's original suggestion was made in October 1954 in an article in Politique Étrangère (Paris) ; see Foltz, op. cit., pp. 66, 75.

[65] On the OCRS, see Zartman, The Sahara . . . , op. cit., pp. 26-31.

[66] See Thompson, "Dahomey," op. cit., pp. 249-57; Jeune Afrique, April 2, 1962; Monde diplomatique, August 1964; Note de Conjoncture, No. 9, Moniteur Africain (Dakar), March 1962.

[67] Radio Brazzaville, April 6, 1960.

[68] Apithy letter and interview, La Semaine en Afrique Occidentale (Dahomey), February 7, 1959.

[69] Radio Lomé, March 22, 1962.

[70] Wolfers, op. cit., p. 28. See also Ernst Haas, Regional Integration and National Policy (New York: Carnegie Endowment for International Peace, 1957 [International Conciliation Series No. 513]), p. 430; Gabriel d'Arboussier, L'Afrique vers l'unité (Paris: St-Paul, 1961), p. 54; and, generally, Amitai Etzioni, Political Unification (New York: Holt, Rinehart & Winston, 1965).

4 CONCLUSIONS, TRENDS, AND PATTERNS OF DEVELOPMENT

Three conclusions are presented here. One seeks to gather together previous points into a summary description of the developing nature of Western African foreign policy. The next is an attempt to apply experiences inside and outside the area to the development of regional unity, an approach designed to reconcile Western Africa's major ideological goals. The third is a projective analysis, dealing with trends and changes that may be expected in intra-African policy.

DEVELOPING FOREIGN POLICY

The realization is slowly spreading that development is a process that covers the whole range of human activity, and that economic development—although most easily measurable in finite terms—is a meaningless concept if divorced from social and political development. This is not the place to argue this thesis, nor does its acceptance preclude separate study of the economic, social, or political *aspects* of one complex development process. The point is simply that in the political side of development there is a legitimate field of study, understood within the context of other aspects, and that inside this field, in turn, there is the need to devote attention to international politics and foreign policy. It is a simple truth that new nations must develop a foreign policy; it does not step full-blown from the head of state. It may also be assumed that, under the pressure of need and practice, foreign policy does develop, at an undetermined and variable rate. There is a basis, therefore, for speaking of the "development" of foreign policies, and for seeking to identify their characteristics in such an area of new nations as Western Africa. What follows is therefore not a study of developed foreign policy, or an attempt to compare Western Africa's foreign relations with those of other areas. This is a task left to students who wish to define developed foreign policy and then compare the two. By the same token, it is possible that the foreign relations of other developing areas exhibit different characteristics. A description of these characteristics is the task of students of these areas; and when it is done, fruitful comparisons may also be made.[1]

As a part of political development, foreign-policy development is affected by the process of nation-building. International relations is the study of power relations among states, and states in Western Africa are going concerns, interested in their self-preservation and capable of carrying out policy with one another. In this, Western Africa differs little from other areas, but such similarities are only apparent and superficial. The state in Western Africa is only partially a "sovereign territorial group." [2] Sovereignty, as the highest formal or legal fiction behind authority, provides the formal framework within which to carry out a foreign policy. Some African states (particularly the revolutionary-idealists), however, tend to regard conformity to a standard of conduct, that may be called "Africanity," as a higher source of authority, much as Bodin regarded sovereignty as subject to a higher source found in divine law. By seeking to change the governments—without actually conquering the territory—of other states, they challenge the sovereign right of states to govern their own affairs, and in this view they find a philosophical basis for subversion and for challenging domestic policies. Territoriality too is dubious, for in every Western African state some stretch of boundary is also a legal fiction. The area's boundaries in general are lines which have more concreteness on a small-scale map than as limits separating the states' control of land and people. This is not to suggest that the nonterritorial state is Africa's contribution to a new form of international relations; instead, the developing aspect of the state is emphasized by its continuing efforts to constitute a territorial unit. But it is the "group" nature of the state's population that is even more dubious. The nation is not yet "an organized aggregate," with "a pattern of solidarity and cooperation" or a system of integrated operations and perspectives (identities).[3] Allegiance is still owed to the traditional nation or tribe; control of the state is not felt equally among all its people; enrollment of the people in the governmental process (including the determination of interests) is still inchoate, and even the definition of *citizen* and *expatriate* is cloudy.

Intra-African relations are still carried on primarily among party leaders rather than among governments acting in the name of states representing people. This is merely to say that the transition in the unit of interest and identification from party to state to nation is not complete. Western African foreign policy has left the colonial stage and is no longer carried out exclusively for the interests and aspirations of revolutionary political movements seeking to overthrow established governments; it has entered into the sovereign stage, designed to further the interests and aspirations of the state in dealing with other sovereign states. Yet elements of both stages still exist side by side in many countries. Ghana is perhaps the best example of the dualism. Nkrumah's behavior is largely explained by the fact that he regards himself as the head of a revolutionary political party as well as the head of a sovereign state. Guinea, Mali, and Algeria frequently display similar tendencies. Such behavior is characteristic of the revolutionary-idealist states, and is a natural carryover from colonial times—a fact that explains the high incidence of political warfare, internal violence, and subversion. Conversely, the conventional-realist foreign policy is the one which has shown the most successful transition from a party to a state basis. Western African foreign policy is thus intimately related to political development and nation-building, in that the state—both as an actor in international relations and as a basis for foreign policy—needs development.

A second key concept of international relations is power: capability to achieve a goal in a particular situation. Western African states' capability of achieving any foreign policy goal is extremely limited. The elements of state power, on which this capability is based, are underdeveloped; the instruments of national policy, by which this capability is exercised, are limited; the distribution of power, among states of relatively equal—if low—capability, is highly diffused. Essentially, power arises from a situational, psychological relationship, and can be exercised in many ways: directly between individuals on the basis of personality or pleas; indirectly between individuals through threat, slogans, purchase, or reason; indirectly between decision-making elites through public opinion or pressure groups; or directly between states through economic aid, diplomatic support, sanctions, or force. All involve the use of real or implied gratifications or deprivations. The status of elements, instruments, and distribution of power in Western Africa means that the possibilities of deprivation or gratification are slim.[4] Ideological approbation can be extended or withheld (justifying slogans can be used to condemn or condone); trade can be cut (borders can be closed, often ineffectively); military threats can be made (with varying degrees of credibility). But the list stops there. Sanctions and force are either disallowed or impractical; domestic public opinion and pressure groups have little weight in decision-making process and foreign leaders frequently have little access to them; the possibilities for aid are insignificant; purchase, reason, and support, in a bargaining process, are rarely used because there are few clear goals, flexible policies, and national-interest criteria to which they can be applied. Finally, the informational input on which capability must be based is small. As reality replaces slogans, as information replaces feelings, and as the elements of state power are developed, the states of Western Africa can increase their capability in international relations. At present, there is very little possibility of one state influencing another's foreign policy, except through ideological appeals.

A third characteristic of developing foreign policies, then, is the primacy of ideology. Having no power but only trampled rights,[5] having fallen under the domination of stronger states, and having overthrown the colonial system largely by manipulation of slogans and by default, Western African states attempt to reject international relations based on power and speak of a new era, one no longer characterized by the domination of the stronger over the weak. This Fanonistic revisionism,[6] which in one form or another characterizes most Western African states' views of international relations, depends on the creation and acceptance of a system of values that denigrates power, inhibits its use, and establishes rights. Because the existence of power, influence, and even domination cannot be denied, it must be disarmed, and the prohibitions and rights must be codified into an accepted value construct that can govern action and explain events. This is the role of ideology. Ideology is pseudoscience or ultrascience in that it seeks to explain and order events and roles into meaningful patterns, to describe cause and effect, and to prescribe conforming action.[7] It puts the stamp of authority on extrarealistic sequators, that is, on a system of internal logic derived from premises which bear a selective, not a rigorous, relation to reality. Thus ideology is a source of power, or an antidote to the power Western Africa fears and does not have.

The initial frame of reference for these hypotheses is Africa's relation to the external world, but the ideology is all-pervasive. In intra-African relations, ideology not only includes the prominent goal-values of independence, unity, and development; it also gives them a generally accepted order of priority: independence over unity and development, independence and development over unity. It further surrounds these values with an accepted mythology: the right of independence, the basic unity of the African personality or the African people, the right to development. Ideology, then, shapes the perception of events, serves to justify action, and limits the choices of ends and means. Obviously, its effect is more strongly felt in revolutionary-idealist states, where the place of ideology is more important. But ideology plays an influential role even among the conventional-realist states. Of course, no claim is made here that there is a single African ideology (some different, if related, types of ideologies have already been outlined) but ideology has an unusually large role in Western Africa in determining attitudes and reactions, and there is a high value placed on the fact of "having an ideology."

The role of ideology leads into a fourth characteristic of developing Western African foreign policy: its searching nature. Ideology, goals, policies, and events have the common characteristic of seeking satisfying definitions. There is a search for an ideology, a search for a definition of *unity*, a search for national interests. The attempt to "find an ideology" is part of a powerfully felt need, with many ramifications, that is characteristic of political development. In foreign policy, the search for a definition of *unity* has been seen to be particularly instructive. It took place on all levels. The continental search led through many "groups" and conferences to the summit at Addis Ababa. During the course of the search, new issues appeared which accentuated ideological differences and the states reconceived unity as a search for ideologically compatible allies. In the meantime, there was a good deal of experimentation with regional definitions of *unity*, taking the form of a search for institutions that could reconcile unity and independence. It would be condescending to shrug off these attempts as ritualistic or worthless. They have been an important part of Western Africa's learning process, by which the area became more familiar with the real content of independence and unity. The negative results are scarcely surprising; independence and unity are difficult values to reconcile. The positive effects of these experiments are not the less real to the foreign policy-makers of Western Africa because they are hard to measure.

It is in this searching process that the characteristics of a foreign policy suitable to the Western African scene may be developed. The following section suggests one of these in regard to the three primary goals already mentioned. Others may arise; there is no suggestion implied that Western African foreign policy need rediscover all the conventional patterns of foreign policy operative in other parts of the world and find them advantageous. So far, military alliances appear to be unsuitable to Western Africa's needs, whereas temporary international pressure groups geared to a few common stands—although not completely successful—have been the predominant mode of alliance policy. A satisfactory approach to problems such as diplomatic representation, boundary disputes, the status of migrant or "international" populations, the common development of natural resources and interstate transportation lines, and the control of subversion has yet to be formulated. It is to be hoped that the searching process, which has already attacked some of these problems, will continue to focus on them until adequate answers are found.

A corollary of the searching process is the predominance of ad hoc policy-making in the present stage of development. Developing Western Africa is still looking for institutions of government. States in the area have experimented with a number of innovations, particularly regarding the relationship between government and party, and a number of constitutions have been altered during the few years of independence as new institutional roles and relations are tried. But the states must keep on governing while their institutional experiments are being carried out, and the policy-making in the transitional stage creates its own patterns and—eventually—its own habits. Until policy-making patterns are habitualized, policy remains ad hoc. The danger of forming habits before one is sure of, or ready for, them is sometimes recognized, creating a healthy wariness that underlies Western Africa's apparent fear of supranational institutions.

Unfortunately, Western Africa's policy is not only ad hoc in form; it often tends to be ad hoc in content as well. Despite the claim by some leaders that their decisions are based on the unshakable principles formulated by their party, policy is frequently unstable and subject to rapid change. Too often it is made on the basis of incomplete evidence, chance meetings, and accidental stimuli, and without much awareness of state interests. Ad hoc policy makes predictability difficult, thus increasing the tactical difficulties of allies and enemies, and also favoring a vicious circle of ad hoc policy-making. In such a situation, the development of mutual respect for obligations or commitments and stable organizations of alliance and cooperation, becomes difficult.

The final characteristic of Western Africa's developing international relations is their instability. What is referred to here is, of course, not the current myth that Africa is a continent of unstable government, internal and external disorder, and anarchy. In fact, the governments of Africa have been remarkably stable when considered alongside the problems they face; disorder and insecurity are local exceptions, not national rules, and the use of external violence has been seen to be minimal; and anarchy on any level—domestic or international—is rare indeed. Instead, instability in Western African foreign affairs involves the lack of permanence in affinities and commitments, and the lack of control over events. Alliances themselves have been seen to be an innately unstable stage in international relations, when states waver unsteadily between independent action and unification. In Western Africa, many alliances are even more unstable, because there are frequently no clear interests involved to hold them together; thus they tend to be based on the policy stands and issues of the moment, at the mercy of changing situations and events. Because government and opposition have little awareness or consensus concerning interests, and because both forces tend to define themselves in terms of a total image of roles and policies, a change in government almost invariably brings a change in alignments. Political underdevelopment can also be characterized as a low degree of control over events, a trait that is evident in Western African foreign policy. Because the states have not yet had the time or the experience to develop a coherent foreign policy, new events are not judged within the framework of continuing policy; instead, they may set off a new policy stand or reaction. When all the situational influences are taken into acount, there are usually few courses open to a state. Events, then, tend to have the upper hand over Africans' choice in foreign relations, leaving Western Africa, in foreign policy as in other aspects of development, deeply engaged in a still unsuccessful struggle to dominate its environment.

The reflection of these characteristics, in Western Africa as in many other developing regions,[8] is a special type of international-relations system. Unlike the more traditional models of balance-of-power, bipolar, hierarchial or supranational systems,[9] the African system is one of mobile relations carried out within certain limits imposed by ideology and environment. Western Africa has had its proto-balance-of-power period (1959-63), when alliances and counteralliances were formed and expanded to check one another's growing power (usually measured in the few terms open to member states: solidarity and slogans). This alliance race dissolved in the OAU, without by any means ending the ideological conflicts on which it was based. But since 1963 Western Africa has avoided permanent alliances, for the several reasons suggested above, and instead has fallen back on the more basic characteristic of international relations: temporary coincidence of policy on the issue of the moment. There is no assurance that, under the impact of an exceptionally strong situational stimulus, these coincidences might not again harden into firmer patterns of solidarity, such as groups and alliances. There is, however, the likelihood that, in the present stage of foreign-policy development, even these patterns would be only situational and, hence, temporary. Without firm or credible commitments to alliance, a balance-of-power or bipolar system cannot evolve. Without consensus on institutions and values of solidarity, a hierarchial or supranational system cannot be created. Hence, Africa retains its system of limited, mobile relations. It may be noted, however, that there is a certain unity to this system, just as a certain independence of its members is preserved. This unity is real, even if it does not have institutions, a flag, or a common policy; it is the interactional unity of a system, not the monolithic unity of union or agreement.[10] Its reality can be judged by its common characteristics, interrelations, and effects. In its search for *African unity*, Western Africa appears to have evolved a new type of definition that it did not consciously seek to create: the unity of independent African states interacting in a system of international relations.

PATTERNS OF REGIONAL UNITY

One fact of Western African relations is the continuing existence of the sixteen sovereign states. Not only have attempts at unification broken down; they have never reached a stage that would really test any institutions of unification. This should scarcely be surprising when it is remembered that independence has generally been the primary goal of Western African political forces. Touré's dictum—"We prefer independence in poverty to servitude in riches"—shows the primacy of independence over development,[11] and the history of all countries but Senegal and Soudan (Mali) reveals the primacy of independence over unity. Yet the values of unity and development are strong. Unity has come to be defined as unity of action and harmonization of policies among independent states, within limits imposed by state sovereignty, state ideology, and separate state leadership. Vague on the continental level, where this definition was nevertheless ratified, such unity becomes increasingly meaningful as the number of states involved is reduced and their similarities—material, historical, and ideological—increase. This consideration suggests the rising importance of regional unity, a conclusion reinforced by the exigencies of the third value: development. Rational utilization of scarce resources, increased chances of attracting foreign aid and investment, and the possibility of taking advantage of common geographic features are all favored by cooperation among neighbors. The past few years have also shown that some measure of external policy cooperation and internal development harmonization can be achieved within a regional framework.

Regional cooperation is the middle road between equally inconclusive arguments for unification and against balkanization, on one hand, and those for state autarky and against actions that limit its sovereignty, on the other. Western African states endowed with natural resources may be capable of achieving industrial development on the basis of foreign aid and their own internal demand, although the result would be suboptimal industry oriented toward the small national market and held in place by a high protective tariff wall.[12] The smaller, poorer states have no such chance, yet union with a richer state is no answer to their problem, for they would then simply be poor provinces, good for exploitation but without independent political means of attracting aid and attention. In the Cold War competition, a poor area can have greater chances of attracting aid as an independent state than as a disinherited province of some large state;[13] its attractive powers are maximized when it pools resources and bargaining power with a richer neighbor, while retaining its own sovereignty as a lever in negotiations. As part of Morocco, Mauritania would simply be a poor part of a larger kingdom, placing its scarce resources at the disposal of that part of the country with the greatest promise for development: the northern coastal zone of agriculture and industry. From an economic point of view, Mauritania's large iron deposits would simply put it in a colonial relation to Morocco. But as a member of a regional unit, in which the continuing existence of the unit itself becomes a value to defend and each member brings its resources into coordinated use, Mauritania would be in a stronger position to demand its share of cooperative benefits while contributing to the common exploitation of resources that could benefit all. Regional cooperation among sovereign states can maximize the values of independence, unity and development, and avoid the problems inherent in both nationalist isolation and ambitious unification.

Identification of the proper conditions is crucial. Most important is identification of the region, centered on core areas of population, economic activity, and influence. Preconditions of unity, dynamic ingredients leading to regionalism and background, neutral, and dysfunctional conditions should also be understood. This section will examine the possibilities of regional unity in Western Africa, borrowing from studies of attempts to create pluralistic security communities in other areas of the world and other times in history, and from the past experiences of the area.[14] Although no claim is made for the predictability of such efforts, it is likely that Western Africa can benefit from these examples and their lessons and characteristics.

Certain conditions which had often been considered as essential for the establishment of an amalgamated security community [turn] . . . out to be helpful to that end but not essential to it. Such helpful but nonessential condition [include] . . . previous administrative and/or dynastic union; ethnic or linguistic assimilation; strong economic ties; and foreign military threats.[15]

Although a number of regions, variously defined (such as the Maghreb, the West African Customs, Postal, and Monetary Union within the OCAM and former AOF, the Entente, or the Mali Federation), fit the first and second background conditions, economic ties throughout these regions are highly variant while foreign military threats, as has been seen, are nearly nonexistent. It is fortunate that past experience shows these background conditions to be nonessential, for future possibilities of regional cooperation would be limited indeed if they were tied to past experiences, and would be further reduced in Western Africa if they had to await foreign military threats. Instead, the interest here is in exploring future development that could bring about regional cooperation.

There are some conditions that appear to be neutral or ambiguous in their effects. One is "early direct popular support." [16] The studies of a Princeton group noted that active popular support came only at a later stage, when, however, it tended to play an important role. The weaknesses of Western African public opinion have been noted, along with the ability of leaders to arouse popular support for diverse policies in terms of general ideological slogans. The prevalence of the undefined term *unity* in the Western African political vocabulary sets the stage for its use in support of regional cooperation, but it may be a long time before a fully developed public opinion is able to exercise enough influence to be a constant ingredient in the area's politics.[17] The Princeton study also noted ambiguity in the importance of political appeals used to sell the idea of pluralistic integration.[18] The strengthening of an existing or emerging sociocultural community, the promise of greater equality and greater power, the prospect of increased specific rights and liberties, and the defense of existing privileges were used (in that order).

The terms in which early references to unity in Africa have been couched tend to confirm the list of appeals and their ranking. Unity appeals have already been buttressed by reference to "African personality" (in Nkrumah's language) and by reasoning in terms of the "Arab Maghreb" and the "Negro-African or Negro-Berber nation" (in the words of North African leaders and Senghor, respectively). There has been no attempt to sentimentalize cultural attachment to any intermediate regions between the state and the West African area, although West Africa, like "West Arabia" (translation of "Maghreb"), has been used as a reference symbol. Promises of greater power, at least in international negotiations, have been used to justify regional cooperation, in as diverse appeals as Nkrumah's Pan-Africanist programs, the combined action of the eighteen associated members of the European Common Market in dealing with the Inner Six in Europe and of the four members of the Entente in negotiating multilateral agreements with France. In fact, the entire drive for unity can be seen as a defensive action designed to assert and maintain more effectively African independence and identity against colonial, neocolonial, and Western (Euro-modern) encroachment. Promises of greater equality and demands for specific rights also buttress appeals for unity, although these promises and demands are couched in foreign-policy terms; Western Africa's approach to external relations is still frequently in general terms of denied equality for the race, state, and people, and trampled rights that must be restored and assuaged by reparations. It is significant that these appeals have all been made in the name of the collectivity—continent, region, or nation—and are either directed outward, to justify demands or a cooperative approach, or directed back to the speaker himself and his political circle, to rationalize their own actions. Usually, the appeals have not yet been directed inward to the people of the nation, to further the idea of regional cooperation. Again, this phenomenon is explained by the nature of decision-making and public opinion in the area.

A final ambiguous condition for regional cooperation is a change in significant political strata. Obviously, on a prima facie level of analysis, a change in elites can either help or hinder integration, depending on the attitudes toward unity of the incumbents and their replacements. Deeper analysis can bring more detail to this judgment. The Princeton group notes that an increase in political participation by a formerly passive group, the closure of access to an established elite, the failure of a significant group to adjust to loss of dominance, and a realignment of political forces to block integration are all dysfunctional aspects of political dynamics in integrating countries, whereas the arrival of a new generation, a realignment of political forces in favor of integration, and an increase in elite willingness to compromise are all helpful changes.[19] These two sets of conditions may be summarized in three ways: integration tends to bring about a realignment of political forces; integration tends to be brought about by a change (partial or complete) in the political elites and not merely a change in the ideas of an established elite; and integration is accomplished most easily when local demanding groups which have to be satisfied are known and stable. What is the effect of these conditions on Western African regional cooperation?

Both the conditions and the previous attempts at cooperation and alliance in the area suggest that the present Western African leadership is relatively fixed in its general foreign-policy values; with few exceptions, these guidelines include passive justification of, but not active impetus toward, unity. The impetus, and the consequent adoption of a policy of pluralistic integration, must then come from new blood in the elite circle. Such figures as Albert Tevoedjre of Dahomey and Abderrahim Bouabid of Morocco are likely candidates; Doudou Gueye and Mohammed Masmoudi have already returned to the ruling circles in Senegal and Tunisia. Entry can come by co-option, or, where access to the ruling circle is closed, by the death of the leader(s) or the overthrow of the government. In general, those states in which political elites reinforce themselves with new blood and new ideas have a better chance of moving toward regional cooperation than states with a closed inner circle. Furthermore, increased regional cooperation is unlikely as long as most of the area's George Washington figures still head their states' governments (although this is not to say that the replacements will necessarily turn to a policy of integration). The Dahomeyan *coup* probably increased possibilities of Benin cooperation and the Togolese *coup* was followed by Togo's membership in the UAM, but the royal succession in Morocco has not altered state policy toward Maghreb unity. The George Washington figure is usually too deeply committed to a symbolic position of leadership and to a limited range of policy options to be willing or able to share affective or policy-making primacy. The Guinea-Mali experience in cooperation is a good example of such problems. The third condition appears less relevant to Western Africa, for few new demanding groups of significance are likely to appear. However, the dissatisfied modern group of unemployed bourgeoisie and proletariat (to use terms which are becoming real in Western Africa) can become an exception of increasing importance; its effect depends on whether this group can come to a realization that its problems can find solution within a regional framework—if indeed they can—or whether it will fall back on ultranationalist symbols of dissatisfaction that include making scapegoats of neighboring states. In 1963 Dahomeyan reactions to the Entente and Algerian reactions to Morocco provide examples of the latter danger, while the attitude of the Moroccan opposition to Algeria is a partial example of a more positive effect. In each case, national politics, and the relation of the dissatisfied group to the government, are also important factors.

The crucial starting point for regional cooperation lies in the existence of cores of strength. The core concept does not conflict with the Western African reality of diffused political power or a balance-of-power effect within the region. Instead, pluralistic integration presupposes the existence of several political centers capable of compromise, cooperation, and bargaining for advantage. Although defined primarily in terms of nonpolitical conditions, including such items as population, economic activity, communications, and trade patterns, the basis of the core concept also includes political "power grids" or zones of influence.[20] Identification of core areas begins with location of definable regions of high populations density, centered on modernizing urban centers with surrounding farmland. One such is the coastal band of the Maghreb that stretches from the western Atlas mountains through Morocco and Algeria to the sahel region on Tunisia's eastern Mediterranean shore. A second concentration along the Benin Coast is less regularly shaped; it begins on the Camerounian border and extends westward across Nigeria, Dahomey, and Togo toward the western border of Ghana, with two major northward prolongations: one extending through Ghana to the Mossi country of central Upper Volta, and the other extending across Nigeria northwest along the Niger River into western Niger and northeast across the Niger River into the northern region of Nigeria and the southern borderlands of Niger. Adjacent to this "Benin" concentration is a smaller region of dense population in central Ivory Coast from Abidjan to Bouaké. Another region comprises a hundred-mile-deep coastal belt from Conakry southward across Sierra Leone toward the eastern Liberian border. Finally, a well-populated zone includes western Senegal, Gambia, and northern Portuguese Guinea. Lesser concentrations are located in two parts of Mali; along the inland delta of the Niger and around Bamako.

Working on the basis of the core area of population concentration, there is no difficulty in identifying other characteristics of the Maghreb region. The entire populated area from Safi to Tunis is serviced by a standard-gauge railroad in good working condition; standard-gauge spurs cross the Moroccan plains from Marrakesh to Tangier and reach into the desert at Colomb-Bechar and Biskra, and a narrow-gauge rail network covers northern Tunisia and eastern Algeria. The populated area of the three countries is also united by an extensive network of paved roads, some of which cross the Atlas barrier into regions of economic activity but lesser population. Bus and trucking industries are active within and among all three states. A telephone cable runs through the three capitals and other major cities. Airline service within the region is skeletal, but there the number and distribution of airfields, personnel, and equipment in the three national airlines would allow expansion and coordination of service as needed. The most important freight transportation link among the three states is coastal shipping. The region is well equipped with ports scattered along its entire coast, Casablanca being the largest. Once commodities reach port, the road and rail systems spread them throughout the countryside. Morocco and Algeria have a particularly important place in each other's trade, with Tunisia as a lesser trading partner of both. There is also a significant interchange of migrant labor between Algeria and its two neighbors.

Two other material factors aid conception of the Maghreb region. Only Morocco has important hydroelectric installations; the other two countries depend on thermal production of electricity, but Algeria can produce and sell either natural gas or electric energy to both neighbors at rates which benefit all three countries. A bilateral agreement between Algeria and Tunisia has already restored the connection between the two states' national electric grids. The other material factor is the location of important mineral deposits in border areas or in areas where economical exploitation requires regional cooperation. The most striking cases are the new oilfields at al-Borma in the disputed boundary zone between Tunisia and Algeria (now placed under joint sovereignty by bilateral agreement) and the iron fields near Tindouf in the disputed boundary zone between Morocco and Algeria (where conflicting claims have prevented exploitation). A number of unworked mineral deposits are also located in the contested Bechar region, and iron and phosphate deposits are found astride the Algero-Tunisian border. Broader cultural—including religious, ethnic, and linguistic—elements of similarity among the Maghreb peoples also strengthen the material characteristics of the core area.

Other core areas, although identifiable, are less obvious. The largest West African population region is the Benin complex, including parts of Nigeria, Dahomey, Togo, Ghana, and also Niger and upper Volta. Economic and communications factors would suggest including Ivory Coast as well, although its population concentrations form an "island" separated from the main complex. But the Abidjan-Niger railway (which is laid only to Ouagadougou) is an important trade line serving the region from the coast to the interior; the Benin-Niger railroad (which is laid only to Parakou), the Togolese railroad, and the well-developed Nigerian Railways network perform the same function. Connecting these lines are paved and all-weather dirt roads that lead from the northern railheads to Niamey, a network of paved and all-weather dirt roads in Nigeria and southern Niger, and a paved coastal road from Sekondi-Takoradi to Lagos. There is also an all-weather road network in Ghana with paved stretches in the southern half of the country. The major break in the road system is found along the northern and western Ghanaian border, although the inland road from Accra to Abidjan is paved for about half its length. Despite the variable quality of roads, trucks and busses ply the entire region frequently, if not regularly. Roads in the region are open throughout the year, but the navigable stretch of the Niger River south of Niamey is too low to bear traffic between May and September. Elsewhere, rivers are of little importance to interstate traffic, although the Niger-Benue system is usable within Nigeria. Airline and telephone service in the Benin region is also developing to overcome colonial patterns of division between former British and French territories.

The same pattern of coastal trade evident in the Maghreb is present along the Benin Coast, and the absence of natural harbors has been remedied by construction of modern port facilities at Abidjan, Sekondi-Takoradi, Tema, Lomé, Cotonou, Lagos, and Port Harcourt. Another important characteristic of the region's trade is the widespread activity of such itinerant traders as Hausamen and Dioulas. Also significant, although difficult to judge by official figures, is the traditional trade, which antedates the legal restrictions that now cause it to be qualified as smuggling. This trade follows distinct lateral patterns along the coast and vertical patterns between the coast and the savannah. A final pattern of movement within the region involves labor migration. From the populated regions of Upper Volta and northern Nigeria a stream of labor flows continually across the Poor Middle Belt to the cities and plantations of the coast; the movement is generally due south, with the exception of those Nigerians who migrate southwest to English-speaking Ghana, and is largely self-contained within the Benin region. There are a few cases of common development possibilities. The lower Niger River (which waters Niger, Dahomey, and Nigeria) and the Mono River between Dahomey and Togo have already been the subject of regional negotiations. Regional use of hydroelectric power from Ghana's Volta River project is also a possibility; the only other hydroelectric sources are in eastern Ivory Coast and northern Nigeria, and fossil fuels for thermoelectric power—except for Nigerian oil—are rare. In the social and cultural fields there is no need to pretend that the Benin states form a homogeneous region of traditional nationalities or modern (European) languages, and it would be idle to debate whether the multiplicity of the former or the sharp dichotomy of the latter makes for the greater difficulty in cooperation.

The third region is the most difficult to justify. The two remaining population cores, along the west Guinea coast and around Cape Verde, are not contiguous, and the lesser population zones in Mali are even more widely scattered. The only transportation line of international significance is the Dakar-Niger railroad, which does have the important effect of tying the western Malian population centers with the port of Dakar. The Conakry-Niger railway is in poor condition and, even when extended by dirt road and by the navigable reaches of the upper Niger River to Bamako, is not a major trade route. The upper Niger and lower Senegal rivers are open to traffic to Mali only in the latter half of the year, and the dirt roads from Senegal to Mali and Guinea are extremely difficult to travel all year around; a poor dirt road connects Conakry with Freetown and Monrovia along the coast. Land transportation in the region is in great need of development. Sea transportation is slightly more satisfactory, for the capitals of the five coastal states all have port facilities, with Dakar and Freetown far in the lead in volume of trade. Freetown, Robertsport, Monrovia, and Buchanan are cut off from their Guinean hinterland by mountain barriers and political borders. Commercial relations between Senegal and Mauritania are more highly developed, owing to the existence of paved roads and rail and river lines.

The region corresponds to Senghor's Senegal River Union plus Sierra Leone and Liberia, and is in reality two subregions, with communications

between them much in need of development. There are other patterns, however, which reinforce the unity of the region. Population migration flows westward from Guinea and Mali into the Casamance farmlands of Senegal, and
then back again after the peanut crop is harvested. Traditional trade, princi-
pally in cattle, moves southward from the Malian savannah and the Guinean
highlands to the coast as far away as Liberia, and northward from Mali through
Mauritania. In some other respects the region is unpromising: there are no
developed energy resources, and prospects in Guinea, Senegal, and Mali are
few and expensive; the rich iron deposits in either end of the region—Fort
Gouraud in Mauritania and Mount Nimba in Guinea and Liberia—are of
commercial, not industrial, interest to the states concerned.

A final problem in the definition of the regions lies in the relation between
Mali and the Benin core. Traditional trade in fish, cattle, and kola nuts, and
the extension of the populated zone northwestward along the Niger River
have long turned central and eastern Mali's face south toward the Benin
Coast rather than west toward Senegal and Guinea. This pattern was reinforced when Ivory Coast and Upper Volta undertook replacing Dakar as the
supply route to Mali. The cause of this shift was political; Mali's need is
for an outlet to the sea, but not for any particular outlet. Furthermore, the
concept of cores and regions does not by any means imply a closed frontier
between regions. The problem of defining the region does not exist between
the Maghreb and West Africa. Despite traditional trade and modern roads
across the Sahara, the desert does form a wide frontier, and there is also a
general trend of depopulation of Algerian cases and migration toward the
coastal area. Patterns of population, trade, communications, and other factors
indicate that it is possible to conceive of three Western African regions—
which may be called for convenience Maghreb, Benin, and Soudan—the
characteristics of which lend themselves to mutually beneficial cooperation
among member states.

Seven preconditions to integration can be identified; most of them are based
on the findings of the Princeton group. The first concerns the need for compatibility in the major values held by the politically relevant strata. In the
absence of pre-existent ideological harmony, this compatibility may be
achieved "by a tacit agreement to deprive of political significance any incompatible values that might remain." [21] An example of this depolitization
process is the devaluation of ideological purity among the radicals and, to a
lesser extent, the moderates of the continent in order to permit agreement on
unity at Addis Ababa. Because ideology is a pattern of values governing
action, and depolitization or devaluation means the lowering of incompatible
values on the scale of importance, this precondition implies the elevation of
unity as specifically applied to regional cooperation. This value is already
deemed important in Tunisia and Algeria, in Senegal, in the four Entente
states, and in Ghana (although here not in reference to the Benin region).
Interpretation of values referring to domestic politicoeconomic systems—
primarily the definition of African Socialism—however, varies widely within

the three regions and is high on the individual states' lists. As long as Houphouet-Boigny has his bet with Ghana over paths to development, as long as Guinea and Mali scorn Senegal's brand of African Socialism, and as long as Algeria denigrates Morocco's bourgeois monarchy, the precondition is not fulfilled. It must be noted in passing that compatibility of values does not imply identity of values, but the cooperative coexistence of individual states' systems and values.

The second, and corollary, precondition is that regional integration must satisfy goals other than unity. As long as other aims are paramount and require energies for which cooperation has to compete, the conditions for regionalism are not present. To a certain extent, this precondition depends on state leaders' perception of their own goals. Morocco and Algeria have regarded their border dispute as insoluble by cooperation, for Algeria has not appeared to be interested in negotiation and the border claims of the two states overlap. Algeria and Tunisia however, have perceived *their* border dispute as an opportunity for cooperation, open to solution by the establishment of a common zone in the conflict area. In the Soudanese region of West Africa, there are fewer such competing goals; but in the Benin region, again, the separate development of Ghana and Ivory Coast—and the leadership rivalry between their two heads of state—illustrates the need for this precondition. The Benin problems appear to be more difficult to solve than those of the Maghreb.

The third precondition, one of great importance, is the expectation of joint rewards. These rewards should take the form of a down payment before substantial burdens are imposed; but they must also be of a continuing nature, so that there may be no danger that early dissatisfaction will lead to withdrawal before firm patterns of cooperation are established.[22] In the Maghreb, expectations have been aroused by such serious studies as those of the United Nations Economic Commission for Africa and the Tunisian Secretariat of State for Orientation (already cited); in the Soudanese region, the United Nations performed a similar service in its study of cooperative advantages around the Senegal River, and the Dahomeyan government has established a study group with a similar purpose (but fewer means) for the Benin Union. Technical conferences (such as the July 1962 conference on the harmonization of industrial development which brought to Niamey most states in the Benin region, plus Mali), even though without immediately apparent results, are also beneficial. There seems to be little difficulty in making regional plans that will bring out possibilities for mutual benefits. The decision to choose those projects that will provide a down payment for cooperation is a political one that can be bargained for and made by the states involved. Once the expectation of benefit is clearly perceived, it can have the important side effect of bringing in support from formerly uncommitted leaders and facilitating the political realignment necessary to cooperation. The Dahomeyan and Voltaic leaders' shift of support from the Mali Federation to the Entente in 1959, on the basis of economic needs, is an example of this process.

The fourth precondition is that of personal mobility within the region. It is because of this need that the migration, movement, and unhindered entry of persons, already noted as characteristics of the core areas, is so important, and that boundary disputes and border closings are especially detrimental to cooperation. Natural patterns in the three regions can be strengthened by liberal legislation on the status of expatriates and by liberal administration of border regulations. It should be noted, however, that the purpose is not to weaken a neighboring state's hold on its border regions, but to foster patterns of mobility that reach the communications and decision-making center in the capital.

The fifth precondition is that of institutionalized common services to assure a multiplicity and balance of transactions. To some extent, a beginning has been made in the existing trade patterns, and in the Western African organizations that deal with them. But much more remains to be done. Western African common services inherited from the colonial period have tended to break down rather than endure; after reconstitution, they have tended to falter frequently. Even such an obviously beneficial arrangement as the Niger-Dahomeyan transportation organization (OCDN) fell to pieces in 1963 over a relatively insignificant dispute. The breakdown of beneficial common services has had its positive side, however, for it has made members learn, by experience, the problems of isolation and the value of cooperation. The pattern has been encouraging; many interrupted common services have been restored, although often in a new form and after a long wait. The creation of common services within the regions lies at the heart of cooperative efforts and is a task of high priority.

The sixth precondition involves the existence of mutually predictable behavior. Predictability begins with acquaintance and familiarity among decision-makers, and broadens to include common ideologies or values for action, similar images of self and environment, and a common way of life. Although the members of the elites of many Western African states know one another intimately, familiarity and understanding drop sharply when they cross from French- to English-speaking territories. African leaders are fast getting to know each other, but this does not guarantee predictability. Also necessary is the removal of many characteristics of foreign-policy underdevelopment that have already been noted. Appreciation of mutual obligations, national interest, and other states' needs and systems all need to develop as preconditions of mutual confidence and predictability of behavior. Broadly understood, a common way of life, based on past experiences and present needs, already exists within each region. Much similarity also exists among African leaders' views of the external world and international relations, however widely their specific policy reactions to these perceptions may vary. The area in greatest need of development is the detailed awareness—beyond the level of slogans—of these common features, in order to heighten already existent familiarity and predictability.

The seventh precondition is a substantial increase in capabilities, in three different fields. Markedly superior economic growth (compared to that of the recent past or of neighboring areas), an increase in the elements of state power, and a greater competence in controlling state behavior and redirecting its attention are all necessary.[23] Integration develops from strength, not from efforts to escape weakness. However, in few Western African states has there been an economic upswing since independence. A boom in a country such as Ivory Coast may be encouraging, but generally worsened conditions elsewhere in the region tend to counteract this advantage. Even were the development of Ivory Coast to continue, it might only serve to convince its leaders of the rightness of their individual course and the lack of necessity for regional cooperation. On the other hand, the development of governmental techniques and political stability does increase capabilities and allows decision-making elites to opt for greater cooperation. The redistribution of economic benefits and the increase in popular participation following the withdrawal of colonial elites, however, may give an illusion of growth, national averages notwithstanding. Thus, the effect of this condition on Western Africa's regions is ambiguous, although not totally negative if capabilities are understood in a sense broader than that of more economic development.

A review of the seven preconditions necessary for regional integration indicates that Western Africa is well on the way to fulfilling only one: that of mobility. In terms of the other preconditions, the Maghreb is closest to the point of being a region, making progress in the satisfaction of goals, the expectation of rewards, and the creation of common services, and needing much more in the compatibility of values, the predictability of behavior, and the increase of capacities. The Soudanese region is advanced in terms of compatibility of the values, the satisfaction of goals, and the predictability of behavior, but progress remains to be made in the expectation of rewards, the creation of common services, and the increase of capabilities. Besides the alien culture area of Sierra Leone and Liberia, which will probably resist integration until it has already been begun by other states in the area, the main problem appears to be the difference in values and political systems from Senegal and Mauritania to Guinea and Mali—although changes can occur rapidly.

The Benin region is the least-developed, although there is a high attainment of preconditions among the Entente states. The obstacle to greater cooperation in this region seems to be the existence of a number of subregional groups or units—the Entente, the Nigerian Federation, and Ghana—each of which is satisfied with its own system and pattern of development. Greatest attention should be focused on problems of the compatibility of values, the satisfaction of goals, the extension of common services, and the predictability of behavior.

After the development of preconditions, there are other dynamic ingredients which go into the creation of regional cooperation. One is the development of a distinctive way of life as a response to an external challenge that is not military but cultural. This challenge is deeply felt in Western Africa, but it is perceived to be coming from outside Africa, largely from Western modernism. The feeling is an ingredient in Africa's process of discovering itself and defining its identity, but it has little direct reference to regionalism. Different attitudes toward the metropole, predominant ties with a single European country, and the continual conflict between the desire to be modern and the effort to remain African all diffuse efforts toward a common, distinctive way of life in face of external challenge. The development of philosophers, historians, writers, and journalists who can stimulate awareness of cultural characteristics (common and particularistic, be it noted) is a long-term process.

A second dynamic ingredient refers to a rise in local demands. "The issue of political integration . . . arose primarily when people demanded greater capabilities . . . from the governments. . . . Integration . . . [was] first considered as [a] possible means to further these ends," rather than as an end in itself.[24] Certainly the much-cited revolution of rising expectations—to the extent that it is a reality in Western Africa—puts pressure on governments to increase their capabilities, although the realization that capabilities can be strengthened through regional cooperation depends on the perception and values of the leaders. Once public commitments are made to the goal of unity and to the search for ways to attain it, and once expectations of joint rewards are raised, the pressures of dissatisfaction can help provide an impetus toward regional integration.

Finally, a full evaluation of the situation must also include two dysfunctional conditions. One is excessive burdens on the governing units or decreased capabilities to deal with outstanding problems. This condition differs from the last-mentioned dynamic ingredient, in that the dysfunctional situation arises when the government allows itself to be overrun by burdens, problems, and demands instead of maintaining its responsiveness toward them and its ability to control its behavior. If current demands and goals are such that they cannot be solved by regional cooperation, integration must await their solution and the return of stability. If the revolution of rising expectations is overwhelmed by its own offspring and successor, the revolution of falling satisfactions, the possibilities of a government turning its attention to long-range planning and cooperation may easily be swallowed up by the short-term need to stop unrest and remain in power.[25] The second dysfunctional condition is the increase of ethnic, linguistic, cultural, or other particularistic differentiation; this may be restated as the rise of subregional nationalism.[26] There is some evidence of an increase of particularism within Western African states, for the progress of nation-building throughout the area increases competition among centers of identification, interest, and justification. Some of this is beneficial to interest-based cooperation among sovereign units, but the line between helpful and hindering effects does not seem susceptible to theoretical or empirical determination.

If successful regional cooperation is to take place in Western Africa, the past experiences of the region and of other areas suggest that preceding conditions will be part of the process. This review does not indicate whether the most effective approach would be to strengthen the conditions in which some progress has already been made or to press efforts on all fronts. It appears likely, from past experiences, that progress in one field can reinforce advances in related fields, although the effects in certain particularly dysfunctional fields can reverse the movement. It is important, in any case, to note that the consolidation of the national unit, and its responsive attention to its own problems, is not necessarily a barrier, but can be an aid, to cooperation. The prospective challenges of development, within the framework of unity and independence, are so great in the entire area that there is no such thing as success in meeting them. Given the increased chances of aid being granted to grouped needs, and the possibility of maximizing scarce resources and avoiding duplication through the pooling of capabilities, regionalism does appear to provide the most economical way of attaining responsiveness.

TRENDS AND PATTERNS

The preceding chapters have, for the most part, dealt with an analysis of the past ten years of Western African relations, with little attempt to conjecture on the durability of these patterns. During these years, change has taken place; indeed, the tense of the very word *developing* suggests that change is a predominant characteristic of the African scene. The first set of conclusions indicated the broad characteristics of developing foreign policy in Western Africa. These characteristics all appear to be susceptible to change in details but they are unlikely to undergo major alterations in their general form, at least in the short run. The second set of conclusions suggested a major line of development that could occur, with guidelines for identifying the direction of change (some of which is already taking place). The present section will examine some of the major features already discussed—both general and detailed—with the specific purpose of ascertaining trends, patterns, and projections into the immediate future.

It is a refreshing opportunity to be able to suggest that not all the characteristics of Western Africa are likely to change. The state can be accepted as a permanent feature; past opportunities for the absorption of new states— the Mali Federation, the Tunisian offer of co-citizenship to Algeria, the UAS, the change of government in Togo, and Gambian independence negotiations— and continuing efforts of party governments to build a viable state and nation point to the durability of the state in both the concept and the reality of intra-African relations. Similarly, the mobile system of international relations within the continental framework of the OAU reflects forces that are deeper and stronger than most of those that might rise to oppose it. The myth of unity, general susceptibility to minimal notions of what constitutes admissible African conduct, and the African capability for absorbing outside influences and turning them to Africa's own purposes are all broad forces that work in favor of continuation of the present system. African wariness of fixed alignments and alliances, and the policy-making characteristics which have made it difficult for them to remain in such alliances for very long, are narrower forces which are likely to remain operative.

These reflections are not meant to exclude attempts to create such alliances or efforts to disrupt the mobile system and supplant it with a supranational, balance-of-power, or bipolar system; rather, it is suggested that these attempts will fail, whatever their momentary effects might be. The only change of any durability might be the change to a concert system, in which consensus is high, problems are brought to a common arbitration agency for solution, and action aimed toward the external world is marked by a high degree of solidarity. Such a system can come into existence without any substantial changes in the institutions of the OAU. But it too seems unlikely. If African ideological divisions are not deep enough to cause firm, competing alliances, they are nevertheless deep enough to keep the OAU from attaining the effectiveness of a concert system, and *a fortiori*, a supranational system. Nor does the OAU appear to be in danger of disappearing as the universal framework for the mobile African system.[27] It can attain varying degrees of effectiveness but, like the Arab League, it has become somewhat of a sacred value; it may be boycotted, bypassed, dominated or divided by factions, but it seems likely to remain. This situation would suggest that the Maghreb will continue to maintain its membership in the OAU, in the African mobile system, and in an active pattern of interaction with West Africa. Membership in both Arab and African organizations—and in both systems—gives North Africa alternatives, allies, and counterweights. As long as neither organization attempts to impose exclusiveness on its members, there seems no reason for the Maghreb to cease being both African and Arab—just as the United States is both Hemispheric and Atlantic.

Another durable feature of Western Africa is the primacy of ideology. In fact, it is likely that the search for ideology will intensify, and that ideology will continue to hold an important place in the determination of the state's national interests. Ideology is not only a pseudoscience; it is a figleaf over reality. Its premises are extrarealistic because it rejects present reality and seeks to point a way to a future ideal. When reality becomes acceptable, or when it has been reshaped according to the values (and sometimes the methods) indicated by the ideology, the ideology itself is no longer as necessary as it was before. Africans are a long way from accepting their reality, and the revolutionary-idealists are further away than the rest. If, as present trends and conditions indicate, the revolution of rising expectations is giving birth only to a revolution of falling satisfactions, reality is becoming less— not more—acceptable, and ideology is becoming more necessary to the Western African. Furthermore, if present ideologies are incapable of explaining, ordering, and prescribing satisfactorily—that is, if they lose all touch with reality—they only contribute to the increase of dissatisfaction, rejection, and revolution. In such a case, both opponent and incumbent ideologies are pushed to resort to internal violence and coercion to keep their following—techniques that are not necessary if the ideology is satisfying and voluntarily accepted. Foreign scapegoats and external distractions are foreign-policy corollaries that have frequently been used at such times. To Western Africa, all this represents a change only in degree.

A third constant element is the low incidence of power. It does not appear that Western Africa will be in a position, in the short run, to make substantial increases in its foreign-policy capabilities, by perfecting either the elements of state power or the instruments of foreign policy. Although there is a great likelihood that the advances will be highly unequal from state to state, the direct effects of resultant power differential seems limited to two areas: prestige and the increased possibility of serving as a core area and stimulus to regional cooperation. It would be intriguing to speculate on the effects that Ghana's Volta River project, Nigeria's growing population, or Algeria's oil production might have on these states' relations with their neighbors; although each increases the capabilities, none puts the state so far ahead of the developing capabilities of its neighbors as to cause major shifts in the power distribution in the area.

In addition to these constant elements—if continuing change can be called a constant—there are also some likely new ingredients. Perhaps the most important and the most problematic concerns internal systems of government. Two omens of change are certain: the death of the George Washingtons and the rise of modernistic dissatisfaction. To understand the effects of these events, another certainty must be added: the decrease of formal ties with the metropole. To begin with the third element, the proponent of "complete" independence is right when he sees accession to sovereignty as only one step in the attainment of independence (although he is on less firm ground when he believes "total" independence to be possible, or misses the fact that sovereignty is crucial to free choice, as Algeria, Guinea, or Mali show). After formal independence come further steps, such as the achievement of republican status in the Commonwealth countries, the cancellation of metropolitan defense responsibilities and the evacuation of colonial troops, the loosening of preferential market conditions, and the diversification of trade. Whatever ties of aid, culture, and sentiment remain, there is a widening of the material distance between metropole and ex-colony.

Another step in this process is the death of the national George Washington. Whatever his political difficulties with the metropole may have been during the struggle for independence, he is likely to be closer to the metropole by training, experience, and past loyalties than his successor. (Indeed, in only two decades some states in the area may be ruled by *sabras,* people born after independence.) Although the second generation will be farther from the real and imagined abuses of colonialism, the experiences of the colonial rule will have been established in the historical myths of the country. There is already evidence to indicate that the arrival of a second generation can produce varied results, not all of them marked by a radical shift. The second generation in Morocco and Sierra Leone has continued the policies and attitudes of the first, and the "second generation" of Togo and Dahomey had actually had a closer relation to the colonial administration than the one it replaced. A more likely effect of generational succession on intra-African politics will be a loosening of established patterns, an increase in the mobility of states within the system of relations, and a growing awareness of the national bases and needs of state policy.

To this effect must be added the third change: the increased pressure of dissatisfied groups that have been trained for, but excluded from, the benefits of independence and modernization—the young middle class and proletariat, many of them underemployed or unemployed. To the extent that national development policies or regional integration are perceived to be (and are, in fact) realistic answers to this challenge, such pressures can be stimuli to realistic national-interest policies. It is more likely, however, that the pressures of dissatisfaction will lead to revolutionary-idealist policies and government and hence to a shift of the center of gravity in Western African relations toward what may loosely be termed *the left*. Although such dissatisfaction may cause the overthrow of unsuccessful conventional-realist governments, there is no attempt here to predict a wave of *coups* sweeping across Western Africa, or to suggest that revolution is the only means of shifting the center of gravity. Even counterrevolutionary regimes may turn to radical foreign policies to draw the attention of both public and opposition away from domestic ills and conservative domestic policies; and, as the center of gravity moves, moderate regimes may feel obligated to follow. Morocco, Tunisia, and Ivory Coast have already given examples of this effect from time to time. On the other hand, conventional-realist regimes are not set up by revolution. They grow. The fact that their approach is essentially evolutionary, however, does not preclude their growing out of an originally revolutionary government, when the revolution has "worn off." In fact, the natural process of revolution seems to include settling down, accepting reality, and digesting the changes it has made.[28] Hence, although this is a process of undetermined length, there is also the possibility that present revolutionary-idealist regimes will gradually moderate and stabilize—or face overthrow by counterrevolutions. The general effects of these changes can be summarized as an increase in the mobility characteristics of the system and a shift in the "average" Western African attitude in the radical direction.

Such a projection must remain general for two reasons: first, neither the shift nor the mobility characteristics imply the attainment of the regional consensus necessary for the adoption of positive programs; and, second, the revolutionary-idealists do not propose many precise, positive measures. Instead, they favor stands on current policy questions, and these attitudes are usually couched in negative terms of *condemn, oppose,* and *deplore.* In such past crises as the Congo problem in 1960-61 and 1964, the Olympio assassination, the Mauritanian question, the Algerian war, Bizerte, and the Algero-Moroccan war, Western African states' positions were largely drawn up for or against someone else's actions, and the few positive proposals were never capable of gathering sufficient support or solving the problem. At their most effective, these stands inhibited any new approach and left the problem to be dealt with by the forces already causing it. There is no reason to expect the above-mentioned changes to alter this pattern, nor does it appear possible to draw any direct relation between the already-noted characteristics of shift and mobility, and the progress of Western Africa toward regional cooperation. An increase in revolutionary-idealist regimes may slightly increase chances for regional cooperation if it reduces ideological friction among governments in the region, and it may decrease these chances if it channels more attention into ideological explanations for real problems than into realistic efforts to overcome them. Similarly, continued mobility makes commitments to cooperate unstable, but it also makes obstacles temporary.

The other potential changes are more precise. One concerns a change in the capacity for external violence, and its effect on the inhibition of war. It has been seen that external violence has been excluded from Western African policies by the absence of means, by the fact that potential ends can be pursued more economically by political methods, by current values (which prohibit the use of military force against other Western African states), and by the area's relation to the Cold War. It has also been maintained that, although none of these conditions alone is sufficient to exclude war, they are mutually supporting and—until now—effective. What would happen if the first condition were altered by the massive importation of arms? Obviously, if armaments increased beyond the prestige-raising level, all other conditions would be brought into question. The government would appear to have decided that political means were inadequate and that military means were not too expensive; it would have judged its goal as being more important than the inhibitions on "un-African" conduct; and the probable source of the arms from one Cold War protagonist or another would reflect a change in the relation of Western Africa to the world system.[29] Thus, in a sense, to pose the question is to answer it; in this sense, the real question is whether the already-mentioned conditions would prevent the arms order from being placed. In general, the discussion has suggested that it has and would. It is the exceptions, however, that are important. A small arms race has already taken place in Western Africa, between Morocco and Algeria. The military situation was, in part, a colonial heritage, connected with the Algerian war, but it was aggravated by postwar Moroccan and Algerian arms shipments, from ultimate sources mainly in NATO countries and the Soviet Union, respectively. Hence, Algeria and Morocco inherited and maintained large armies which, under the impetus of a serious border problem, made war possible. But the other Western African states are in a different situation. They would have to build their armies deliberately, taking the first provocatory step themselves, for the military differential in the area is small except along the Algerian Saharan border (and there a large army is unwieldy). Thus even the Somali experience is not parallel, for a large Ethiopian army already existed in the conflict area. The only possible parallel would be for a neighbor to consider Ghana's paramilitary forces as part of the Ghanaian army, which from any point of view—past or theoretical—seems far-fetched. Hence the chances of a unilateral military buildup remain small, and the chances of a subversive attempt—modeled on the Congo situation and leading to a similar result—appear equally small in Western Africa.

The second potential change concerns boundaries. It has been seen that many states have vague aspirations toward neighboring areas, but that these are lesser foreign-policy goals, and that most boundary problems concern undelineated or undemarcated borders. It has also been seen that these problems arise in the process of nation-building, as the state expands its control to its theoretical frontiers and tries to consolidate its natural unit. But as the state increases its control over its territory and population and develops its power and capacity for government, what are the chances that it will seek to unify tribes partially within its borders or embark on a campaign of conquest in the name of a historical empire? The chances seem dangerously great.[30] A state tends to bring its ends and means into harmony; when its means increase, former low-priority goals rise in importance. Successful integration of one part of a tribe into the national life may well give rise to tribal demands to be reunited with fellow tribesmen if life is not as good on the other side. New "relatives" may be discovered in the process and, most broadly, the growing state may end up seeing its manifest destiny in the boundaries of past empires. Western Africa is no more immune from such sentimental temptations than are states elsewhere in the world: in fact, the pronouncements of Al-Fassi in Morocco show that such ideas are already present. However, it does not appear that any states will have the means to carry out such a policy in the near future, nor that the nation-building process will be completed so rapidly as to give rise to the ends, nor, finally, that the above-mentioned inhibitions on war will cease to limit such contingencies in the short run.

So far, nothing has suggested the likelihood of another 1963—the year of greatest importance to intra-African relations, because of the breakdown of alliances, the formation of the OAU, and the shift in the nature of the African system. Instead, the discussion has suggested that the results of 1963 are likely to last for awhile. Superficial observers may see in every new event a unique situation upsetting past patterns; our suggestion would be to wait and see if, in fact, the event is not another transient ingredient in the mobile system. It seems to be the habit of writers of books on Africa to begin with a citation of the Roman's opinion that "something new was always coming out of Africa." Our aim here has been to suggest that Western Africa's bag of surprises is not bottomless and that there may be some more lasting characteristics, patterns, and trends susceptible of analysis and understanding.

NOTES

[1] Somewhat similar work done in other areas includes Leonard Binder, *The Ideological Revolution in the Middle East* (New York: Wiley, 1964); Charles D. Creameans, *The Arabs and the World* (New York: Praeger, 1963); John C. Campbell, *Defense of the Middle East* (New York: Praeger, 1960); also William C. Johnstone, *Burma's Foreign Policy* (Cambridge, Mass.: Harvard U.P., 1963); and Russell Fifield, *The Diplomacy of Southeast Asia, 1945-1958* (New York: Harper, 1958).

[2] Harold D. Lasswell and Abraham Kaplan, *Power and Society* (New Haven: Yale U.P., 1950), p. 181, cf. p. 177.

[3] *Ibid.*, pp. 30-31.

[4] *Ibid.*, pp. 74-76, 98; Annette Baker Fox, *The Power of Small States* (Chicago: U. of Chicago Press, 1959), p. 3.

[5] See Ali Mazrui, "The United Nations and Some African Political Attitudes," *International Organizations,* XVIII, 3 (Summer 1964), 499-520.

[6] See Franz Fanon, *Les Damnés de la terre* (Paris: Maspero, 1961).

[7] See David E. Apter (ed.) *Ideology and Discontent* (New York: Free Press, 1964), pp. 26, 29-30. The late Dorothy Padmore, in an interview, explained that her husband, George Padmore, had an analytical mind and knew Africans in general, and hence could draw conclusions rapidly and easily even in the absence of detailed evidence or new facts—an implicit testimony to the use of ideology to explain events.

[8] For discussions of other developing systems, see Binder, *op. cit.,* Chap. 9, and Michael Brecher, "International Relations and Asian Studies: The Subordinate State System of Southern Asia," in *World Politics,* XV, 2 (January 1963), 213-35.

[9] Discussions of these systems are found in Morton A. Kaplan, *System and Process in International Relations* (New York: Wiley, 1957), and Richard N. Rosecrance, *Action and Reaction in World Politics* (Boston: Little, Brown, 1963).

[10] Note that the semantics of unity, union, and unification is a problem that has distracted other unity movements; see Arnold Zurcher, *The Struggle to Unite Europe* (New York. New York U.P., 1958), p. 29.

[11] Touré also clearly showed the primacy of independence over unity when he said: "For the Guinean people, the reconquest of African unity is subordinate to that of national sovereignty, i.e. the independence of our people" (AFP-G, November 19, 1958). Although Senegal and Soudan opted for unity before independence, the collapse of the Mali Federation showed the eventual primacy of independence over unity.

[12] See Reginald Herbold Green, "The Development and Use of Multipurpose Economic Institutions in Africa," paper presented to the first Congress of Africanists, Accra, December 1962.

[13] Note that the cause of dissidence in new nations—e.g., Morocco (1958-59), Algeria (1963-64), Sudan (1964-65), and many others—has often been the central government's neglect of "disinherited" regions.

[14] The most frequently cited work is Karl W. Deutsch, *et al., Political Community and the North Atlantic Area* (Princeton, N.J.: Princeton U.P., 1957), referred to as "the Princeton study." Other works used in this section are Karl W. Deutsch, *Nationalism and Social Communication* (New York: Wiley, 1953); Ernst B. Haas, "The Challenge of Regionalism" in Stanley Hoffmann (ed.), *Contemporary Theory in International Relations* (Englewood Cliffs, N.J.: Prentice-Hall, Inc., 1960), pp. 223-39; L. P. Green and T. J. D. Fair, *Development in Africa* (Johannesburg: Witwatersrand U.P., 1962); T. J. D. Fair, "A Regional Approach to Economic Development in Kenya," *South African Geographical Journal,* LIV (1963), 55-77; Norman J. G. Pounds and Sue Simons Ball "Core Areas and the Development of the European States System," *Annals of the Association of*

American Geographers, LIV, 1 (March 1964), 24-40; Amatai Etzioni, *Political Unification* (New York: Holt, Rinehart & Winston, 1965).

[15] Deutsch, *et al., op. cit.*, p. 44.

[16] *Ibid.*, p. 93; Haas, in Hoffmann (ed.), *op. cit.*, p. 236.

[17] According to minimum per capita standards of mass communications suggested by UNESCO, only Algeria, Liberia, Morocco, Senegal, and Tunisia even approach minimum levels in radio receiving facilities, and none of the Western African states have adequate newspaper, cinema, or television facilities; at present growth rates, it would take Africa as long as seventy years to reach certain minimum levels, Wilbur Schramm, *Mass Media and National Development* (Stanford: Stanford U.P., 1964), pp. 94, 113, 275-77.

[18] Deutsch, *et al., op. cit.*, pp. 97-100.

[19] *Ibid.*, pp. 52, 61, 63-64, 86, 88, 94.

[20] The notion of political grids is an intriguing framework for further research and comes from Fred G. Burke, *Africa's Quest for Order* (Englewood Cliffs, N.J.: Pentice-Hall, Inc., 1964), pp. 37-42. Research could also be done on the idea of market areas; see Paul Bohannan, *Africa and Africans* (Garden City, N.Y.: The Natural History Press, 1964), p. 216. Some information is available in Paul Bohannan, *Markets in Africa* (Chicago: Northwestern U.P., 1962), pp. 250-54 (Mossi), 350-59 (Niger Fulani), 685-92 (Koforidua).

[21] Deutsch, *et al., op. cit.*, p. 46; see also p. 90.

[22] *Ibid.*, pp. 49, 71, 95-96; Haas, in Hoffmann (ed.), *op. cit.*, p. 236.

[23] Deutsch, *et al., op. cit.*, pp. 39-40, 51, 57.

[24] *Ibid.*, p. 87; see pp. 85-88; Haas, in Hoffmann (ed.), *op. cit.*, p. 236.

[25] In addition to points previously discussed, this situation was a major element in the absence of closer integration between Guinea and Mali, particularly in 1960-63.

[26] See Deutsch, *et al.*, pp. 62-63, also pp. 59, 94. Another impeding force can be the vested interests of suboptimal national industry; see Green, *op. cit.*

[27] See I. William Zartman, "Characteristics of Developing Foreign Policies in Former French Africa," in William H. Lewis (ed.), *French-Speaking Africa: The Search for Identity* (New York: Walker, 1965). Moderate and radical disappointment with the OAU in 1965 led to the reinforcement of the OCAM (ex-UAM) and discussions among Algeria, Guinea, and Mali on the formation of a radical counteralliance. These moves do not invalidate these conclusions. Egypt made a similar threat, in September 1962, to leave the Arab League, but returned soon afterward, to continue the mobile pattern of relations in the Middle East.

[28] The best treatment of revolution is still Crane Brinton, *The Anatomy of Revolution* (Englewood Cliffs, N.J.: Prentice-Hall, Inc., 1952).

[29] In addition to the elements noted, increased arms supplies depend on the receivers' financial capability and absorption capability, the suppliers' willingness, and the nature of the threat—all of which in reality generally tend to inhibit a sudden rise of military capabilities; H. Roberts Coward, *Military Technology in Developing Countries* (Cambridge, Mass.: Massachusetts Institute of Technology, 1964 [Series C/64-5]), pp. 14-15, 29-41. Arnold Rivkin presents an opposing view: "The situation is ripe for a dozen India-Pakistan situations where military aid to one party in a local dispute will eventually cause a grievance in a rival country. If, as is likely, the competing country turns elsewhere for military assistance, then an armaments race is set into motion between African states and indirectly between the United States and the Communist bloc—or perhaps the UAR" (*West Africa*, January 16, 1960). See also Arnold Rivkin, *Africa and the West* (New York: Praeger, 1962), and Max F. Millikan and Donald L. M. Blackmer (eds.), *The Emerging Nations* (Boston: Little, Brown, 1961), esp. pp. 110-14.

[30] See official commentary on the 1960 constitution of Ghana, noted in Jean Buchmann, *L'Afrique noire indépendante* (Paris: Pichon et Durand-Anzias, 1962), p. 164.

INDEX

Conferences, Parties, and Tribes are listed under those headings